# THE CIVIL RIGHTS OF HOMELESS PEOPLE

# MODERN APPLICATIONS OF SOCIAL WORK

*An Aldine de Gruyter Series of Texts and Monographs*

SERIES EDITOR

## James K. Whittaker

Paul Adams and Kristine E. Nelson (eds.), **Reinventing Human Services: Community and Family Centered Practice**

Ralph E. Anderson and Irl Carter, **Human Behavior in the Social Environment: A Social Systems Approach** (fourth edition)

Richard P. Barth, Mark Courtney, Jill Duerr Berrick, and Vicky Albert, **From Child Abuse to Permanency Planning: Child Welfare Services Pathways and Placements**

Kathleen Ell and Helen Northen, **Families and Health Care: Psychosocial Practice**

Marian Fatout, **Models for Change in Social Group Work**

Mark W. Fraser, Peter J. Pecora, and David A. Haapala, **Families in Crisis: The Impact of Intensive Family Preservation Services**

James Garbarino, **Children and Families in the Social Environment** (second edition)

James Garbarino, and Associates, **Special Children—Special Risks: The Maltreatment of Children with Disabilities**

James Garbarino, and Associates, **Troubled Youth, Troubled Families: Understanding Families At-Risk for Adolescent Maltreatment**

Roberta R. Greene, **Social Work with the Aged and Their Families**

Roberta R. Greene, **Human Behavior Theory: A Diversity Framework**

Roberta R. Greene and Paul H. Ephross, **Human Behavior Theory and Social Work Practice**

André Ivanoff, Betty J. Blythe, and Tony Tripodi, **Involuntary Clients in Social Work Practice: A Research-Based Approach**

Paul K. H. Kim (ed.), **Serving the Elderly: Skills for Practice**

Jill Kinney, David A. Haapala, and Charlotte Booth, **Keeping Families Together: The Homebuilders Model**

Robert M. Moroney, **Social Policy and Social Work: Critical Essays on the Welfare State**

Peter J. Pecora, Mark W. Fraser, Kristine Nelson, Jacqueline McCroskey, and William Meezan, **Evaluating Family-Based Services**

Peter J. Pecora, James K. Whittaker, Anthony N. Maluccio, Richard P. Barth, and Robert D. Plotnick, **The Child Welfare Challenge: Policy, Practice, and Research**

John R. Schuerman, Tina L. Rzepnicki, and Julia H. Littell, **Putting Families First: An Experiment in Family Preservation**

Madeline R. Stoner, **The Civil Rights of Homeless People: Law, Social Policy, and Social Work Practice**

Harry H. Vorrath and Larry K. Brendtro, **Positive Peer Culture (Second Edition)**

Betsy S. Vourlekis and Roberta R. Greene (eds). **Social Work Case Management**

James K. Whittaker, and Associates, **Reaching High-Risk Families: Intensive Family Preservation in Human Services**

# THE CIVIL RIGHTS OF HOMELESS PEOPLE
Law, Social Policy, and Social Work Practice

MADELEINE R. STONER

ALDINE DE GRUYTER

New York

## ABOUT THE AUTHOR

**Madeleine Stoner** is Associate Professor at the University of Southern California, School of Social Work. She began to work with homeless mentally ill women in 1972 when she was Director of Health and Welfare at the Urban League of Philadelphia.

A frequently cited homeless advocate, she served on the City of Santa Monica Task Force on Homelessness, and has worked directly with numerous homeless agencies and people.

Her previous work has made critical breakthroughs in analyzing the problem of homelessness. Her book, *Inventing a Non-Homeless Future: A Public Policy Agenda for Preventing Homelessness,* challenged the growing shelter system. An earlier article, "The Plight of Homeless Women," was the first to call attention to the increasing number of homeless women in the United States.

ALDINE DE GRUYTER
A division of Walter de Gruyter, Inc.
200 Saw Mill River Road
Hawthorne, New York 10532

This publication is printed on acid free paper ∞

**Library of Congress Cataloging-in-Publication Data**
Stoner, Madeleine R.
    The civil rights of homeless people  :  law, social policy and social work practice  /  Madeleine R. Stoner.
       p.  cm.  —  Modern Applications of Social Work
    Includes biographical references and index.
    ISBN 0-202-30513-9 (cloth  :  acid-free paper).  —  ISBN 0-202-30514-7 (pbk.  :  acid-free paper)
    1. Homeless persons—Legal status, laws, etc.—United States. 2. Homeless persons—Civil rights—United States. 3. Homeless persons—Government policy—United States. 4. Social work with the homeless—United States. I. Title. II. Series.
KF3742.S76  1995
342.73'087—dc20
[347.30287]
                                   94-49386
                                     CIP

Manufactured in the United States of America

10  9  8  7  6  5  4  3  2  1

# CONTENTS

## 12    THE LIMITATIONS OF JUDICIAL ADVOCACY

# ACKNOWLEDGMENTS

Acknowledging the many people, past and present, who help an author complete a book is a humbling task that reminds us of our strong dependence upon so many important others. My most direct and constant sources of support came from Lori Sandovaal and Ruth Britten. Lori is our most capable Research Assistant at the University of Southern California Social Work Research Center. Although she is responsible for social work research, she was more than competent as a legal researcher in locating the judicial cases cited in this book. Ruth Britten, the librarian in the School of Social Work, was "on-line" before computer searches were even possible. The new technology has only added to her willingness and ability to provide sources and references.

I owe a debt of gratitude to all of the lawyers who tried cases representing homeless people during the past decade. Two of these stand out for me. Gary Blasi, who exemplifies those lawyers who are committed to social justice for disempowered people, read my manuscript and offered substantive suggestions. He also steered me in the right direction to launch my research for this book. Although I have not worked with Robert Myers, I acknowledge his work in the field of homeless litigation, in particular the fact that he resigned from his position as City Attorney in Santa Monica on the principle that he could not enforce an anti-homeless encampment law that was unconstitutional and unjust, in his opinion.

The National Law Center on Homelessness and Poverty outline of homeless litigation served as the primary reference for this book. It would have taken me far longer to complete my research if I did not have access to the work of the Center. The presence of such an effective organization at the national level offers a powerful resource and voice for homeless people. I am proud to be a member of this organization.

Raymond Albert, M.S.W., J.D., responded to my requests for information about the Bryn Mawr Graduate School of Social Work and Social Research Law and Social Policy program, as well as his knowledge about law and social work collaboration. His own career embodies the interprofessional paradigm suggested in this book.

Bruce Jansson, my colleague at the University of Southern California, advanced my understanding of social policy by identifying a wider range of social policy practice tasks and skills for social workers. This encouraged me to return to my earlier convictions about the value of judicial policy practice.

Finally, it is the right time and opportunity to acknowledge two people from my past who influenced my deep commitment to the profession of social work and its values. Bernard Ross, as Director of the Bryn Mawr Graduate School of Social Work and Social Research, had the foresight to assign me to the Lighthouse Settlement as a master's degree student when I would have preferred an internship at a more traditional planning agency. He also demonstrated great foresight when he began the Law and Social Policy Program at Bryn Mawr. Edward Sparer, J.D. taught me how to combine legal and social policy analyses in my quest for social justice. I am proud that I am one of the many students who studied with him at the University of Pennsylvania Law School, and even prouder that I have retained his ideals of practice.

# PREFACE

My work on this book has completed a personal circle in my social work career. As a student intern in 1967, I was a welfare rights organizer at the once proud, but now defunct, Lighthouse Settlement. Every aspect of this work required extensive collaboration with staff lawyers of the Community Legal Services Corporation. That experience convinced me of the importance of using the courts in the press for social change and equality in American social policy and social welfare institutions.

As equal partners in direct service to our clients, as well as organizers and advocates, we brought valuable and complementary knowledge and skills to our work. I focused on personal counseling and building an organization of welfare recipients to challenge unfair denials of benefits and other inequities in the public welfare system. My legal counterpart defined the constitutional and statutory rights of our clients. We both stood with them in their encounters with public welfare officials. Together, we facilitated the competence of welfare recipients to function more autonomously in every aspect of their lives. We were privileged to witness the personal and political empowerment of people who never before thought that they had any recourse to justice.

It was very clear then that poverty, welfare reform, and racial discrimination were so complex that every human service profession was compelled to join forces to reverse long standing institutional patterns of inequity and indignity against welfare recipients, poor families, and African Americans. We focused mostly on African American people at that time because they were viewed as the welfare cheats and drains on the system, even though more white people received public assistance benefits. Even today, the epithets "welfare queens" and "welfare cheats" operate as racist codes.

Political support for law and social justice was extremely strong then. The Community Legal Services Corporation was well funded as a central component of the Economic Opportunity Act. Its staff consisted of many of the brightest young lawyers in the nation who fervently believed that their representation of poor people through direct services and class action litigation could reverse discriminatory institutional patterns. The interest in using the courts as instruments of social change was so pervasive among young lawyers that even the most traditional private legal firms were compelled to expand their *pro bono* staff, hours, and resources to recruit and retain some of the best and brightest young lawyers.

It seemed entirely logical that I should study poverty law during my doctoral program, and I was privileged to take classes with Edward Sparer at the University of Pennsylvania Law School. His personal career embodied the ideals of law and social justice. In his work at Mobilization for Youth, the National Welfare Rights Organization, and the Community Legal Services Corporation of the Office of Economic Opportunity, he developed many strategic approaches to apply the principles of the United States Constitution to the lives of the most disadvantaged Americans. This educational experience firmly planted my perspective on the value of judicial approaches to social policy.

The history of the demise of the War on Poverty after 1973 is a well-documented matter of record. By 1981, the Community Legal Services Corporation was dismantled after 8 years of gradual withdrawal of resources. This occurred as part of the overall reductions in social services and income maintenance programs in the 1980s. It is no accident that mass homelessness emerged so rapidly at that same time! The withdrawal of a secure safety net promulgated a new form of poverty. The truly poor became the devastated poor. Contemporary policy analysts frequently note that homelessness is *the* face of poverty in the last decades of the century.

My personal involvement with homeless people began in 1973 when people were discharged from state mental hospitals under the deinstitutionalization movement. Even then we turned to the courts in our efforts to close down unlicensed boarding houses because of their abusive treatment of residents. We succeeded and eventually most board and care homes for mentally ill people operated under regulatory statutes and contracts. Moreover, many new rights of mental patients became codified in judicial and legislative law at that time.

I left the United States to live and work in England. When I returned in 1980 I was disheartened to observe that antiwelfare attitudes had intensified to a revised welfare reform movement based upon the same negative stereotypes of welfare recipients that we had challenged 20 years earlier in the welfare rights movement. I was even more disturbed by the spread of homelessness across the nation.

I joined the rush of vocal and compassionate advocates who decried this injustice and degradation of American citizens. We focused on the travesty and immorality of the problem and fought for shelter to ameliorate the problem. After several years of effective advocacy that resulted in shelter and other emergency assistance, many of us realized that we had helped to establish a new service delivery system, the shelter system. Our concern was that the new system was inferior to any previous safety net provisions and that it was in danger of becoming a permanent social welfare institution. We also observed that our focus on emergency assistance diverted the attention of policy makers and concerned citizens from developing permanent solutions to homelessness. To address this new problem, I wrote *Inventing a Non-Homeless Future: A Public Policy Agenda for Preventing Homelessness* in 1989.

As one of the many advocates who began to despair over the national failure to provide long-term solutions and the increasing tide of anti-homeless activity in cities across the United States, I searched for the cup that remained half-full. This was the record of successful impact litigation that preserved the fundamental rights of homeless people to social entitlements and constitutional protections in their own country. My discovery renewed my enthusiasm and sense of possibility about solutions to the problem of homelessness.

I realized yet again that the energy directed to achieving social justice and equality through the courts so fervently espoused in the welfare rights and antipoverty movements had remained intact. It was clear that the only substantive gains in ameliorating the personal and public problems of homelessness emanated from judicial decisions and the labors of attorneys and teams of advocates who brought actions to the courts.

During a 10-year period, over 1000 class action lawsuits challenged antihomeless practices and laws. This impressive record was possible despite the demise of the Community Legal Services Corporation. Privately funded public interest legal organizations, operating with skeletal staff and resources, assumed responsibilities for major constitutional challenges representing the civil rights of homeless people. Foremost among these are the National Law Center on Homelessness and Poverty, the Legal Aid Society Homeless Family Rights Project in New York City, Legal Aid Societies across the nation, the Western Center on Law and Poverty, the Inner City Law Project in Los Angeles, and the Community for Creative Non-Violence in Washington, D.C. In Los Angeles, public interest law firms, together with several private law firms that provided *pro bono* contributions, formed the Homeless Litigation Team. Lawyers from private law firms also continued their *pro bono* work and Robert Hayes, a member of a prestigious New York City firm, devoted most of his time to homeless litigation. The homeless problem will not be solved until a comprehensive plan of housing, services, and income maintenance is put into place. In the interim, the court mandates and fines facilitated by so many legal actions have goaded political leaders and citizens to consider permanent solutions to the proliferation of homelessness.

This book describes the work of public interest lawyers and their colleagues from other human service fields to demonstrate the efficacy of seeking judicial solutions to the social problems that confront all of society, and comprise the major focus of social welfare practice and theory. A secondary purpose of the book is to add to the relatively sparse body of literature on social work and law.

## Legal Content in Social Work Education

It is becoming increasingly clear that the problems that people bring to lawyers and social workers frequently overlap. Recent literature in the fields of child welfare, mental and physical health, and general clinical practice demonstrates the growing interaction between the professions. More social workers and lawyers in public and private settings are demonstrating an interest in developing sociolegal approaches to the solution of personal and public problems.

However, there is a notable dearth of opportunities to integrate professional content in the preparatory curricula of both professions. Twelve universities offer dual-degree programs that lead to the J.D. and M.S.W. degrees in which students can complete 5 years of work in four. This represents a significant advance because only two such programs existed in 1976. Students apply to these programs by completing separate forms for the law and social work schools. Admission to each program is determined by separate criteria without any consultation between the schools.

Bryn Mawr College School of Social Work and Social Research offers a unique Law and Social Policy program. This is a postmaster's degree program designed for professionals in social work, other human service professions, public administration, or policy analysis. Students may apply to the program at three critical periods in their education: (1) after completion of a master's degree program, (2) after completion of 1 year in Bryn Mawr's masters in social service program as joint-degree students, and (3) in conjunction with their application to the Bryn Mawr master's program, also as joint-degree students. No other program like this exists.

Columbia University's Graduate School of Social Work has developed a field internship model of law and social work collaboration. In partnership with a local union, law and social work students collaborate in dispute resolution and in solving client problems. The law students handle the legal grievances and the social work students provide services and counseling. The unique feature of this program is the interdisciplinary seminar for joint exploration of the legal and social concepts and perspectives that arise in their experiences.

A precedent for this emanated in the 1960s when the Columbia University School of Social Work housed the Center on Social Welfare Policy and Law that organized many of the major class action suits on behalf of welfare recipients and other categories of poor people. It is interesting to note that the School of Social Work agreed to sponsor the Center only after Columbia's Law School rejected the idea.

Both the joint law and social work programs and the Bryn Mawr model offer obvious strengths and weaknesses. Completion of a legal curriculum and a social work curriculum offers no guarantee that graduates will readily integrate the knowledge obtained in each school. Courses of study are designed independently to satisfy different professional criteria. No university joint degree program offers even one integrative seminar during the course of study. Integration is left entirely up to students. Moreover, only one university has designated a faculty/administrator position for coordination between the two professional schools.

The Bryn Mawr program in Social Policy and Law maximizes opportunities for integration in class and field internships. However, most students who are interested in both professions opt for the joint-degree programs because they end up with two separate degrees. Bryn Mawr students complete one master's level degree and the legal component of their education provides them with the equivalent of a certificate of competence. Students remain ambivalent about whether the extra credential is worth their time and frequently opt to spend 4 years in a joint-degree program.

Bryn Mawr conducted two surveys of legal content in social work curricula, in 1983 and 1985. The first survey was sent to every undergraduate and graduate school of social work in the United States. Fifty percent of the graduate programs and 30% of the undergraduate programs returned the questionnaire. The second survey was sent to a randomly selected subset of 50 graduate and undergraduate programs that participated in the first survey. Twenty-five programs responded. Dr. Raymond Albert, the director of the program, reported the analysis of the findings at the Annual Program Meeting of the Council on Social Work Education in 1991. The report noted the following trends:

Most social policy courses attempt to cover an array of sociolegal topics in mental health, child welfare, family law, adoption, divorce, and custody. Their primary concern is providing a general view of the various legal environments for social service.

A few courses incorporated law and social policy content within the larger context of social work advocacy viewing law as a function of social work practice on behalf of clients. Most social policy courses focus on social welfare legislation or policy as a context for social service delivery. They are less likely to include the judicial context of the social services.

Two courses specifically teach dispute resolution processes and techniques viewing mediation as a viable social work function.

Most courses do address the social worker as witness and social worker–lawyer collaboration. When they address the social reform role of social work they emphasize legislative advocacy. A few courses include specific content on state regulation of social work practice. One school teaches a special course on divorce and custody that involves the law; and one school offers a course entitled "Law and Society," which covers issues related to the social functions of the law. Only a few schools suggested that they teach basic legal research skills.

Despite the sparse number of law and social work courses offered, all respondents highly valued the importance of conveying basic knowledge about law and the legal system. Most of the courses that are available are offered as electives. More opportunities for collaborative learning occur in interdisciplinary field placements than in classes.

Bryn Mawr also found that a wide range of law-related topics was covered in continuing education programs. This suggested that social work alumni are not only seeking supplemental legal knowledge and skills but are signaling the importance of incorporating this content into current master's and undergraduate curricula.

The demanding curricular requirements for social work and law students do not leave much space for new courses. There is, however, scope for adding components to existing courses. I have written this book as a supplementary text for social policy courses in both professions. Because it identifies the critical policy issues that cut across most policy arenas, it serves as an illustration of the application of judicial approaches to the implementation of social policy.

Legal and social work practitioners may find the book useful on two levels. It surveys and identifies the key legal decisions related to homeless people. It also offers exemplars of sociolegal collaboration.

# INTRODUCTION

## The Quest for Social Justice in Law and Social Work

Society today is built around entitlement. The automobile dealer has his franchise, the doctor and lawyer their professional licenses. Many of the most important of these entitlements flow from government subsidies to farmers and businessmen . . . social security pensions for individuals. . . . To the recipients they are essentials, fully deserved, and in no sense a form of charity. It is only the poor whose entitlements . . . have not been effectively enforced.

This is not the opinion of the liberal left critics of 1990 welfare–workfare reform efforts but that of the Supreme Court in 1970 cited by Justice William Brennan for the majority in *Goldberg v. Kelly*.[1] This opinion has compelled the welfare lawyers of the 1980s and 1990s to keep alive the spirit and intent of the tradition of advocacy law by pressing for the enforcement of essential entitlements of homeless people.

This book reminds all social workers and other human service practitioners, public administrators, and social policy analysts that some of the most significant rights of homeless people have been established in the courts during the past two decades by reviewing the numerous cases that have been tried on behalf of homeless litigants. It adds a note of optimism to the seemingly insoluble problem of mass homelessness by illuminating the heritage of seeking judicial solutions to social injustice that once flourished and still does. In noting that the advances of welfare rights lawyers of the 1960s have continued in the arena of homelessness, the book is a rarity because it is written in praise of lawyers.

The purposes of this book are twofold. It demonstrates the value and efficacy of collaboration between the social work and legal professions in the quest for social change and equity in its focus on the treatment of equality as a central value of the legal and social systems. Policy practitioners, working within a theoretical perspective and value framework of empowerment, beneficence, and justice, must frequently turn to the legal system to achieve these ends.[2] They must forge collaboration, not

1

only within their immediate circle, but also among the scores of public officials, activists, and lawyers whose interests intersect their own.

Contemporary social workers are more apt to perceive their role in the legal system in terms of their client referrals, seeking personal liability protection and supplying expert testimony. They are also aware of the legal controls on practice, such as mandated reporting of domestic violence and involuntary commitment criteria. Social work advocacy for individual clients within the legal system also plays a prominent role in practice. The advance of advocacy in social work practice has identified the necessity of political activity in the hearing rooms, committee rooms, and conference rooms where public policy is written. It is equally important to claim skills in the legal research necessary for the preparation of briefs, monitoring the enforcement and implementation of laws, codes, and ordinances. Effective policy practice in the contemporary legal environment governing human services should include skills in legal analysis and legal reasoning, how to read a judicial opinion, how to interpret a statute, and how to analyze regulations and the structure of policy implementation.

Public interest lawyers frequently turn to those whose claim to expertise lies in their knowledge of individuals, groups, communities, and social service delivery systems for the knowledge and insight that they need to develop legal arguments. They also seek information about the laws that govern the social services and impact on social problems. Social workers are uniquely positioned to assess how responsive policies and delivery systems are to the private and public problems of their clients.

Collaborative interprofessional initiatives are rapidly spreading across the nation in service delivery systems and on university campuses. This is more than a mere trend. It reflects increasing acknowledgment that the social problems encountered throughout the world are too complex and interrelated to justify single ameliorative efforts.

Existing models for interprofessional collaboration illustrate the potential for expanded partnerships both in direct and indirect services. Although each profession brings different perspectives to social issues, respect for their differences can strengthen their combined efforts.

The second purpose of the book is to document legal challenges to preserve the civil rights of homeless persons in the United States.

The proliferation of mass homelessness in the United States has been accompanied by a growing movement that focuses on the social problem that homelessness reflects, rather than the private problems of homeless people. The occurrence and definition of social movements are difficult to track. We frequently note the existence of a movement only retrospectively when it is well under way. It is equally difficult to identify the precise moment in history when organized grievances transform themselves into social movements directed to the mobilization of resources, solutions, power, and constitutional rights.[3] Despite such elusiveness, it is by now quite clear that thousands of individuals, communities, and organizations across the United States have engaged in an impressive variety of activities "to help the homeless."

Activists in the homeless movement include those who work in soup kitchens, organize outdoor feeding programs, work in shelters, and donate professional services like health care, legal advice, personal counseling, and tutoring. Others engage in political and social action intended to gain more services and resources for homeless people; and many of these activists address their efforts to advocating changes in social and economic policies that would either prevent or end the problem of homelessness.

Much of the homeless movement has necessarily related to the provision of emergency food and shelter, as well as more permanent personal provisions. However, even those individuals and organizations that have been most directly involved with service delivery have directed their efforts toward advocacy. What has been clear since the landmark *Callahan v. Carey* judicial decision of 1980 granting the right to shelter for homeless people in New York City is that legal advocacy for homeless people in the courts has wrought the most substantive victories within the homeless movement.[4] Lawyers have also played an important role by analyzing and interpreting existing federal, state, and local laws and regulations that guarantee homeless persons certain rights and benefits such as food, medical care, disability, and veteran's benefits, as well as education for homeless children, and public and emergency assistance. As cities continue to respond to mass homelessness by attempting to legislate homeless people out of sight and out of mind, advocates have challenged antihomeless laws and actions in court. The impact of these advocacy efforts has been possible only because it has been part of the mass homeless rights movement that has evolved since 1981.

The impressive docket of homeless impact litigation serves as an important reminder to all social policy practitioners that social and institutional change efforts can be advanced by strategic use of the law. Even direct service practitioners need to understand both the procedure and substance of laws governing their clients, as well as how and when to consult lawyers as a routine part of their work.

These court challenges, although successful, have wrought only partial victories. There can be no complete victories until the public and private sectors offer solutions to the root problems of homeless people: poverty, lack of affordable housing, unemployment, racism, and under-resourced social services. Many constitutional protections are predicated on the protection of property rights. The homeless lack conventional property. This constrains the limits of the judicial intervention and remains the most challenging test for legal advocates in their quest to guarantee rights for homeless people.[5]

## The Denial of Constitutional Rights to Homeless People

Without identifiable property, homeless people have been denied access to nearly every fundamental human right guaranteed by the United States Constitution in different parts of the United States. Their lack of a permanent address rendered them ineligible for receipt of public assistance benefits and food stamps. They were disenfranchised for the same reason. Use of public spaces such as parks, benches, and lavatories was denied. Few legal guarantees of minimal food and shelter existed in any jurisdiction. The most tragic denial of rights was to be found in domestic law. Once families became homeless, public welfare departments frequently took children away from their parents. First amendment protections of free speech were denied as municipalities sought to curtail begging. Freedom of movement, so basic to values of human freedom, has been denied through antihomeless ordinances prohibiting vagrancy and loitering, as well as homeless arrest campaigns.[6]

Social welfare historians have noted the exact parallels between contemporary antihomeless laws and the Elizabethan Poor Laws of sixteenth-century England. More than 200 statutes punishing vagrancy existed in England between the seventeenth century and the beginning of the twentieth century. These laws, directed at vagrants, beggars, and transients displaced after the demise of feudalism, increased proportionately with the number of displaced persons.[7]

In Colonial America, similar sanctions followed the British model and continued during the eighteenth and nineteenth centuries. Colonial governments applied these laws to involuntary servants. They authorized punishment for rogues and idle people as a mechanism for supplying the labor needs of the colonies. The Articles of Confederation excluded paupers from the right to enter and exit any state and from other privileges of immunity granted to other citizens.[8] The Great Depression in the United States brought the first official challenges to efforts to exclude the itinerant poor.

This wholesale assault on constitutional protection and human rights has formed the central thrust for the homeless movement. Activists ranging from service providers, politicians, academics, and lawyers have rallied around the inequities that accompany homelessness. The result has been a wide ranging docket of case law and litigation arguing to reinstate personal rights to homeless people. Over 1000 reported decisions involving homelessness have been delivered since 1980.[9] The basic intent of every lawsuit has been to build a foundation of legal guarantees that the condition of homelessness is neither a civil nor a criminal offense. The central focus of all litigation on homeless issues has been on government responsibility for creating and alleviating the conditions that characterize homelessness.

A nationwide cohort of lawyers in private practice or public interest legal agencies, along with larger advocacy organizations like the National Law Center on Homelessness and Poverty, the Western Center on Law and Poverty, the American Civil Liberties Union, and the National Coalition for the Homeless, has steadily and vigilantly brought class-based lawsuits to the courts to restore fundamental rights to homeless people. Despite the enormity of legal activity, most lawsuits have focused on three problems: challenges to the availability and adequacy of public assistance, the right to keep a family together, and the right to shelter.[10] Other litigation, much of which is pending in the courts, has challenged the burgeoning antihomeless ordinances and municipal codes prohibiting encampments, sleeping in public places, panhandling, loitering, and vagrancy.

Lawyers, and judges, have based much of their arguments upholding homeless people's rights to public assistance, family preservation, and shelter on Article I, Section 8 of the United States Constitution that gives the federal government the power to "provide for the general welfare."[11] Historically, the federal government did not honor this provision until the Supreme Court ruled that the protective mantle of economic insurances of the Social Security Act, passed in 1935, was constitutional and that Congress had the power to enact the law.[12]

A wider range of class-based lawsuits upholding the rights of homeless people does not readily lend itself to classification. These lawsuits have focused on such disparate issues as the right to beg, to gather in public places, to vote, and to travel freely, freedom from search and seizure of property, children's rights to attend school, the right to sleep outdoors and even the right to gather uneaten food from trash collections.

The critical arguments in most cases have rested on the exercise of fundamental civil rights under the Equal Protection Clause of the Fourteenth Amendment, which guarantees all persons equality and due process under the law. Contemporary equal protection analysis focuses on the fit between government actions that discriminate against individuals and the purposes such actions are intended to follow.[13] By demonstrating that local, state and federal actions discriminated against homeless people as a class, legal advocates have identified homeless people as a "suspect" classification under the Equal Protection Clause. To determine whether a law or government action violates the guarantee of equal protection, it is necessary to determine whether the law or action discriminates against a suspect, or quasisuspect, class of people, or impinges on the exercise of a fundamental or important right. If a suspect class, or a fundamental right is involved, the law or action will be subject to strict scrutiny.

Court decisions have classified the following population statuses as suspect and, therefore, subject to protective scrutiny: race and national origin, legitimacy, and alienage. Many homeless people fall into one or more of these suspect classifications, so there has been little conflict in applying equal protections to them.[14]

A further provision of the Equal Protection Clause is that a right must be found in the Constitution to be considered a fundamental right. Such a right need not be explicitly stated in the Constitution. It may be implied. For example, the Equal Protection Clause was applied to those states that had issued 1-year residency requirements for receipt of Aid to Families with Dependent Children (AFDC). The Court found that the concepts of personal liberty require that all citizens be free to travel and that rules or regulations that restrict such movement are unconstitutional.[15]

Homeless arrest campaigns for sleeping in public places and encampments have been challenged under the Eighth Amendment to the Constitution. These challenges have claimed that arrests for public inebriation, narcotics use without the possession of same, and other forms of involuntary conduct constitute cruel and unusual punishment. Other legal challenges have been based upon the right to freedom of speech, freedom to travel, due process, and equal protection.[16]

Advocates challenging antihomeless laws in the courts have tended to rely on rights that are explicitly, or implicitly, found in the Constitution because these are identified as fundamental rights. Many government antihomeless laws and actions that have impinged upon important but not fundamental rights have been more difficult to defend. Indeed, many have gone unchallenged because of this legal distinction. Among those important nonfundamental rights are health care, employment, the means to support one's children, and the right to live where one chooses.

Despite this distinction, the courts have ruled that certain important nonfundamental rights may be sustained if they are consistent with a legitimate government purpose. Access to public education is one example of an important right. *Plyler v. Doe* stated,

> Public education is not a right granted to individuals by the Constitution.
> But neither is it merely some governmental benefit indistinguishable from

other forms of welfare legislation. . . . The American people have always regarded education and the acquisition of knowledge as matters of supreme importance.[17]

Homeless legal advocates have drawn upon this consideration of important rights in arguing to keep homeless children enrolled in school.

Any respectable analysis of civil rights must be founded on a theory of law and justice. It is clear that advocates who have attempted to protect and preserve the civil rights of homeless people have relied on John Rawls's persuasive theory of justice. This theory presupposes not only that people have rights but that one right among all is fundamental. This right is a clear conception of the right to equality, the right to equal concern and respect. This conception of equality has been used to interpret the Equal Protection Amendment of the United States Constitution in ruling against discriminatory laws and practices directed at numerous minority groups in the nation.[18]

Until the root causes of homelessness in the nation are addressed through long-term solutions, efforts to assure that homelessness cannot be criminalized out of existence remain central responses to the problem. Indeed, food and shelter, the proverbial "three hots and a cot," may be less critical, despite Maslow's identification of "a hierarchy of needs."[19]

## The Plan of the Book

This book surveys court challenges to antihomeless laws, ordinances, and other actions such as homeless sweeps and arrest campaigns that have occurred across the nation. It identifies court rulings that have sought to protect the civil and constitutional rights of homeless people and presents an analysis of the issues involved in each case. In some instances, lawyers have interpreted existing laws and regulations relevant to homeless persons without litigation. The book identifies these as well.

Two parts divide the book. The first reviews litigation that has either restored or guaranteed homeless persons their citizenship entitlements to human services, housing and shelter, income, child welfare, education, health care, psychiatric treatment and counseling services, and voting. The second part reviews a growing body of litigation attempting to reverse the current national trend to criminalize homeless people by prohibiting them from using public spaces or soliciting charity.

Because many advocates have attempted to challenge four types of antihomeless actions, Part II emphasizes these efforts. They are anti-panhandling codes, antisleeping codes, antiloitering codes, and vagrancy codes.[20]

Chapter 1 presents a summary analysis of the use of the courts for legislation of social policy, highlighting the history of such advocacy law, as well as the more recent history of homeless advocacy law. Included in the chapter is an explanation and description of the structure of the United States judicial system. It is important to be reminded that the political principle of the separation of powers embedded in the United States system of government restricts the application of judicial law to instances where the legislature takes no action.

Succeeding chapters identify the docket of court decisions affirming the rights of homeless people. These chapters also attempt to analyze the policy issues and compromises involved in every case.

Each chapter begins with an explication of the central policy issues that affect homeless people in the relevant service sector. The review of the policy issues related to homelessness serves as a reminder that the personal and public problems of homeless people inevitably reflect failures in every American social policy sector. These sections of the book offer students and teachers of general social policy analysis an opportunity to apply their study to a deeper understanding of contemporary homelessness issues.

The chapters proceed to describe and analyze the litigation in an effort to illustrate successful homeless advocacy arguments.

The final chapter explores issues related to the implementation of legal decisions and judicial policy making. The translation of law into action remains a major focus of scholarly research. It is interesting to note that most of this research has emanated from political and social scientists rather than legal scholars.[21] In the field of social welfare, policy implementation studies have focused far more on legislative implementation than any other source of law. This chapter will add a new dimension to considerations of social policy implementation.

Every legal decision and strategy described in this book has been presented in a style that makes it possible for nonlawyers to understand and apply legal creativity. The use of legal terminology has been carefully explained and limited. Readers may wish to consult a legal dictionary, or even a general one, if any terms are confusing. It will be useful to all policy practitioners, homeless advocates, organizations, citizens groups, and service providers. As individuals and community groups gather across the United States in efforts to "do something about the homeless," they increasingly turn to legal experts for guidance on strategy and tactics.

Students of social work and related professions, as well as law students engaged in the study of law and social policy, will find this book a useful case study of the application of judicial law to social problems. It will extend their understanding of how the legal and human service professions interact in their mutual goals of ensuring equal protection and rights under the law.

This book is intended for use in the seemingly endless struggle to respond to homelessness and to intelligently challenge the growing numbers of business people, homeowners, and general citizens who are unsympathetic to homeless people and are attempting to legislate homeless people out of their backyards.

People who work directly with homeless people in any capacity will also find the explication of the rights of homeless persons in this book helpful. Information and referral services are a fundamental part of any homeless service provider's responsibilities, whatever their job classification. Knowledge of the rights of homeless persons under the law is as useful as any resource directory, or personal file of referral sources to workers.

The book does not attempt to emulate legal scholarship. Its intent is twofold: (1) to identify laws, potential legal positions and strategies that can help advocates better understand areas and theories of law in their efforts to challenge the onslaught of antihomeless activity across the nation; (2) and, to demonstrate how the interaction of law and social policy practice advances entitlement, equity, and empowerment goals.

Legal advocacy has made a substantial contribution to the lives of homeless people. However, all legal advocates allege that they are part of the larger social movement on behalf homeless people. Litigators have consistently built "teams" among those concerned with homelessness that have raised issues and educated both the public and individual decision makers.[22]

Social workers have played prominent roles on these teams. They have contributed their knowledge of the laws and policies governing social services, and the organizational and institutional structures of social service delivery systems to the process of developing the central arguments and strategies of legal briefs. Impact litigation and policy advocacy complement community organizing, media work, administrative and legislative advocacy, and direct service.

Legal advocates also bemoan the fact that far too few homeless people have emerged as activists in this movement. All participants in the homeless movement will gain important knowledge and skills by having access to legal positions and strategies that have ameliorated the struggles of homeless people. They will also gain added appreciation for the potential of the law as a powerful instrument for social and institutional change in the face of resistance by legislative and political forces.

One final caveat is necessary for effective use of this book. The state of the law protecting homeless people is inevitably in flux. Many challenges to antihomeless ordinances are pending. These cases are subject to continuous litigation because cities, states, and federal agencies are simply not addressing the root causes of homelessness. Moreover, court decisions are subject to challenges in their own jurisdictions, as well as higher courts. It is, therefore, impossible to identify a fixed body of law on the subject. It is, however, more possible to identify the many cases protecting homeless people that have been decided by the courts and to analyze the issues involved in these court actions.

## Notes and References

1.  *Goldberg v. Kelly* Supreme Court of the United States (U.S., Jan. 10, 1969).

2.  Jansson defines policy practice as "efforts to influence the development, enactment, implementation, or assessment of social policies," Bruce S. Jansson, *Social Policy: From Theory to Policy Practice*, 2nd ed. (Pacific Grove, CA: Brooks/Cole, 1994), 8.

3.  John McCarthy and Mayer Zald, "Resource Mobilization and Social Movements: A Partial Theory," *American Journal of Sociology* 82(6):1212–1241. Charles Tilley, *From Mobilization to Revolution* (Reading, MA: Addison-Wesley, 1978).

4.  *Callahan et al.* v. *Carey et al.*, No. 42582/79. Supreme Court of the State of New York.

5.  John Blau, *The Visible Poor: Homelessness in the United States* (New York: Oxford University Press, 1992), 107.

6.  Harry Simon, "Towns without Pity: A Constitutional and Historical Analysis of Official Efforts to Drive Homeless Persons from American Cities," *Tulane Law Review*, 66(4):649–651 (March, 1992).

7.  Sidney Webb and Beatrice Webb, *English Local Government: English Poor Law History*, 350 n. 1 (1927); Harry Simon, "Towns without Pity: A Constitutional and Historical Analysis of Official Efforts to Drive Homeless Persons from American Cities," *Tulane Law Review*, 66:(4)637–640 (March, 1992).

8.  Ronald Takaki, *A Different Mirror: A History of Multicultural America* (Boston: Little, Brown, 1993), 54.

9.  National Housing Law Project, *Annotated Bibliography of Selected Cases and Other Material Involving Homelessness*, National Clearinghouse for Legal Services, Inc., 407 South Dearborn Street, Suite 400, Chicago, Illinois 60605 (No. 45, 055C0 Working Draft, September 1992), unpublished manuscript.

10.  Blau, 103.

11.  U.S. Constitution, Article I, Section 8; for a full discussion of the general welfare provision see Andrea Saltzman and Kathleen Proch, *Law in Social Work Practice* (Chicago: Nelson-Hall, 1990), 106–121.

12.  *Halvering v. Davis*, 301 U.S. 619 (1972).

13. Simon, "Towns without Pity," 664.

14. The term "suspect" refers not to people but to political and social actions that tend to be discriminatory. Saltzman and Proch, *Law in Social Work Practice*, 112–119.

15. *Shapiro v. Thompson*, 394 U.S. 618 (1969).

16. *Robinson v. California*, 370 U.S. 660, 666 (1962); *Powell v. Texas* 392 U.S. 514 (1969).

17. *Plyler v. Doe*, 457 U.S. 202 (1982).

18. Ronald Dworkin, *Taking Rights Seriously* (Cambridge, MA: Harvard University Press, 1977), xii.

19. Abraham Maslow, *Motivation and Personality* (New York: Harper & Row, 1954). Maslow delineated five categories of needs: (1) physiology/ecology, (2) safety/security, (3) affect/belonging, (4) esteem/identity, and (5) self-actualization. Some hold that Maslow's hierarchy is additive in that one need has to be satisfied before another need can be worked on.

20. National Law Center on Homelessness and Poverty, *Go Directly to Jail: A Report Analyzing Anti-Homeless Ordinances* (Washington, D.C., December 1991), 3.

21. Harry P. Stumpf, *American Judicial Politics* (New York: Harcourt, Brace Jovanovich, 1988), 454.

22. Judge Robert C. Coates, *A Street Is Not a Home: Solving America's Homeless Dilemma* (Buffalo: Prometheus Books, 1990), 286.

# THE ROLE OF THE COURTS IN
# FORMULATING SOCIAL POLICY

## The Structure of the Legal System

The legal system is comprised of the numerous governmental entities that produce laws. The American legal system encompasses administrative, legislative, and judicial law. All three are produced, administered, and enforced by different branches of the government. Social policy may be formulated by administrators, legislators, and judges.

Legislative law is produced by the federal, state, and local elected legislative bodies throughout the nation: the U.S. Congress, state legislatures, and county and city governing bodies. All of these laws are codified into administrative law that is written by the bureaus and agencies that are charged with promulgating regulations. The Department of Health and Human Services, for example, is responsible for promulgating all regulations governing health and human service laws enacted by the Congress and the President.[1] Similarly, the Department of Housing and Urban Development regulates housing legislation. Each state and local governing body has a corollary system for administrative rule making.

Constitutions are general documents that provide the framework for all laws and government procedures. Although constitutions are generally drafted by separate conventions, they are classified as legislative law because they must be ratified by a legislative body.

Judicial law is produced in two ways. Courts, in the process of resolving disputes, may determine the meaning and scope of a constitutional provision, statute, regulation, or any other form of law. This process of interpreting existing laws is defined as *construction*. When courts engage in construction, they, in effect, formulate laws and policies.

Courts also make laws when confronted by a dispute that involves a unique problem or fact that is not addressed by any existing constitutional provision, legislation, or regulation. Over the years, court decisions on such matters have evolved into a large body of law on a wide range of subjects such as professional malpractice and liability for injury. Judicial law that emanates in this way is referred to as common law.

Judicial decisions influence both the disputing parties and those who follow. Judicial decisions are held to be binding in subsequent cases when they formulate a general principle necessary to the decision of the issue between the litigants. Nevertheless, many judges derive widely diverging conclusions on the same or related issues, so that case law continually evolves.[2]

Responsibility for the enforcement of legislative, administrative, and judicial law rests with the Department of Justice. The Department may file legal actions in the courts, or employ more aggressive strategies in efforts to enforce the law.

## Social Change and the Courts

There are strict limits on the court's authority to make law. The role of the courts, and their limitations on political activity, has been the subject of major debate since the establishment of the American nation. Prevailing wisdom about courts and judges is capsulized by the term "judicial restraint," which rejects judicial intervention without strictly construed authority. It emphasizes democracy, the rule of law, and decision making driven by legal rather than political methods. Judges are charged with making legal rather than political decisions.

This principle was exemplified by the controversy surrounding President Franklin Delano Roosevelt's appointments to the United States Supreme Court. Many landmark court decisions such as *Brown v. the Board of Education*, desegregating public schools, and *Roe v. Wade*, legalizing abortion via a woman's right to privacy, have stimulated heated clashes among political and legal scholars about the legitimacy of the court's jurisdiction. Public acceptance of government by judiciary does not allow the courts the scope of action available to a legislative majority. Charles Houston, the pioneer of applying the law as "social engineering," taught and inspired a generation of civil rights lawyers to exercise the strategy of seeking outcomes that a democratic majority will not legislate for itself, but that judges will tolerate as constitutional protections.[3]

For most of the past 30 years, the Court has adopted a political role in determining controversial issues like abortion and the death penalty. Earlier courts, and more recently the conservative Court appointed under Presidents Reagan and Bush, have been predisposed to decide technical legal questions, rather than moral dilemmas.[4] However, even the current conservative justices have not practiced judicial restraint. They have actively used the Supreme Court to invalidate legislation to eliminate environmental or safety restrictions on business, or to stop government intrusions into the economy and protect personal property rights. Conservative justices have tended to invalidate legislation when the civil rights issue has been campaign finance reform, bias-motivated crime, or affirmative action. Free speech rights have been seriously undercut, and a person can be executed without a hearing even though there is credible new proof of innocence, if the proof is not discovered soon enough after the trial.

The historic record reveals that judicial activism to protect individual rights and personal freedom, usually favored by people with a liberal political persuasion, was prevalent in only two periods, from 1937 to 1944 and from 1961 to 1973. But judicial activism in favor of other goals has been present since 1803 when Chief Justice John Marshall introduced judicial review, which is not mentioned in the Constitution. Whether dominated by conservatives or liberals, the Supreme Court plays a major role in American politics and culture. The central issue is no longer whether judicial activism is appropriate, but on what issues and in favor of which groups or segments of society it will be selectively employed.[5]

Major differences exist between the process and rights granted to the judiciary, legislature, and administration. Courts, unlike administrative agencies and legislative bodies, can never make laws. They may interpret law only when they are in the course of resolving a dispute that is brought before them for deliberation. Administrators and legislators can make decisions based upon their values and beliefs about what is right and wrong. They may also make laws on the basis of a whim, in response to interest groups, political expediency, and public opinion. Courts may make law only on the basis of what is known as "common law reasoning." This is a process of reasoning by analogy that occurs when a court searches for existing case law with facts that are analogous to the case being presented. This is known as "precedent," and judges are required to follow precedent in deciding cases before them.

Finally, courts are limited in the kinds of decisions they are authorized to make. They cannot establish social programs. They cannot appropriate money. They cannot mandate regulatory programs such as licensing laws. They cannot mandate what must be done. They can determine that certain actions are done improperly and what the consequences are when they decide that such actions are inconsistent with a law. However, they cannot direct what proper action should be taken.

In spite of these limitations, the courts can and do wield a powerful influence on other law making bodies. For example, the court decisions that local or state governments have an obligation to provide shelter for homeless people have compelled governing bodies and administrative agencies to appropriate money and establish shelter programs.

The broadest influence of the courts lies in their authority to interpret the Constitution. A precedent, like a regulation, may be overruled by legislation, unless it interprets the Constitution. The courts are the only legal entity that is granted this interpretive authority.

## The Court Hierarchy

The American court system is federal with more than 50 state court systems. These are organized hierarchically with "trial" courts and "appellate courts" in each system. Each has distinct functions.

Trial courts resolve disputes that are brought before them in a "case" or a "suit." Nearly all cases begin in a trial court. Trial courts never initiate cases. They decide only cases that are brought before them by persons who have a real interest in the case.

Federal trial courts may resolve disputes only when the parties are from different states, or, more important, where federal government jurisdiction is involved. State trial courts usually have subject jurisdiction over every kind of case.

Appellate courts are used when parties believe that a trial court made an erroneous decision. Appealing parties generally cannot question the facts decided by a trial court. They can argue that the trial court made a legal error in the way it decided the facts or applied the law. In both the federal and in most state systems, there are two levels of appellate courts: a "court of appeals," which is an intermediate court, and a "supreme court," which is the court of last resort. A court of appeals must hear all cases that are brought before it, whereas a supreme court has discretion to accept or refuse a case. This decision must be based upon the supreme court's determination concerning the importance of a case, not whether it disagrees with the lower court's decision.

Because the state and federal courts systems are parallel, cases do not go back and forth from one system to another. Parties may never appeal from a state trial court to a federal appeals court. However, if a party is not satisfied with the decision of a state supreme court, he or she may seek review in the United States Supreme Court, but only if the case involves a federal question. Most cases are filed, and remain, in state court systems.

The term "parties" refers to all petitioners and respondents in court pleadings. This excludes all other participants: the judge, the jury, and the attorneys. Participants may be individuals, government entities, private associations, or corporations. In some cases, commonly known as "class actions" or "representative suits," one or more named parties act as representatives of unnamed parties who are similarly situated to the named parties. If the named parties prevail in their suit, the unnamed parties also prevail. If they lose, the unnamed parties also lose and may never be able to bring suit on their own behalf.

In some class-action suits, the named party may have a smaller stake in the outcome of a hearing but is identified as the named party for technical reasons. In such a case, the party who has the larger stake is named as the "real party in interest." For example, child support payment cases may be brought against a parent, but the child is the "real party in interest."

People who have a legitimate and direct interest in a case may not be named as the party of interest, but they may be given "party" status by the court, or a statute. For example, the biological father in an adoption case is not usually named as a party, but is granted party status.

All parties, named or granted party status, must be served with all pleadings and other important documents, must be notified of all hearings, and have a right to be heard at all hearings. Unnamed class members may also be entitled to notice and to be heard.[6]

The basic principle of the court system is that when government is working properly, the executive and legislative branches pass laws that address social problems. Only when such leadership is found lacking and problems mount, do social needs get addressed in the courts. Ironically, it is this insulation of the courts from politics that gives it the power to act. Powerful conservative forces that prevent the legislatures from responding to social problems do not have the same access to the courts. Judges, who hold office longer than legislators, are more impervious to political pressures. They also carry more legitimacy and are less subject to criticism by conservative political forces.

## Limitiations of Legal Advocacy

Nevertheless, apparent limitations persist in any effort to use litigation as an advocacy tool. The most obvious are the limited legal service resources needed to investigate and try cases. Without the public resource of legal services, reliance on *pro bono* attorneys is random and unreliable. Growing judicial conservatism may make all future litigation pointless. The complexity of the court system means that all litigation is lengthy. For homeless people, the loss of time during their crisis may spell the loss of life. Finally, litigation about social problems seeks relief

as institutional reform, rather than individual damages. Findings granting the right to shelter, income, or schools will not specify standards
or levels of benefits. These remain the purview of administrators and
legislators.

Ethical and political tensions in advocacy for disadvantaged people
are ever present. The act of representing others may produce a domination in which lawyers and organizers dictate what others need, thereby
reproducing subordination of poor clients. This concern of critical legal
studies scholars is offset by the question of what lawyers who wish to
fight economic and social injustice can do besides resort to the courts.
When movements are relatively weak and constituents have little or no
power, appeals to constitutional protections offer brighter prospects for
results than other strategies.

The intrinsic tension underlying social need and scarce resources in
faltering economies also limits the outcomes of advocacy. On the other
hand, advocacy on many fronts is more necessary when governments
and private citizens reduce benefits and entitlements.

Despite these limitations, litigation has proven to be a uniquely effective tool in promoting the rights of homeless people. Furthermore, the
homeless have been, and probably will continue to be, an ineffective
political constituency. This renders legal channels the best available
method to address the problem.[7]

### History of Advocacy Law

Homeless advocates are continuing a tradition that dates back to the
progressive-era lawyers and, before that, the Legal Aid Society (LAS).
LAS was formed in 1876 to provide free legal assistance to poor immigrants. Most cases involved employers who refused to pay agreed upon
wages. LAS lawyers consistently preferred to settle all cases out of court
because this was cheaper and less time consuming than going to trial.
The progressive-era lawyers served the labor and women's reform
movements by defending state labor and public health laws from court
challenges. These lawyers, the most famous being Louis Brandeis,
worked closely with progressive reformers who frequently conducted
the research necessary for writing briefs. Many of these reformers were
the settlement house workers who represent the vanguard of social
work advocacy in the United States.

During the 1930s, 1940s, and 1950s, the left-wing Lawyer's Guild and
civil rights lawyers, most notably the NAACP Legal Defense and Educational Fund, kept the tradition of advocacy law alive. Charles Hamilton

Houston, charged with rebuilding Howard University Law School in the early 1930s, proclaimed the objective of training "social engineers." The impressive body of civil rights law that evolved during these decades was largely built by the professional legal cadre that Houston taught and inspired. These lawyers influenced the opinion that civil rights law could form the legal basis for welfare entitlements.

The earliest welfare rights advocates, led by the originator of welfare rights law Edward Sparer, J.D., argued that poor people could be considered a class requiring federal judicial protection from unequal treatment by states and localities. As director of Mobilization for Youth, Sparer rejected the strategy of "maximum feasible participation of the poor" representation through neighborhood law offices opting, instead, for a centralized independent legal staff free to select cases on the basis of long-term strategy and major social implications. This concept evolved into the establishment of the federally funded Community Legal Services Corporation.

Initially, Sparer considered a two-tier model of legal service delivery combining day-to-day advocacy for individual clients with strategic litigation. In this model neighborhood lawyers and social workers would provide routine legal services, and impact litigation would be handled by specialists working with community-based organizations. He realized, however, that neighborhood law offices were not equipped to concentrate on the strategic planning he envisioned for litigation that involved larger class actions. Inundated with hundreds of clients whose problems required individual representation, it was necessary to develop a separate organization to formulate and implement comprehensive legal strategies.

To implement this, he founded the Center on Social Welfare Policy and Law at the Columbia University School of Social Work after Columbia Law School rejected his idea. At the new Center, Sparer and Richard Cloward integrated the activities of lawyers and social workers serving the poor. They focused on welfare litigation for the growing poverty law movement, a strategy designed to bring the confusing system of federal and state funding and administration created by the Social Security Act of 1935 under the scrutiny of federal law. When Sparer joined the faculty of the University of Pennsylvania Law School, he founded a similar law and social policy program there with Sylvia Law, the Health Law Project.

The welfare rights lawyers of the 1960s understood that advocacy law makes an impact only when it is accompanied by a social movement. The gains made in the courts on behalf of welfare recipients could not have been achieved without the political organizing strategies engaged in by the National Welfare Rights Organization and its local affiliates.

Lawyers, welfare rights organizers, and many social workers convinced recipients that their poverty was a matter of injustice and a civil rights issue rather than an individual character flaw or failing.

The combined efforts of the welfare rights lawyers and the welfare rights organizations concentrated on two fronts: one was the welfare system and the other was the courts. By adopting a "crisis strategy" they organized to flood the welfare system with special grants requests and, if they were denied, "fair hearing" requests. Their hope was to overburden the administration of public welfare as a way of bringing pressure for a reform that would raise the standard grant and thus reduce the need for special grants.

In the courts, several Supreme Court decisions resulted in major triumphs. Lawyers in the South challenged common practices that expelled women from the welfare rolls during seasons when low wage workers were needed, and ending welfare grants when women received male visitors by showing that these practices were disproportionately used against African Americans. In 1968, Southern welfare lawyers won their first major Supreme Court decision in *King v. Smith*, which held that such procedures violated the Social Security Act. In the North, the first major legal victory came 1 year later in the *Shapiro v. Thompson* ruling that welfare recipients are entitled to hearings before their benefits are cut or reduced. This case inspired Charles Reich's notion that a welfare benefit should be considered property, like a house, automobile, bank account, or license, and was entitled to the same legal protections against search and seizure without due process. This case was followed by "Operation Nevada," in which dozens of welfare rights organizers, lawyers, and law students worked to force Nevada to rescind welfare benefit cutoffs. They used a range of tactics including demonstrations, fair hearings, and teach-ins on welfare rights.

The gains made by welfare lawyers derived from *procedural* due process arguments. The courts were holding that once a benefit had been granted, a recipient had a right not to have it taken away arbitrarily or inequitably. At the peak of the welfare reform movement, welfare lawyers were beginning to press *substantive* due process claims to get the courts to rule that a minimum level of economic security was a right on its own merits. However, they met with no success on this issue. They could not persuade the Supreme Court that limiting the maximum AFDC benefit per family discriminated against children in large families. Nor could they persuade the Court that low AFDC benefits, compared to old-age benefits, constituted racial discrimination because of the disproportionate number of minority families who relied on AFDC.

By the early 1970s, the political climate turned conservative. The National Welfare Rights Organization declined in size and energy; politicians launched an antiwelfare and antitax backlash, and President Nixon appointed more conservative judges to the Supreme Court and other courts in the federal judiciary system. It is interesting to note that the changes in the welfare system advocated in the 1990s, known as "welfare reform," were introduced by Senator Daniel Patrick Moynihan under the Nixon Administration.

Advocacy law remained stagnant as successive Presidential administrations gradually dismantled the Community Legal Services Corporation, which saw its final demise under Ronald Reagan. The next discernible wave of welfare law advocacy emerged in the beginning of the 1980s as advocates turned their attention to the rights of growing legions of homeless people.[8]

## Use of the Legal System by Homeless Advocates

Homeless advocates have turned to the courts to fill the political vacuum created by homelessness. When it became apparent that federal, state, and local governments were not addressing the growing problem of homelessness across the United States, advocates turned to the courts where, by default, many serious grievances have been redressed. Paralleling the growth of homelessness, litigation about homelessness on dockets across the United States has grown dramatically.

The federal legal system has been the least open to homeless litigation. The U.S. Supreme Court has never acknowledged the existence of a "right to shelter." In *Lindsey v. Normet* (1972) the Supreme Court stated that the Constitution cannot provide remedies for every type of social and economic problem.[9] This is the basis for the federal government's refusal to specify a national standard of adequate benefit for AFDC recipients.[10]

Perhaps even more central to understanding the reluctance of federal courts to rule on homeless rights is the fact that most constitutional protections are based on property rights. The very condition of homelessness means that there is no property ownership, even though advocates define personal possessions and effects, including clothing and shopping carts, as property.

These constraints on the federal courts, along with a growing reluctance of federal court judges appointed by conservative Republican presidents to intervene on behalf of the poor and minorities, led public interest lawyers to turn away from federal courts to the state level during the 1970s. Moreover, the U.S. Supreme Court began to articulate a deference to states' rights, leaving the state courts open to class-based litigation on behalf of people affected by social problems. Finally, state courts have presented a more direct jurisdiction because litigation has been introduced on behalf of homeless residents in the states. Federal courts restrict their jurisdiction to issues between states.

Legal advocates have relied on class-action, or impact litigation, naming one or more parties as representatives of cohorts of homeless people. They have based most of their arguments on behalf of homeless people on the Equal Protection Clause of the Fourteenth Amendment identifying them as a "suspect," and therefore protected, class. Under the Equal Protection Clause, courts must put government to the test of justifying group-based distinctions by demonstrating that discrimination is rationally related to a legitimate government function. To implement equal protection, the courts have specified certain populations as "suspect" based upon historical patterns of discrimination.

Homeless litigators have identified their clients as being in one, or more, of the "suspect" classifications identified under the Equal Protection Clause. Lawyers have also identified homeless people as a new "suspect" classification entitled to equal protection of fundamental Constitutional rights.

Other cases have drawn on previous court rulings that important but nonfundamental rights pertain to homeless clients.[11] No clear pattern exists relating to which state courts have been used for litigation. Decisions have been handed down from trial courts, as well as appellate courts. Lawyers, and their clients, have a clear interest in appearing before trial courts and winning their cases at that level. This saves time, money, and other valuable resources.

An early analysis of approaches to litigation by homeless advocates explained that

> Homeless advocacy has occurred on two levels: 1) service cases, and, 2) impact litigation. In service cases lawyers may represent individuals with individual problems. However, if an entire system refuses to provide legally mandated assistance, any amount of individual advocacy will be in vain. In response, Legal Aid and public interest attorneys have filed legal challenges to system-wide denials of rights to the homeless. This latter is called impact litigation.[12]

One strategy worth noting is the reliance of lawyers on other homeless advocates, social policy practitioners, and experts, as well as homeless people, in developing their briefs. Lawyers regularly note that their efforts in the courts have been part of the wider homeless movement. These collaborative efforts provided more than material for legal briefs. They brought a collective energy to each case that was tried in the courts, the momentum of which stimulated media interest and political pressure. They acted as one part of a broader movement to protect the rights of homeless people, to serve them and to challenge the nationwide avalanche of antihomeless statutes, ordinances, and provisions.

Another key strategy employed by homeless litigators has been the development of a detailed knowledge and sensitivity to the local welfare, shelter, and health systems designated to help the indigent in every state. With the help of direct line public welfare workers as well as sophisticated social policy analysts, they have mastered the political and institutional contexts of the judicial jurisdictions in which they have brought court actions.

They have also cultivated the media in efforts to gain public support for their clients. Conversely, they have sought to learn about the realities of life on the streets to bring evidence such as affidavits, exhibits, and testimony to the courts.

Homeless litigation in the United States followed World War II when vagrancy and loitering laws became the object of criticism. During the 1960s and early 1970s numerous state and federal decisions overturned loitering and vagrancy laws as discrimination against the poor. They also used the grounds that they punished status or condition, which amounted to cruel or unusual punishment.[13]

Litigators have applied several legal techniques and theories. Case decisions have challenged bureaucratic, or administrative, interpretations of state constitutions and statutes that cause harm and deny homeless people certain rights, in spite of the intent of the laws to help people. These challenges have been in the form of extraordinary writs, requests for injunctive relief, or mandamus. They have sought prohibitory injunctions refraining actions, as well as mandatory injunctions compelling action. A writ of mandamus is a legal remedy commanding a government official to perform a duty imposed by law.[14] In litigation for the homeless, a mandatory injunction or a writ of mandamus can order governments to comply with their legal duties, but only an injunction can provide detailed specifications about what an action should entail.

Lawyers challenging governmental activities can rely on extraordinary writs. Plaintiffs seeking an injunction must establish four elements: (1) a violation of a clear legal right, or imminent threat of same, (2) threat of irreparable injury, (3) no adequate legal remedy, and (4) a balance of equities in his or her favor. Judges may deny injunctive relief if it is not in the public interest. Homeless people frequently question their legal rights and experience threats against their rights, as well as injury. Their lawyers have relied on establishing that their homeless clients have encountered these four elements.[15]

In 1972, *Papachristou v. City of Jacksonville*, tried in the United States

Supreme Court, Jackonsville's vagrancy ordinance was overturned on due process grounds. In this action, eight people convicted under Jacksonsville's vagrancy ordinance challenged the law. The State of Florida Supreme Court unanimously stated that the ordinance was vague and, therefore, failed to give fair notice of prohibited conduct. This indefiniteness encouraged arbitrary arrests and convictions. Recalling the history of antivagrancy laws, the Court condemned them as "archaic classifications." The Court also noted that Jacksonsville's ordinance criminalized innocent activities such as wandering and strolling. The landmark decision warned that all vagrancy laws were aimed against poor and undesirable people, thus applying the rule of law unevenly.

At the higher level, the United States Supreme Court struck down a California loitering statute that punished failure by any person wandering the street to produce credible identification when requested to do so by a police officer. The Supreme Court held that this statute was too vague. This decision upheld the *Papachristou* decision.[16]

However, the clear and apparent launching of homeless litigation as part of a social movement strategy to obtain rights for homeless people is marked by *Callahan v. Carey* filed in New York by Robert M. Hayes in October 1979 citing the need for emergency relief for Robert Callahan and two other plaintiffs. Callahan was a 54-year-old resident of New York City who was solely dependent on the Men's Shelter for lodging. According to the brief, he had virtually no income or property and was unable to provide for himself. However, he was not before the court on a disorderly conduct charge and this made his case unique among poor and itinerant people who entered the justice system.

The Callahan case did not reach trial until January 1981 and the final judgment was entered in August 1981 in the form of a Consent Decree. This now famous decree set forth the terms and conditions under which required shelter was to be offered to homeless men. The city later agreed to include homeless women in the decree. The decree stipulated decent bedding, adequate supervision and security, minimal staffing levels, requirements for storage of clients' belongings, and regular monitoring by city compliance officers and outside observers.[17]

The drama and horror of the large New York City shelters and armories demonstrate how the Callahan Consent Decree was implemented. New York City met its obligation to provide shelter. It has failed to meet the standards and spent the better part of 5 years challenging the Consent Decree. Nevertheless, the City continues to recognize its obligation to provide shelter and is currently attempting to replace its decrepit shelter system with permanent housing for homeless people.

The New York case foreshadowed many class action lawsuits on behalf of homeless people in municipalities across the United States. These legal actions have covered the wide range of indignities heaped on homeless men, women, and children. Many have resulted in victories. Other cases, pending before the courts, have served to stall implementation of antihomeless laws pending court decisions. For example, the City of Santa Monica enacted an antiencampment law in 1992. It could not enforce this law because of an outstanding lawsuit challenging its constitutionality. When the law was found to be unconstitutional, the City of Santa Monica was forced to comply with the terms of the decision, including the establishment of a viable alternative to the camps.

In such instances, the lengthiness of court actions has proven to be a political tactic, intended or otherwise, allowing homeless people and their advocates opportunities to organize against antihomeless laws and policies.

Most lawsuits brought on behalf of homeless people can be categorized by litigation objectives. Much litigation has sought to break down barriers to assistance. Other actions have focused on the right to shelter. The adequacy of income maintenance has been another legal concern. The rights to vote, beg, sleep, and sit in public parks have become an increasing subject of litigation as local governments engage in a trend to banish the homeless from their communities in the name of public health and safety. Concern for mentally ill homeless people remains a subject for the courts, as does support for the stability and integrity of homeless families. The following chapters are classified by this typology.

Despite the many strengths and victories of legal advocacy on behalf of homeless people, this strategy retains inherent constraints. Foremost among these limits is the fact that many states do not have statutes or codes that could provide the basis for developing class-action suits. Litigation is also time consuming, frequently involving years of research and litigation. Finally, the implementation of legal decisions is often less satisfactory than the outcome of a favorable court decision would indicate. The case study of the quality of New York City's shelters, discussed at length in Chapter 2, bears this out.[18]

As antihomeless sentiments continue to find their way into the law, legal advocates working in coalitions with social workers, other organizers, sympathetic local officials, business people, residents, and homeless people are continuing to work together to challenge antihomeless legislation and to press for *real* solutions to homelessness.

All homeless advocates and service providers acknowledge that the underlying conditions of homelessness can be addressed only partially by legal advocacy. Legal tactics alone cannot resolve the fundamental problems that are at the root of homelessness. In the absence of legislation, however, they have preserved the fundamental constitutional protections threatened by the status of homelessness. Litigation has also served curative purposes by ameliorating the hardships of homeless Americans.


## Notes and References

1.   U.S. Congress. *Administrative Procedure Act*. P.L.404, 79th. Cong., 2nd. Sess., 11 June 1946. The Administrative Procedure Act spells out the procedures for the promulgation of federal regulations.

2.   Raymond Albert, *Law and Social Work Practice* (New York: Springer, 1986), 16–17.

3.   Mark Tushnet, *Making Civil Rights Law: Thurgood Marshall and the Supreme Court, 1936–1961* (New York: Oxford University Press, 1994).

4.   Robert Giuffra, "The High Court's Low Profile," *The New York Times* June 19, 1993, A 15.

5.   David Kairys, *With Liberty and Justice for Some* (Philadelphia: New Press, 1993).

6.   Saltzman and Proch, *Law in Social Work Practice*, 6–37 (Introduction, Note 11).

7.   Kim Hopper and L. Stuart Cox, "Litigation in Advocacy for the Homeless: The Case of New York City," in Jon Erickson and Charles Wilhelm, eds. *Housing the Homeless* (Rutgers, NJ: Center for Urban Policy, 1986),301–314.

8.   Martha F. Davis, *Brutal Need: Lawyers and the Welfare Rights Movement, 1960–1973* (New Haven: Yale University Press, (1994).

9.   *Lindsey v. Normet*, 405 U.S., 56 (1972); Geoffrey Mort, "Establishing a Right to Shelter for the Homeless," *Brooklyn Law Review*, 50:939–994 (Summer 1984).

10.   *Rosado v. Wyman*, 397 U.S. 397 (1970); *Dandridge v. Williamson* 397 U.S. 471 (1970).

11.   The Equal Protection Clause and the designation of fundamental and important rights are discussed in the introduction.

12.   Judge Robert C. Coates, *A Street Is Not a Home: Solving America's Homeless Dilemma* (Buffalo: Prometheus Books, 1990), 286.

13.   Simon, "Towns without Pity," 642 (Introduction, Note 6).

14.   Coates, *A Street Is Not a Home*, 287 (Introduction Note 22).

15.   *Ibid.*, 287–288.

16.   These cases are discussed in Simon, "Towns without Pity," 643–645 (Introduction, Note 6); the *Papachristou v. City of Jacksonsville* is also described in *Go Directly to Jail: A Report Analyzing Anti-Homeless Ordinances*, National Law Center on Homelessness and Poverty, 918 F Street NW, Suite 412, Washington, D.C. 20004, December 1991, p. A–8.

17.   For a detailed description of *Callahan v. Carey*, see Hopper and Cox, "The Case of New York City," 303–320.

18.   Michael Fabricant and Irwin Epstein, "Legal and Welfare Rights Advocacy: Complementary Approaches in Organizing on Behalf of the Homeless," *The Urban and Social Change Review*, 17(1):15–20 (Winter 1984).

# I

## ENTITLEMENTS OF
## HOMELESS PEOPLE

Part I reviews litigation that has attempted to restore and preserve entitlements to cash or in-kind services for homeless people. It also reviews other actions related to threats to citizenship entitlements of homeless people, specifically education and voting. Cash and service programs include public assistance, old age security pensions, Medicaid, child welfare, vouchers for food stamps, aid to the blind and disabled, subsidized housing, Unemployment Insurance, Worker's Compensation, and emergency assistance. Established under the Social Security Act of 1935, these entitlements were considered fundamental rights of citizenship and the responsibility of federal, state, and local governments. After more than a half-century of experimentation and expansion of these entitlements under the Social Security Act, a more conservative political climate has permitted federal, state, and local governments to devolve these responsibilities onto private individuals, families, religious organizations, and nonsectarian charitable organizations in the belief this is the more appropriate mechanism for social service delivery and income relief.

Although not articulated in the Social Security Act, education is also considered an entitlement of citizenship. Homeless children have frequently been denied access to schools because of the uncertainty of their residence.

Contemporary support for such euphemistic "welfare reform" transcends political and ideological partisan lines. In the years since the passage of the Omnibus Reconciliation Act of 1981 we have witnessed massive devastation of income and service programs intended to provide a residual "safety net" for the poorest American citizens. For many, there is no longer any "safety net."

Homeless people exemplify the failure of the social safety net envisioned in the Social Security Act. They represent the new face of poverty at the millennium. Not only have they suffered from the withdrawal of the "safety net," they have also experienced widespread denial of their entitlement to safety net income and in-kind benefits for a variety of reasons identified in this part.

Perhaps the only positive outcome of this retreat from the welfare state ideology has been the mobilization of professional social workers and other human service practitioners as effective advocates for their abandoned clients. Some segments of the profession are returning to the prominence of their predecessors in the settlement movement and the War on Poverty.

In their effort to play a more prominent and effective role in social welfare policy formulation, they have been reminded of the importance of collaboration with attorneys. This contributed to the vigorous litigation campaign to restore to homeless people their rights of social citizenship, identified by T.H. Marshall.[1]

### Note

1.   T.H. Marshall, *Citizenship and Social Class* (Cambridge: Cambridge University Press, 1950).

# 2

## THE RIGHT TO SHELTER AND
## EMERGENCY ASSISTANCE

### Is Shelter a Right?

Despite the fact that thousands of emergency shelters now operate throughout the United States, New York and West Virginia are the only state jurisdictions that have identified the right to shelter within their constitutions. The *Callahan* consent decree planted the right to shelter more firmly in New York than in West Virginia.

New York City, as the first and only major city to shelter the homeless on demand, spends $7.2 billion on social services—more than the entire budgets of 21 states. Approximately $500 million goes toward housing homeless people.[1]

The New York City strategy of litigating for a right to shelter on demand was unique and the results of the consent decree have rendered the City a laboratory of homeless policy and advocacy for all cities. Over the decade, numerous contempt charges have been filed against the City for failing to comply with the consent decree. On August 4, 1993, a State Supreme Court judge in Manhattan imposed new fines on New York City and officials for contempt of court by failing to comply with court orders to serve homeless people.[2] The state's appellate court upheld this contempt ruling in May 1994.

More recently, a New York state court judge held New York City in contempt for leaving more than 100 homeless families a night sleeping on tables, chairs, and the floor of a city office while they waited 2 months for shelter. The judge also approved $2.5 million in fines to be paid by the city to thousands of homeless families who had overnight stays between September 1991 and December 1993. The judge went even further and ordered New York City to pay fines directly to families if it fails to shelter them in the future. Each family is entitled to $50 for the first overnight in the office and $100 for every night thereafter.[3]

New York City was granted partial relief from its obligation to provide shelter on demand when governor Mario Cuomo issued a state rule

29

allowing it to let homeless families wait for shelter and services for two or more nights. The new ruling does not nullify the city's obligation. Proponents contend that it provides greater flexibility so that they can be more careful in serving the families. Advocates counter that the rule reflects a clear attempt to scale back government's commitment to the homeless. The rule will undoubtedly be challenged in court.

Most cities rejected the strategy of creating an entitlement to shelter. They relied, instead, on charitable and nonprofit groups to provide shelter on an unplanned basis. In Washington, D.C., the City Council repealed the Overnight Shelter Act that granted the right to shelter.[4] Homeless advocates in Philadelphia abandoned their efforts to enforce a right to shelter, despite the fact that a 1982 consent decree required that the Department of Welfare provide emergency shelter for the city's homeless people. They argued that homeless people need more than shelter.[5] Only 10 cases have appeared on court dockets across the United States involving state and federal provisions to require provision of shelter, housing, or income sufficient to secure them.[6]

In December 1979, the New York Supreme Court granted homeless men a preliminary injunction requiring New York City to provide beds for all homeless men who requested shelter. The Court based its decision on its acknowledgment of a legal right to shelter citing provisions of the New York Constitution, the State Social Services Laws, and the City's Administrative Code that mandate the provision of shelter.

The plaintiffs based much of their case on the Equal Protection Clause of the United States Constitution. However, the Court stated that existing provisions were so clear that no consideration of equal protection was necessary.

After the Court delivered its decision, it issued a temporary injunction requiring New York State and the City to provide shelter that included clean bedding, wholesome board, adequate security and supervision to any person who applied for shelter at the New York City Men's Shelter located in New York's Bowery. The temporary injunction applied until the case concluded the trial stage.

The significance of the preliminary order was its specification of minimum standards for shelter. However, the City opened a large shelter for men in a deserted psychiatric hospital called the Keener Building. From the outset, no efforts to comply with the standards of the court order were apparent. The City transported homeless men by bus to the Keener Building, an extraordinarily lengthy trip. The new facility filled so rapidly that its capacity for 180 people stretched beyond 625 within months of the court order. No professional staff were assigned to the Keener Building. It was operated solely by inexperienced "institutional aides." Violence, illness, disorder, and neglect soon characterized the Keener Shelter.

Robert Hayes, who tried the *Callahan* case, filed a second class-action brief in April 1980 on behalf of a group of men at the Keener Shelter. This case never reached litigation because it was settled on the eve of the trial. The City agreed to triple its funding for the Keener Shelter and to provide professional social workers, as well as medical and psychiatric resources, at the facility.

When the *Callahan v. Carey* case reached the trial stage in January 1981, over 1 year after the preliminary injunction was granted, it was settled after 7 months of negotiations in the judge's chambers. The basis for the settlement was the plaintiff's agreement to withdraw the demand that shelters be "community-based." The settlement resulted in a final judgment that set forth a consent decree citing the terms and conditions under which shelter would be offered to homeless men.

The Mayor of New York City later agreed to include homeless women under the terms of the consent decree. When it became clear that shelters for women were not meeting the qualitative standards set by *Callahan*, *Eldredge v. Koch* was filed on behalf of homeless women against the Mayor of the City of New York and the Commissioner of the Human Resources Administration. The plaintiffs contended that the defendants violated the Equal Protection Clause of the United States Constitution by not applying the terms of the consent decree to women. The State Supreme Court ruled that the City had no rational basis for setting standards for the homeless applicable only to shelters for men and affirmed that the *Callahan* decree applied equally to women.[7]

The consent decree established a right to shelter on demand that carried the force of law. It also specified more clearly what decent bedding and adequate supervision and security meant. It set minimum staffing levels, designated that arrangements be made for storage of client's belongings, and provided for regular monitoring of compliance by outside observers.

The escalating numbers of homeless people that began in the early years of the 1980s resulted in a lack of beds to meet requests for emergency shelter. Robert Hayes, continuing as lawyer for the plaintiffs, returned to court twice to force the City to comply with the consent decree when City officials complained that they had run out of shelter space. Each time, the City opened more shelters. Unfortunately, as more shelters opened the standards stipulated in the consent decree were ignored. As a result, the ignominy of New York City's large shelters deterred many homeless people from coming off the streets.[8]

Current New York City policy on homelessness continues to honor the right to shelter on demand. The dangers and dilapidation of the large public shelters located in armories and decrepit hotels became both a problem and an embarrassment to City officials. This resulted in a redirection of the right to shelter toward placement in rehabilitated apartments. Hence, working under the obligation to provide shelter, New York City is attempting to transfer homeless families from shelters and welfare hotels to permanent housing in public housing projects or rehabilitated apartments.

Some of this policy is attributable to the *McCain v. Koch* decision delivered in 1987. *McCain* challenged the failure of New York City and State to provide safe, suitable, and adequate emergency housing to homeless families with children. The Appellate Division held that the City and the State have a right to provide emergency housing to homeless families under the State's Emergency Assistance for Families program, the federal Social Security Act, State and Federal constitutional guarantees of equal protection, and Article XVIII of the New York State Constitution.

The Appellate Division based its ruling on the State Constitution, which provides that "The aid, care and support of the needy are public concerns and shall be provided by the state and by such of its subdivisions, and in such a manner and by such means, as the legislature may from time to time determine." A partial settlement of the case prohibited future use of unauthorized commercial hotels as emergency shelter for families with children and prohibited multiple-night use of barracks-style shelters for families.[9]

This case vividly demonstrates how the force of law can advance the process of solving social problems even though the process is fraught with troublesome consequences.

Unfortunately an unanticipated consequence of the policy to place homeless families in permanent housing became even more embarrassing to City officials than the squalor of the shelters and welfare hotels. Families who previously would have had to wait for at least 1 year in hotels before gaining space in public housing projects were moved in 1 or 2 months, bypassing nonhomeless families who had been on the waiting list for as much as 10 years.

Housed families, seeking a shortcut to placement in public housing projects, soon began to declare themselves homeless. In the summer of 1990, almost 500 more families asked for shelter than had those in the summer of 1989. This unforeseen consequence of a benign policy prompted the City to revert to requiring families to remain in shelters for 1 year until they could qualify for housing. The immediate result of this decision was a bottleneck of homeless mothers and children in shelters and city offices.

The New York Legal Aid Society's Homeless Family Rights Project filed contempt charges against the City for failing to immediately place families in shelters. The City settled the case by agreeing to place social workers in all 36 City welfare centers to help prevent families from becoming homeless. Unfortunately, the City never honored this agreement because of budget constraints.[10]

West Virginia specified the right to shelter by designating homeless people as "incapacitated adults" under the terms of the West Virginia Social Services for Adults Act that mandates adult protective services. In *Hodge v. Ginsberg*, lawyers reasoned that adults have homes and when they are without homes they are relatively less adult. Therefore, they require government intervention.[11]

The legal justification for the *Hodge v. Ginsberg* decision poses several highly evident conceptual problems. It demeans all homeless people by defining them as "incapacitated adults." No image of a healthy functioning adult who simply cannot afford a home under high market rates exists in this conception. This has meant that West Virginia's right to shelter is not fully developed, so that attempts to prove that homeless people are able-bodied can disqualify them from shelter.

Baltimore County, Maryland remains under an interlocutory order enjoining the county to provide shelter for at least 25 homeless single males in the same manner as shelter is provided to homeless single women. This order resulted from the *Jedlicka v. Baltimore County, Maryland* brought by plaintiffs on behalf of homeless men in 1990.

The plaintiffs sought relief prohibiting the county from closing the Baltimore County Men's Shelter in violation of the state Equal Rights Amendment, the Equal Protection Clause of the Fourteenth Amendment, and the equal protection and due process principles located in Article 24 of the Maryland Declaration of Human Rights and the rights articulated in the Universal Declaration of Human Rights.[12]

Right-to-shelter advocacy has attracted wide interest for the simple reason that it is such a fundamental issue for homeless persons. Nevertheless, legal advocates have found little opportunity for litigation based on existing law. Twenty states lack any statutory basis for a right to shelter. Only 17 state constitutions make any reference to aid for the poor. Six states contain some clear language that can be interpreted as a right to shelter.[13]

St. Louis, Missouri agreed to a consent decree requiring the City to provide services for homeless people as a result of the *Graham v. Schoemel* case. The decree, delivered in the State Circuit Court, included shelter among its designation of services.[14]

Class-action lawsuits tried in the states of New Jersey and Connecticut have also interpreted a right to services and shelter. *Maticka v. Atlantic City* and *Algor v. County of Ocean* established that a statutory, although not a constitutional, right to shelter exists. *Lubetkin v. Hartford* resulted in regulations requiring the provision of aid for homeless people.[15]

The Supreme Court of Montana held that the state's policy of denying general assistance relief to a class of able-bodied persons on the basis of attained age did not pass "constitutional muster." In *Butte Community Union v. Lewis*, the court decided that the state violated the state constitutional guarantee of equal protection by eliminating classes of eligible individuals from public assistance.

In that same year, 1986, the Montana state legislature adopted amendments stipulating that able-bodied people without dependent minor children were eligible for only 2 months of nonmedical general assistance within a 12-month period. The original plaintiff, the Butte Community Union, challenged the new provisions in the District Court where it was determined that the provisions failed to meet the equal protection guarantees under the state constitution. This was later affirmed by the state Supreme Court.[16]

## Legislation on Shelter

Individual cities, counties, and states have declared a statutory right to shelter where no constitutional rights exists.

The Governor of the State of California established a statewide initiative to provide shelter in cold weather. The initiative authorized the state national guard armories to be open as Emergency Cold Weather Shelters for the homeless for 90 continuous days beginning each year on November 1. It also allows the extension of the program for an additional 60 days, a total of 5 months, if local conditions call for it. Cities and counties throughout the State of California have taken advantage of this authorization and have funded cold weather shelter programs. Many have funded extensions up to 60 days.[17]

The State of California has also ceded a right to shelter for homeless AFDC recipients. Prodded by the Western Center on Law and Poverty, legal staff who argued that the fastest growing group of homeless people in the state were single mothers and children, the State Department of Welfare agreed to provide up to 30 days of shelter to AFDC recipients. It also agreed to pay move-in costs when suitable housing was located.

The Western Center did not take this case as far as litigation. As is true in many other legal contests, the threat, or possibility, of litigation can yield decisions, legislative or administrative, favoring the positions of potential litigants. Data produced by the State Department of Welfare and the Western Center on Law and Poverty found that 60,000 children who would have been homeless benefited from the shelter and move-in allowance during the first year of the Homeless Assistance Program.[18]

The District of Columbia, home of the Center for Creative Non-Violence organized by homeless advocate Mitch Snyder, was the center of a major shelter entitlement controversy in 1990. The Council of the District enacted the Emergency Shelter Services for Families Reform Amendment Act of 1987 (the Family Shelter Act). It established a homeless family shelter program that required apartment units with cooking and bathroom facilities, separate sleeping quarters for adults and children, and access to immediate outdoor areas equipped with exercise and play facilities. The law also stipulated that the Mayor not place a homeless family with minor children in a hotel, motel, or other similar shelter arrangement. The Act also directed the District to provide employment counseling, job training, remedial education, mental health counseling, and other social services that would lead toward family independence and stabilization.

Three years after the passage of the Family Shelter Act, individual homeless families and a homeless advocacy organization filed a suit charging the District with noncompliance with the Act. The plaintiffs charged the District with noncompliance with the Family Shelter Act, the Social Security Act, U.S.C. Sections 601 et seq, and the Fifth Amendment to the United States Constitution.

The trial court granted the plaintiffs' claim and dismissed other claims. However, the District of Columbia repealed the Family Shelter Act, which was upheld after a referendum. The court then vacated its injunction on the Family Shelter Claim holding that the statutory language of the Family Shelter Act created a property interest in the plaintiffs for family housing and social services. However, the court removed the entitlement.[19]

While the *Fountain v. Barry* case described above was pending, homeless families in shelters filed a class-action suit against the city alleging that the defendants failed to provide them with adequate 24-hour emergency shelter required under the Emergency Assistance to Families Program. Plaintiff families who were required to leave their rooms each morning moved for a temporary restraining order requiring that the city provide families needing emergency shelter with 24-hour access to their assigned shelter places. The temporary restraining order also required that the city segregate families and single adults in sleeping quarters and bath/shower facilities. The city was also directed to improve family shelters by offering more privacy, smaller shelters, and free transportation to meal sites.

Finally, the plaintiffs filed a motion to amend their original complaint that the use of mass shelters for families violated city housing regulations, and the Overnight Shelter Act prohibited the use of mass shelters for families. The judge dismissed the case without ruling on the amended complaint. As a result, the District of Columbia is still required to shelter families with children with 24-hour access and specified standards. However, no prohibitions against mass shelters exist.[20]

Two federal actions relating to the right to shelter have been filed: one was successful and the other was dismissed. In the first action, plaintiffs sued the Department of Defense to make unused military facilities available as emergency shelter for homeless people. The case was based upon a 1983 federal statute requiring the Department to implement such a policy. Plaintiffs contended that the Department had ignored the statute. The judge granted the plaintiffs' motion for summary judgment, denied the defendants' motion to dismiss the case, and ordered the defendants to issue regulations implementing the shelter program in 1987.[21]

The second action was brought in federal district court in Washington, D.C. to force The Secretary of Health and Human Services to require that the 25 states participating in the emergency assistance to families program actually provide emergency shelter to homeless families. After 2 years of deliberation, the lower court granted the Secretary's motion to dismiss the case.

## Policy Issues Concerning Right to Shelter

The question of whether to press for right-to-shelter laws evoked considerable debate among homeless activists and advocates during the decade of the 1980s. Everyone concerned with the problem of homelessness agreed that food and shelter present the most immediate needs of homeless people. No individuals or organizations questioned the moral imperative to build and operate shelters and soup kitchens in the face of such pitiful need. Nor did they question the existence of a human being's right to shelter.

The controversy focused on a series of wide-ranging issues. These included the following complex questions. Would right-to-shelter laws result in the massive degrading shelters that prevailed in New York City following the consent decree? If homeless people preferred small community-based shelters to large public shelters and traditional missions, would it not be preferable to encourage community groups to establish smaller and more humane shelters? Many expressed distrust and distaste for the bureaucracy of government and preferred that shelters operate within the private voluntary welfare sector. The example of the dangerous and unwelcoming large shelters of New York that never complied with the standards set forth in the Consent Decree and created a formidable bureaucracy loomed urgently before all homeless activists as an example of hostile government compliance with the law.

Others expressed concern that the energy required in fighting for a right to shelter would divert the homeless movement from focusing on long-term solutions to the problem of homelessness.

Activists who devoted their efforts to explaining the causes of homelessness and advocating for permanent solutions nevertheless ceded the need for shelter. They developed a three-tier response to homelessness advocating emergency shelter and assistance, transitional housing, and permanent housing, or what is commonly referred to as a continuum of housing. This scheme satisfied the imperative to respond to the immediacy of the crises confronting homeless people while continuing to press for more complete solutions.[22]

Because of these reservations about right-to-shelter outcomes, minimal litigation followed the New York and West Virginia cases. Nevertheless, the number of shelters and soup kitchens operated by nonprofit and charitable organizations throughout the nation proliferated so rapidly during the 1980s that people began to decry the fact that a "shelter system" had evolved to a point where shelters had become permanent housing for many.[23] Advocates became alarmed that emergency responses were becoming institutionalized so that the shelter system had become the contemporary almshouse replete with the stigma and harshness of the earlier scheme to control transient people.

A dramatic illustration of the resurgence in almshouse provisions occurred in Sacramento, the state capitol of California, where a workhouse was actually established. It operated on indoor relief principles of Poor Law infamy requiring homeless General Relief recipients to live in the Banning Street residence. The Banning Street residence was found to be unconstitutional and closed down immediately after the court decision.[24]

Housing experts, and homeless people themselves, contend that the emphasis on shelter has drained resources that could have been spent on permanent housing and rental subsidies and has impaired the public sector's ability to aid homeless people and control the rising costs of shelter. An increasingly vocal group of advocates and experts has decried the fact that a shelter industry has been created that thrives on keeping people homeless to perpetuate itself.[25]

The bureaucratic horrors of New York City's barracks-style shelters and hotels became a media event focusing on decrying their inhumanity and degradation.[26] This was no accident. Advocates in New York, who continued to press for shelter as a right on demand, used the National

Welfare Rights Organization strategy formulated in the 1960s. The theory employed by the welfare rights organizations was that the enrollment of all eligible people on AFDC would destroy the public assistance system.[27] Homeless advocates anticipated that exposure of the terrible conditions in the shelters would embarrass the City into giving homeless people permanent housing.

To win such sympathy, homeless advocates in New York, as well as other cities that did not press for a legal right to shelter, identified solutions to the homeless problem in overly simplistic terms and slogans. The most common cry of advocates across the nation was "Housing, Housing, Housing"!

More than 70 national organizations sponsored a Housing Now! march and rally in October 1989. The event brought together homeless people, advocates, local and state public officials, church leaders, and others to demand immediate federal action to restore billions of dollars in federal funding that had been cut from the federal budget since 1981 and to emphasize the fact that a permanent solution to homelessness must be based on guaranteeing opportunities for all Americans to enjoy decent and affordable permanent housing.

At a Housing California 1989 State Conference, sponsored by the California Housing Coalition and the California Coalition for Rural Housing, the California "Right to Housing Campaign" was launched. This, too, was a campaign for decent, affordable housing.[28]

Some officials responded with sympathy, most notably Mayor David Dinkins in New York City. Others responded more negatively arguing the homeless people were drug addicts, alcoholics, and welfare cheats who preferred the dole to work and would never function in any type of decent housing. Critics also argued that local government money was being lavished on homeless people and services.

This debate was fueled nationally when President Reagan's appointed Undersecretary responsible for federal welfare oversight, Wayne A. Stanton, viewed a television program that denounced New York City for paying luxury prices for squalid rooms in hotels. The program, *Heartbreak Hotel*, aired in 1986. It also noted that the Federal Government was paying for hotel stays of more than 30 days, even though families were living in them for 1 or more years. Stanton announced that the Government would pay for only 30-day hotel stays. Fortunately, the Congress delayed the cutoff, but the threat remained in place so that families were frequently evicted from the hotels.

Contemporary advocates, including those in New York City, have backed off from pressing for a right to shelter on demand. The New York City Commission on the Homeless, under the direction of Andrew Cuomo, recommended that the City withdraw from shelter provision and let nonprofit groups develop and run small social service programs for the homeless. The report also recommended that only those with no other options should be sheltered. Furthermore, the Commission suggested that only those who tried to help themselves should be given permanent apartments, e.g., addicts in treatment, the mentally ill accepting care, and neglectful mothers who attended parenting classes.[29]

A similar report issued by the City Santa Monica Task Force on Homelessness in 1991 recommended an array of proposed housing projects that would reflect a continuum of services. The Task Force noted that the design of such a continuum should avoid situations where people receive shelter and/or housing support but are forced to return to the streets because they cannot live independently.[30]

Both cities expressed opinions that reflect general thinking across the United States. They advocated the use of small community-based shelters, shelter operation by nonprofit organizations even for publicly funded facilities, and supportive service intervention that starts at the emergency stage and continues through stabilization in permanent housing. Some of the extant proposals include requirements that shelter guests agree to participate in counseling and rehabilitation programs as a condition of acceptance, or pay a small sum for their stay. These approaches have been dubbed "tough love" by their proponents as well as many advocates who oppose them.

Future federal policy indications suggest a similar revamping of the emergency shelter system, which does not eliminate shelters but places them at the beginning of a continuum of services for homeless people. President Clinton issued an executive order in May 1993 directing his Administration to develop a "single coordinated plan for breaking the cycle of homelessness."[31] The federal plan, no matter how limited in scope and financial resources, has been influenced by Andrew Cuomo, who directed the New York Commission on the Homeless, in his position as Assistant Secretary for Community Planning and Development at the United States Department of Housing and Urban Development under the Clinton administration.

The principle of revamping shelter operations toward smaller service-enriched residences seems to ignore the fact that requests for emergency shelter increase every year. The U.S. Conference of Mayors reported that requests for emergency shelter increased in the cities it surveyed by an average of 12% in 1991 with no cities reporting decreases during that period.[32]

Moreover, new municipal housing problems have emerged. Across the United States, an estimated 10 to 15% of people living with acquired immune deficiency syndrome (AIDS) are homeless. This is 2 to 40 times as high as that of the domiciled population.[33] AIDS housing is a new item on the municipal agendas of all cities.

New York City, continuing to operate under shelter upon demand law, has responded to this new problem by allocating the former welfare hotels and Single Room Occupancy hotels (SROs) to homeless persons with AIDS. AIDS activists and other nonprofit organizations have opened a limited amount of special housing, including individual apartments, group homes with on-site drug treatment, and hospices for people who become severely ill.

Other cities, not laboring under a requirement to shelter all homeless people, have also begun to operate ambitious programs. Seattle and Boston have begun programs that feature ideal arrangements such as the use of apartments with the AIDS afflicted scattered throughout the city. The intent of these programs is to provide options that enable people to live independently within a normal mainstream life. Los Angeles, like most cities, has developed a piecemeal arrangement of facilities funded by churches, AIDS organizations, and state and county government. All cities report waiting lists for AIDS housing except New York, which remains bound by its legal responsibility to provide shelter on demand.

Federal legislation has added resources to assist organizations and local governments. In 1990, Congress passed the National Affordable Housing Act, which includes the *Housing Opportunities for Persons with AIDS* program. (HOPWA).[34] This program creates housing resources for those cities hardest hit by the HIV/AIDS epidemic, enabling them to fund a range of programs for people living with HIV disease, including AIDS housing information and coordination of services, short-term supported housing and services, rental assistance, single-room occupancy housing, and community residences and services.

The AIDS epidemic underscores the complexity of any shelter and housing policy for homeless people. Although the Cuomo Commission recommended that the City withdraw from its shelter obligations in favor of smaller service-enriched programs for people who participate in efforts to improve their lives, the AIDS crisis presents situations that do not readily lend themselves to such a selective arrangement. New York officials point out that most nonprofit groups refuse to shelter all people. For instance, most private groups refuse to shelter hard-core drug users. Only the City accepts all requests.

This dilemma between providing shelter on demand, no matter what its quality, and more coordinated selective shelter persists despite growing support for the latter. Beset by every tempest of human misery, municipalities and housing providers need many options. In the final analysis, New York City has become the urban laboratory for experiments in shelter, even though growing numbers of advocates are questioning spending for shelters given severe low-income housing shortages and budget constraints across the nation. Without the Consent Decree, the City would undoubtedly be responding like all other cities in a looser patchwork of shelter and housing policies. Finally, it is noteworthy that no city in the entire nation has developed long-term solutions to homelessness in spite of the fact that they have not labored under the regulatory shelter environment of New York.

## Notes and References

1. Barry Bearak, "Waiting to Die at the AIDS Hotel," *Los Angeles Times* (25 July 1993), A 15.

2. Ian Fischer, "New York City Is Fined on Homeless," *New York Times* (August 5, 1993), A16; Steven Banks, Esq., Legal Aid Society Homeless Family Rights Project, New York, NY.

3. Celia W. Dugger, "Judge Finds New York City in Contempt over Its Care of Homeless Families," *New York Times* (September 28, 1994), A14.

4. *Atchison v. Barry*, Civil Action No. 11987-88 (D.C. Superior Ct. June 25, 1991); D.C. Act 8-228, 37 D.C. Reg. 4815-4823.

5. *Committee for Dignity and Fairness for the Homeless v. Pernsley*, No. 1886 (Pa. Ct. of Comm. Pleas, Philadelphia Cnty, April 29, 1985) (consent decree) (Clearinghouse No. 40, 945).

6. National Housing Law Project, *Annotated Bibliography*, 3–7.

7. *Eldredge v. Koch*, 98 A.D. 2d 675, 469 N.Y.D. 2d 744 (1st. Dept. 1983) (Clearinghouse No. 38, 512).

8. The *Callahan v. Carey* case, and its implementation, are described and analyzed in Hopper and Cox, "Litigation in Advocacy for the Homeless: The Case of New York City" (Chapter 1, Note 7).

9. *McCain v. Koch*, 70 N.Y. 2d 109, 510 N.E. 2d 62, 517 N.Y.S. 2d 918 (N.Y. Ct. App. 1987), *rev'g in part*, 117 A.D. 2d 198. 502 N.Y.S. 2d 720 (1st Dept. 1986) (Clearinghouse No. 40, 919).

10. Celia Dugger, "Housing Setbacks Temper a Mayor's Hopes," *New York Times* (July 5, 1993), 12.

11. *Hodge v. Ginsberg*, 303, S.E. 2d 245 (West Virginia, 1983).

12. *Jedlicka v. Baltimore County, Maryland*, No. 90-CSP-1298 (Md. Cir. Ct., Baltimore Cnty.) (Clearinghouse No. 45, 732); Summarized in National Housing Law Project, *Annotated Bibliography*, 3–4 (Introduction, Note 9).

13. James K. Langdon and Mark A. Kass, "Homelessness in America: Looking for the Right to Shelter," *Columbia Journal of Law and Social Problems* 19(3):307, 332–333 (1985).

14. *Graham v. Schoemehl*, No. 854-00035 Consent Decree, Mo. Cir. Ct. (1987).

15. *Maticka v. Atlantic City* 524 A. 2s 416 (N.J. Superior Court, App. Div., 1987); *Algor v. County of Ocean*, No. Am-388-85T5 (N.J. Superior Court, 23, De-

cember 1985); *Lubetkin v. Hartford*, Connecticut Superior Court filed 4 February 1984; these cases are identified and discussed in Blau, *The Visible Poor: Homelessness in the United States* (Introduction, Note 5).

16. *Butte Community Union v. Lewis*, 745 P. 2d 1128 (Mont. 1987) (Clearinghouse No. 37, 503).

17. City of Santa Monica, The Santa Monica Task Force on Homelessness, *A Call to Action*, City of Santa Monica Community Development Department (December 1991), 40–43.

18. Los Angeles County Department of Public Social Services and State of California Department of Social Services, *Homeless Assistance Program*, 1991.

19. *Fountain v. Barry*, Civ. Action No. 90-1503 (D.C. Super. Ct. Oct. 12, 1990) (Clearinghouse No. 45, 724); National Housing Law Project, *Annotated Bibliography*, 10–11 (Introduction, Note 9).

20. *Walls v. District of Columbia*, Civ. Action No. 7486-90 (D.C. Super. Ct. filed April 22, 1988) (Clearinghouse No. 45, 870); *Walls v. Barry*, No. 1372-88 (D.C. Super. Ct. March 11, 1988); *Walls v. Barry*, No. 1372-88 (D.C. Super. Ct. April 1, 1988).

21. *Bruce v. Department of Defense*, Civ. Action No. 87-0423 (D.D.C. filed Feb. 19, 1987).

22. Nancy K. Kaufman, "Homeless: A Comprehensive Policy Approach," *The Urban and Social Change Review* 17(1):21–26 (Winter 1984). This was the first scholarly article that presented the three-tiered strategy.

23. Madeleine R. Stoner, *Inventing a Non-Homeless Future: A Public Policy Agenda for Preventing Homelessness* (New York: Peter Lang 1989); Shelter Partnership, Inc., *The Short-Term Housing System of Los Angeles County: Serving the Needs of the Homeless: An Analysis of Operating Characteristics and Funding Activity* (Los Angeles: The Shelter Partnership, 1987).

24. *Robbins v. Superior Court* (Sup. Ct., CA), 38 CAL 3r. 199 (1985).

25. Stoner, *Inventing a Non-Homeless Future*.

26. Jonathan Kozol, *Rachel and Her Children: Homeless Families in America* (New York: Crown, 1988).

27. Frances Fox Piven and Richard Cloward, *Poor People's Movements* (New York: Vintage, 1979); Michael Fabricant and Irwin Epstein, "Legal and Welfare Rights Advocacy: Complementary Approaches in Organizing on Behalf of the Homeless," *The Urban and Social Change Review*, 17(1):15–20 (Winter 1983).

28. Shelter Partnership, "Join the California Right to Housing Campaign"; 'Housing Now! A National Call to Action,' *Homeless Reporter*, 1 (May 1989).

29. Celia W. Dugger, "Housing Setbacks Temper a Mayor's Hopes," *New York Times* (July 5, 1993), 12.

30. *The Santa Monica Task Force on Homelessness: A Call to Action*, City of Santa Monica, Community Development Department, Community and Neighborhood Service Division, 1685 Main St., Santa Monica, CA 90401.

31. Celia W. Dugger, "Finding Housing for All Vexes Political Leaders," *New York Times* (6 July 1993), A13.

32. The United States Conference of Mayors, Raymond L. Flynn, Mayor of

Boston, President, *A Status Report on Hunger and Homelessness in America's Cities* (1 28-City survey) (1991).

33.    Center for Disease Control, 1991.

34.    Anita Savio, "7.2 Million in HOPWA Funds Allocated to Los Angeles-LongBeach Metropolitan Region," *Homeless Reporter*, Shelter Partnership, 4:1 (1993).

# 3

# INCOME MAINTENANCE LITIGATION

## The Policy Framework of Income Maintenance

The United States, frequently characterized as a reluctant welfare state, has traditionally organized income maintenance systems to deter all but the most destitute from applying for benefits. Welfare disincentives have compelled people to prove that they are void of any assets or sources of support to qualify for eligibility. The doctrine of less eligibility, first articulated in England at the end of the nineteenth century, applies to all eligibility criteria and benefit determination today. Less eligibility refers to the principle that no public assistance benefit should be equal to the amount of money that can be earned by the lowest wage earned in the labor force. Although homeless people would appear to meet any conceivable designation of destitution, they have been subject to the stringency of welfare policies despite their lack of personal resources.

The National Housing Law Project has identified 35 court cases that have dealt with income entitlements for homeless people. The central thrust of most of these cases has been the verification that federal laws guaranteeing income security pertain to homeless people. Litigation has verified that homeless people are eligible for food stamps, medical care, disability and veteran's benefits, as well as Supplemental Security Income for persons over the age of 65 and Social Security Disability Insurance benefits for disabled persons. Persons in the last two categories do need a permanent residence or address to qualify. None of the other categories of income maintenance requires a permanent address or residence anymore.

The legal docket of advocacy cases involving income maintenance has included four major categories of concern. Cases have been filed contending that the level of public assistance benefits should be consistent with either the general cost of living or the cost of housing. A few cases have addressed local public assistance regulations that limit benefits to able-bodied poor people, or impose work requirements as a condition of eligibility. A third category of cases has involved efforts to remove barriers to access to entitlements such as residency requirements and delays in payment schedules. Other cases have attempted to provide guarantees of emergency assistance. Finally, a few cases have addressed jurisdictional responsibility for provision of general relief assistance.

More litigation has addressed problems associated with General Relief Assistance (GR) than Aid to Families with Dependent Children (AFDC) benefits. General Relief Assistance is the minimum subsistence public assistance benefit available. It is even more vulnerable to the politics of budget cuts than AFDC because its recipients, mostly single adult males, evoke little public sympathy. Indeed, they frequently evoke antipathy associated with stereotypical views that people on relief are lazy and would rather be on the dole than work. Most homeless people rely on this income category. Homeless advocates frequently argue that cuts in the level of GR benefits result in increased homelessness.

AFDC, the higher public assistance benefit, available to families with children, has been the focus of cases that link benefit levels to the cost of living or identify barriers to access and emergency assistance for homeless families.

Four cases have been brought alleging discrimination in Food Stamp allocations against homeless people. Although not an income program, food stamps are classified as an in-kind benefit that is included among income maintenance entitlements.

State governments require county government officials, Boards of Supervisors, or Departments of Welfare to fund and administer GR and AFDC under state statutes and codes in accordance with the Social Security Act.

## Level of AFDC and GR Benefits

The courts have clearly tended to rule in favor of plaintiffs filing for more adequate benefit levels sufficient to maintain fair and humane health and decency.

The most extensive case involving public assistance benefit levels took place in New Jersey in 1989. When the state welfare agency rejected a petition from AFDC and GR recipients (including many homeless persons) requesting that the standard of need of AFDC be revised and a GR standard of need be established to reflect the actual costs of food, shelter, clothing, and other basic necessities, the Appellate Division ruled against the welfare agency.

The Appellate Division held that the New Jersey AFDC and GR statutes require that the welfare department establish realistic standards of need for these programs. The Supreme Court affirmed the Appellate Division and ordered the Department of Health and Human Services (DHS) to establish adequate needs standards for both programs.

DHS appointed a Standard of Need Advisory Committee, which recommended substantial increases in both programs. The committee based the housing component of the needs standard on the Fair Market Rents established by the Department of Housing and Urban Development (HUD). Dissatisfied with the Advisory Committee's recommendations, DHS contracted with a private consulting firm to establish a different formula for determining the housing component. The consultant arecommended a 20% lower standard.

Given the discrepancy between the two standards, a public hearing was held. Those testifying included the New Jersey Public Advocate and prominent national housing consultant and advocate Cushing N. Dolbeare. Both argued that the fair market rents, rather than the methodology used by the consultants, be used in establishing the housing component of the needs standard.

The Dolbeare report contained the central theme of housing advocates relevant to needs standards. It noted that the Fair Market Rent levels have been criticized widely for being too low. They are based on the 45th percentile rate of standard quality units and rents of recent movers. The 1990 Cranston–Gonzales National Affordable Housing Act directs the General Accounting Office to study Fair Market Rents to determine whether they are so low that they impede racial and ethnic integration of predominantly white communities. This statute reinforces advocates' attempts to persuade HUD to increase Fair Market Rents so that they can permit the use of Section 8 certificates in higher-cost neighborhoods and communities.

The DHHS adopted the standard of need recommended by the agency Advisory Committee, rejecting the formula and methodology presented by the private consulting firm.[1]

The significance of the New Jersey petition rests on the fact that it included both AFDC and GR and linked them to every component of the cost of living. Moreover, it addressed the housing component and questioned extant formulas for estimating housing costs.

Most of the lawsuits involving income have addressed the level of benefits as they relate to the cost of living and housing. All cases related to payment levels and standards of need affect recipients' ability to secure housing. A portion of the GR and AFDC benefit includes a shelter allowance. The housing allowance may be in the form of money, vouchers, or vendor payments. Few homeless people can afford to pay for housing and other basic needs with their GR benefit. Similarly, AFDC are insufficient to meet the cost of housing and basic survival needs in most rental markets. In Los Angeles, where one of the nation's highest concentrations of homeless live, 90% of the AFDC benefit level is absorbed by housing payments.

*Burks v. Knudson*, tried in the California Superior Court directly challenged the Alameda County Board of Supervisors ordinance that denied the shelter portion of the GR grants to homeless GR recipients. Plaintiffs argued that the defendant county had no evidence before demonstrating that indigents could meet their nonshelter needs on $146 a month. The plaintiffs further claimed that the ordinance violated state law and their right to privacy guaranteed under the California Constitution.

The court granted a preliminary injunction prohibiting the county from reducing the shelter component of the GR grant for homeless recipients or those whose housing costs were less than the allowance. The court also enjoined the county from adopting a GR vendor pay program "that was not based on a needs study for the different portions of the allowance and locked recipients into inadequate allocations for shelter, food, incidentals, transportation, and clothing and thereby prevents them from meeting basic minimum needs."[2]

In 1992 plaintiff-appellant GR recipients filed a brief challenging Alameda County's interpretation of a statute providing that the county set its GR grants at amounts equal to a certain percentage of the poverty line, in lieu of a needs study. The brief also requested that the county adjust its benefit levels to conform with the adjustments provided under the AFDC statutes. A final decision on this case has not been delivered, but it remains an important precedent for challenging GR benefit levels.[3]

In 1991, *Mendly v. County of Los Angeles* was filed challenging the adequacy of Los Angeles County's GR grant levels, which had been $312 per month since 1988. The county agreed to a settlement that raised the monthly grant levels to a single-person GR household from $312 to $341. The county also agreed to increase the monthly grant levels to an amount corresponding to AFDC households for 5 years.[4]

This decision has not held up under the pressure of county budget cuts. There have been two serious reductions in the GR benefit since the court decision. The first reduced the benefit to $293. The most recent GR cut took effect on September 1, 1993, and cut an additional 27% from the benefit bringing it down to $212 a month. County officials have claimed that the court decision is not binding under the budget reductions forced on the county by the state. They further contend that all public assistance payments are limited to the amounts appropriated by the legislature. The county equally contends that it is justified in going below the minimum grant allowed under state law by maintaining that the free medical care it provides the poor is worth $73 a month.

The Homeless Litigation Team that tried the *Mendly* case requested a preliminary injunction to block the reduction in General Relief welfare payments. The brief was based upon the 1991 Mendly decision. In addition, it contended that the state legislature did not intend counties to include the value of health care.

The Superior Court judge rejected the request, basing her ruling on a 1992 case in Contra Costa County that allows counties to count the total value of services they provide to indigent people, including health care. Despite the Contra Costa case, Los Angeles is the only county in the State of California that includes the value of health care as part of the fulfillment of its obligation to provide general relief.

The inclusion of total services in benefit levels was applied in the *Poverty Resistance Center v. Hart* case. Plaintiffs challenged Yolo County in California when it set its GR allowance at an amount below the minimum shelter cost as determined by its housing survey. The county attempted to justify this action by arguing that it also provided funds for soup kitchens and homeless shelters. The court of appeal reversed the trial court's grant of a demurrer, holding that the county's housing and food allowances were not supported by recorded evidence. The California Supreme Court accepted but then declined to review the case.[5]

The definition of "minimum subsistence" under GR requirements was challenged in San Francisco City and County in *Boehm v. Superior Court*. The court, in this case, held that a county GR reduction was arbitrary and capricious because it was based on a needs study that included only housing and food. The court held that "minimum subsistence . . . at the very least, must include allocations for housing, food, utilities, clothing, transportation and medical care."

The state statute in the Welfare and Institutions Code requiring counties to support indigent residents is so general that the court relied upon decisions from other states and the Universal Declaration of Human rights providing

> Everyone has the right to a standard of living adequate for the health and wellbeing of himself and his family, including food, clothing, housing, medical care and necessary social services, and the right to security in the event of unemployment, sickness, disability, widowhood, old age or other lack of livelihood in circumstances beyond his control.

The court also used the Welfare and Institutions Code, which requires that aid and services be provided "promptly and humanely."[6]

A second case involving the plaintiff Boehm was tried in Merced County, California. It challenged the board of supervisors' reduction of the GR grant level. Lawyers for Boehm argued that the reduction was made without making a factual determination of the minimum subsistence needs in the county. The supervisors based their decision on rec-

ommendations of the county department of human resources, which
were in turn based on an unsubmitted survey comparing GR levels in
nearby counties.

The court of appeal held that the county's action was arbitrary because
the board had not made any factual determination of minimum subsistence needs.[7]

A blind recipient of financial aid to the blind in Nevada brought suit
claiming that his actual needs were $291.16 per month and that the $198
he received was insufficient. He was granted a hearing before the state
welfare board, which found that the $198 was sufficient and interpreted
"actual needs" to mean "need standards developed by the welfare
board," rather than individual recipients.

The plaintiff brought a court action challenging the board's decision.
The lower court affirmed the board's conclusions holding that payments
to the blind were restricted to the amounts appropriated by the legislature to the fund for the blind support, even if such payments did not
meet actual need of a recipient.

The Supreme Court of Nevada reversed the lower court decision holding that the welfare division's definition of "actual need" was unreasonable and that the fact that allowances were based on 1959 standards was
"a disgrace to the State of Nevada."[8]

In Ohio, county residents who were eligible for GR brought a class-
action suit alleging that county officials failed to provide them with
enough assistance to maintain health and decency. The Court of Appeals ruled that the defendants were responsible for providing those
who were eligible for GR with sufficient income to maintain health and
decency. The Supreme Court affirmed the lower court's ruling.[9]

A strong homeless advocacy case was brought before the court in
Dallas County, Texas. Plaintiffs, homeless persons, challenged the General Assistance program administered by Dallas County, which prohibited the distribution of funds to people who were poor and homeless.
Only those people who were poor and had permanent housing were
eligible for assistance. The court required the county to provide shelter
to homeless people and, in a settlement agreement, it was agreed that
"the fact that an applicant is homeless does not disqualify the applicant
from income assistance."[10]

In Sheboygan County, Wisconsin, a class-action suit was filed challenging the county's policy on general welfare payment maximums for
single-member families. The case was settled with the county agreeing
to raise the maximum, review the grant level annually, and provide
written notice of the availability of retroactive relief to class members.[11]

Several lawsuits focused exclusively on AFDC benefit levels relative to
the cost of living. The most recent case, filed in June 1992, is pending in

San Francisco. Plaintiffs challenged the State of California's failure to reevaluate its AFDC "standard of need" to conform with the Family Support Act. The plaintiffs maintain that the AFDC grant will not cover average rent payments in the 11 largest metropolitan areas in the state, including Los Angeles. In Colorado, *Johnson v. Berson,* took the same position, compelling a reevaluation of the standard of need pursuant to the Family Support Act.[12]

An appeal is pending in the District of Columbia after the trial court granted a summary judgment for the defendants. In this case, the plaintiffs challenged a reduction in AFDC benefit levels, contending that the District had violated a local law when the City Council failed to assess the minimum needs of recipients before reducing benefit levels. Plaintiffs further charged that monthly benefit levels did not meet minimum needs, and alleged that the council acted illegally by taking food stamp benefits into account when setting the lower levels, and by failing to consult the Medicare Advisory Board before the reductions. The plaintiffs also challenged the reduction on the grounds that the council failed to give adequate notice of the change denying the opportunity for a fair hearing. The plaintiffs also challenged the fact that the announcement was written in English only.[13]

A major case that addressed the need for adequate shelter, housing, and benefit levels for homeless families and children took place in the State of Massachusetts where the Massachusetts Coalition for the Homeless perceived a conflict between the requirement under General Law 18, Section 2, and the fact that AFDC grant levels paid by Massachusetts were "substantially below the level needed to satisfy the General Law." The court resolved this conflict by requiring that

> if in any year the department concludes that the funds appropriated for AFDC purposes are insufficient to permit it to furnish that level of financial aid which Section 2 directs it to provide, the department has an obligation to bring its inability to comply with the payment level described in Section 2 to the attention of the Legislature and to ask that it appropriate an adequate sum or that it provide some other solution to the dilemma.

The court also noted that the Department of Public Welfare has an obligation under the same General Law to provide sufficient income to permit AFDC parents to live in a home, and not simply provide accommodations to AFDC parents. Although the Massachusetts courts did not go so far as to order the state to provide enough money for AFDC recipients to secure permanent homes, the legislature did increase the grants. More promising was that the state directed housing subsidies to homeless families and families at risk of homelessness. The state also provided money to help people find housing.

Three years after this suit, the Massachusetts Coalition for the Homeless filed a supplemental brief, adding the state Executive Office of Communities and Development and the Executive Office of Administration and Finance as defendants. That complaint sought to require the defendants to "marshall and coordinate all available state and federal housing resources." The state Superior Court granted one part of the plaintiffs' motion for a preliminary injunction enjoining terminations of shelter or shelter benefits because a recipient had been sheltered for 90 days or more. The court did not grant the other claims of the plaintiffs, but it did note that it "had not foreclosed judicial action on the question of housing for AFDC families . . . and ordered that funds be expended for housing provided that there is a careful analysis of what appropriated funds are available."[14]

This case holds great significance for AFDC homeless recipients. It raises key issues about whether, and to what extent, state housing authorities and officials are obligated to target AFDC recipients for housing and housing assistance. The findings held that the state does have the authority to order that public housing authorities give their highest priority rankings to homeless people.[15]

AFDC recipients in New York challenged the state's practice of establishing shelter allowances that were inadequate to pay the cost of housing. They based their case on the State's Social Service Law that directs shelter allowances to be granted to AFDC recipients, and that these allowances should enable parents to bring up their children properly, including support maintenance in the home for one or both parents. The trial court issued a preliminary injunction requiring that the state set shelter allowances at a level commensurate with the cost of housing.

At the appellate level, however, the court reversed the decision holding that the legislative mandate to provide assistance to bring up children properly was subordinate to the legislative mandate setting the amount of the benefit. The Appellate Division based its ruling on the state's Social Services Law directing shelter payments to AFDC recipients by specifying that the shelter amounts be administratively determined to reflect the cost of local rents in different parts of the state.

This case (*Jiggets v. Grinker*) was then taken to the New York Court of Appeals, which reversed the Appellate Division. The higher court held that the Commissioner of Social Services has a statutory duty to establish shelter allowances that reasonably relate to the cost of housing in New York City.

The court also interpreted the Social Services Law as including services that are necessary for each child and its parents in a home-type setting. Referring to appropriation priorities, the court held that the State Commissioner of Social Services has a statutory duty to provide such assistance no matter how the legislature appropriates funds.[16]

This case marked another significant decision because it addressed the question of whether legislative appropriations take precedence over statutory mandates and standards.

A case similar to *Jiggets v. Grinker,* tried in Westchester County, New York, held that the AFDC shelter allowance violated state law requiring the state commissioner of social services to establish shelter allowances that realistically relate to the cost of housing. The court also ruled that county authorities can bring judgment action cases based on this claim. The court distinguished between cases in which county officials challenged decisions made in fair hearings and interpretations of statutes or regulations.

The general tendency of court decisions on the level of benefits for General Relief Assistance and AFDC beneficiaries has clearly been to grant public assistance recipients entitlements to benefit levels that are commensurate with the general cost of living, frequently singling out the cost of housing. Although a few cases have addressed child welfare, the findings on this issue have been more ambiguous. Courts have tended to weigh the general cost of living more favorably than the need to raise children in decent, healthy adequate home-like settings.

One of the more important precedents has occurred in those cases where the courts have held that legislative appropriations do not take precedence over statutory codes and regulations governing the determination of minimum subsistence levels.

Supplemental Security Income (SSI) and Social Security Disability Insurance (SSDI) are other income maintenance resources available to homeless people. People who are over the age of 65 are eligible for SSI. This provides cash benefits up to $368 per month and recipients do not need a permanent address to qualify. SSI can also lead to medical coverage, food stamps, and housing.

Homeless disabled people who have worked in the past may be entitled to SSDI. Cash payments under this program average $555 per month. Applicants do not need a permanent address to qualify. Many severe and persistent mentally ill people rely on SSDI for income, homeless or otherwise.

The State of California legislature created a "special circumstances" program to supplement SSI in 1976. This program was designed to meet "peculiar," and "non-recurring needs," including "unmet shelter needs." The regulations promulgated to implement this statute addressed unmet shelter needs indirectly by allowing homeowners up to $750 to prevent foreclosures and renters a maximum of $300 for deposits necessary to secure new rental housing.

A case was brought before the Alameda County intermediate appellate court requesting that the Department of Social Services take the following steps to implement the legislation: (1) cease denying Special

Circumstances benefits to those without a written notice of eviction or forced move, (2) cease denying benefits for temporary shelter, (3) cease denying benefits to prevent eviction of renters, and (4) provide reasonable notice of the Special Circumstances program to all recipients.

The Court granted the fourth item of the request but denied the first three on the grounds that the Department of Social Services was entitled to administrative interpretation of the statutory phrase "unmet shelter needs." The Court further argued that the Department of Social Services was entitled to deference.[17]

## Work Requirements for Eligibility

The practice of linking work to welfare is at least as ancient as the Elizabethan Poor Laws. Under the Statutes of Labourers, vagrants or transients were confined to designated residences and required to work at specified wages. Under such "indoor relief" practices, vagrants and transients were designated as criminals unless they remained in their assigned abodes and worked at their jobs.[18] As the number of displaced poor rose in sixteenth-century England, the government adopted increasingly harsh punitive laws against vagrants and unemployed indigents and vested responsibility for the poor, as well as unrestrained control over their lives, in local governments.

The American colonial settlers adopted the English Poor Laws and retained the emphasis on linking relief to work requirements. By the eighteenth century every state in the Union enforced vagrancy laws against the unemployed poor that punished idle persons without means of support who, although able-bodied, failed to work.[19]

During the twentieth century, the legal systems empowering local governments to regulate and punish displaced able-bodied poor people began to break down. During the Great Depression, many jurisdictions continued to enforce laws criminalizing paupers and attempted to expel newly arrived poor people. However, many challenges were directed to the official efforts to exclude itinerant poor people. In 1941, *Edwards v. California*, the United States Supreme Court struck down a California law that prohibited the importing of paupers into the state.[20] *Shapiro v. Thompson*, decided in 1969, dealt a further blow to state statutes that predicated the receipt of benefits on the length of residence.[21]

The major emphasis of all welfare programs during the War on Poverty was on linking work and/or job training to eligibility for public assistance, whether GR or AFDC. Under the recently enacted Family Support Act, every state is required to develop a mandatory work requirement and job training program for AFDC recipients. Contemporary thinking continues the linkage between work and welfare so that all efforts to reform welfare in the foreseeable future will feature "workfare" goals and objectives.[22]

This combination of tradition and the current emphasis on connecting work and welfare ("workfare") has directly affected many homeless people. Whether homeless, or at risk of homelessness, the threat of losing public assistance benefits spells the end of the line for many. In response to this peril, legal advocates for the homeless have addressed harsh work requirements for recipients of public assistance.

*Washington v. Board of Supervisors* contested San Diego County's policy of limiting GR for employable recipients to 3 months in any given 12-month period. Initially, the court denied the plaintiffs' motion for a preliminary injunction against the county. The plaintiffs then petitioned for an appellate writ and obtained a stay. The Court of Appeal has held that San Diego County must continue to provide General Relief to employable recipients. The Court of Appeal held that the "injury to the recipients from immediate loss of benefits appears to be considerably greater than the apparent damage suffered by the Board resulting from expenditure of money to fund this program."[23]

Los Angeles County imposed a fixed 60-day penalty for GR recipients who failed to present documentation that they had completed job search requirements. The Legal Aid Foundation of Los Angeles filed suit against the County of Los Angeles in 1991 and the parties reached a settlement in the dispute over the administration of the GR sanctions.

The County agreed to replace the 60-day penalty for each violation of program rules with a new sliding scale of 0 days for the first violation, and 60 days for the third violation. It was also agreed that if a recipient has no violations during the preceding 12 months, he or she starts a clean record on any discipline. Moreover, all recipients were allowed to begin with a "clean record" as of the settlement.

Additional items in the settlement included other changes in the County's GR program. Recipients were allowed to file their monthly reports by the third Thursday of each month and then have their aid immediately reinstated. A new unit was to be established to help disabled recipients qualify for SSI, and the job search requirements were to be amended to allow recipients to "cure" any violation. The County estimated that the settlement of the case increased the GR budget by approximately 21 million dollars annually.[24]

An earlier work/welfare case was tried in Los Angeles County in 1985. *Bannister v. Board of Supervisors of Los Angeles County* directly challenged the County's requirement that GR recipients locate and present written verification of 20 job interviews per month, turn in verification forms, and attend scheduled interviews to be eligible for general relief assistance. All infractions, no matter how minor, resulted in a 60-day denial of all relief, including emergency relief. Plaintiffs alleged that this indiscriminate use of sanctions resulted in approximately 5000 people being forced out into the street, and that such enforced homelessness was a violation of substantive due process and fundamental rights under the state Constitution and state law.

The court ruled that recipients were to be allowed to establish good cause for their failure to comply with the eligibility requirements before the County could impose sanctions on eligibility. This lawsuit compelled the County to modify its GR administrative procedures to conform with court's orders.[25]

*Jennings v. Jones,* also tried in California in 1985, brought an action against the County of Los Angeles alleging that the county violated the federal and state Constitutions by imposing a fixed duration for the suspension of benefits, and that the method of terminating the benefits violated procedural due process.

County welfare policies for GR recipients required them to participate in the county's work assignment, work training, and other self-support programs to receive benefits. Those who did not comply were disqualified from eligibility for GR benefits for a fixed period.

The trial court ruled in favor of the County but the Court of Appeal reversed the lower court holding that the county violated the plaintiffs' procedural rights to due process in refusing to have a knowledgeable caseworker present at the pretermination hearings. The Court of Appeal also ruled that the sanctions imposed by the county violated statutory requirements that services and aid be provided promptly and humanely.[26]

## Food Stamps for Homeless People

Critics of the Food Stamp program point to alleged flaws in the system that enable recipients to be "welfare cheats." Long the target of welfare critics, the program is frequently held up as a sham. Images of middle class people standing in food stamp lines purchasing luxury food items characterize the negative stereotype of the food stamp "welfare cheat." Other stereotypes feature poor people who use their personal funds to purchase drugs and alcohol, and their food stamps to buy basic foodstuff.

These images have worked against homeless people who have been denied food stamps. The federal government did address this issue when it intervened in the state administrative process on behalf of homeless people granting food stamps to residents of shelters. Three court challenges have addressed this problem.

The first case was filed in 1985 in New York as a class action challenging the denial of food stamps to medically disabled homeless people who could not eat the food provided in shelters.

The enactment of federal food stamp legislation on behalf of shelter residents occurred during the case so that a settlement was reached. The settlement went beyond the law by approving awards of retroactive food stamps to the medically disabled plaintiffs.[27]

Five years after this case, *Franklin v. Kelly* was brought in the District of Columbia on behalf of all district residents who were eligible to receive food stamps and who either applied for assistance after 1989, or attempted to. This case is still pending.

The complaint alleges that the District of Columbia government does not provide food stamps within the time periods required by the Food Stamp Act, 5 days for homeless and destitute applicants and 30 days for all other applicants. The complaint also alleges that the District engages in practices that discourage eligible applicants from applying.

The parties entered into a Settlement Agreement in which the District agreed to comply with the Food Stamp Act. The District also agreed to conduct eight studies monitoring its compliance.

One year after the settlement, the plaintiffs filed a motion for summary enforcement of the Settlement Agreement claiming widespread violations of the Agreement. Subsequent to the filing of the plaintiffs' motion, the District issued its monitoring studies indicating that less than 30% of applicants approved for expedited food stamps based upon their indigence received assistance within the required 5-day period. The plaintiffs' motion for enforcement is now pending before the federal District court.[28]

A California case, filed in 1991 by the Western Center on Law and Poverty, appealed a District court decision that California's homeless assistance payments include income for food stamp purposes. The plaintiff-appellees were families with needy children. The central argument in the brief alleged that counting food stamps as part of the special needs payments does not constitute income under the state AFDC program because "they do not repeat indefinitely on a regular basis." The argument held that payments are resources.

The appellees case relied on a 1990 decision in *Massachusetts v. Lyng* that held that "back-to-school" clothing allowances were recurring payments because they were provided on a regular basis. The appellees also argued that the designation of food stamps as income violates the intent and meaning of the Food Stamp Act.[29]

Another case is in the discovery period. This case challenged the refusal of the city, state, and federal governments to provide food stamps to homeless single adults. Since this case was filed, the Homeless Eligibility Clarification Act has been implemented, obviating the need for prospective relief. However, the defendants are being sued for the payment of retroactive benefits. Their motion for a preliminary injunction was denied, and discovery is proceeding.

### Barriers to Access and Receipt of Public Assistance

The general unpopularity of public assistance programs, coupled with pervasive suspicion of recipients, has served as a rationale for imposing barriers and obstacles on recipients. Common among such barriers are payment delays, excessive requirements for verification of eligibility, and unmanageable caseloads that make it difficult, if not impossible, for recipients to interact with administrative personnel. The Department of Public Social Service office in Los Angeles' Skid Row has been reputed to let caseloads go as high as one worker per 1000 clients. Untimely changes in laws and procedures with little notice to recipients also feature prominently among obstacles to receipt of benefits.

Such barriers to access pose formidable obstacles to homeless people who live in a constant state of crisis. With difficult access to emergency relief, as well as regular payments and services, they are more imperiled than domiciled public assistance recipients. Access barriers also place more people at risk of becoming homeless.

More cases involving AFDC recipients have addressed access and barrier issues than those receiving GR.

AFDC recipients challenged the State of California's failure to send them timely notice of a change in the law that reduced their benefits. The District Court ruled in favor of the plaintiffs, but the Ninth Circuit reversed the decision, holding that the state is required to notify recipients of a change in the law only at least 10 days before benefit payments are reduced or overpayments are recovered, and that no prior notice is required. The Court also held that no "grace period" is required under the due process clause before the reduction of AFDC benefits.[30]

In *Pratt v. Wilson*, the court issued a declaratory judgment and held that the federal AFDC statute and regulations preempted California law and that California was therefore prohibited from issuing AFDC checks in an untimely fashion. The court rejected the argument of the defendants that since state funds had not been appropriated, the state constitution and laws prohibited the agency from paying the funds.[31]

A major barrier to eligibility for AFDC benefits lies in limitations on allowable assets. Possession of an automobile, house, jewelry, or any other property frequently disqualifies people who have lost their jobs and have exhausted all cash from qualifying for AFDC benefits. One of the few cases brought at the federal court level addressed this problem. The federal Department of Health and Human Service promulgated a regulation setting a maximum of $1500 on the amount of equity in an automobile that an AFDC recipient could own. We Who Care, an advocacy organization in Maine, filed a class action suit alleging that the regulation violated the Administrative Procedure Act and federal law. The defendants claimed that they had used a 1979 survey of food stamp households to issue the regulation. The data from the survey reported that 96% of food stamp recipients who own cars have an equity value of $1500 or less in the cars. Hence, the upper limit of the automobile asset exclusion was fixed at $1500. The plaintiffs countered that the survey was not part of the administrative record, and therefore the Department of Health and Human Services had no rational basis for promulgating the regulation.

The court stated that because the Department did not provide basic information about the food stamp survey, it was impossible to determine whether reliance on the survey was reasonable. Therefore, the court invalidated the automobile equity regulation.[32]

A case involving both the city and the state of New York involved a demand for prompt emergency issuance of cash benefits, food stamps, and Medicaid cards to persons whose benefits were improperly suspended because of problems in implementing the City's new computerized benefit system. The court issued temporary restraining orders on behalf of all named plaintiffs. A lengthy period of discovery, a motion for class certification, and a preliminary injunction followed. This resulted in a settlement requiring that "back-up" systems be put in place to ensure that eligible AFDC recipients receive their benefits on time, despite any computer-related errors. Moreover, the court ruled that individuals whose benefits are delayed because of any computer-related errors can receive their money and Medicaid cards on the day, or the day after, they were due. Food stamps were ordered to be reissued within 5 days of their due date.[33]

One final case involving complications in receipt of AFDC benefits was not held in favor of recipients. *Savage v. Aronson*, tried in the state of Connecticut, was a class action suit by AFDC recipient families living in emergency housing who challenged the state's 100-day limit on the emergency housing special needs benefit. The plaintiffs based their claim on state statutory language that requires the AFDC program to be administered so that children can remain in their own homes. The trial court invalidated the 100-day limit as inconsistent with this legislation, and also used child welfare laws and the state and federal constitutions as the basis for its decision.

The Connecticut Supreme Court reversed the lower court and held that the regulation limiting special needs emergency housing to 100 days was consistent with the state's statutes and its constitution. The court reasoned that the statute is concerned with conditions for eligibility for aid, and not the extent of the aid that must be provided.[34]

Barriers to general relief assistance were addressed in New York City where plaintiffs in *Robinson v. Grinker* challenged the City's policy and practice of establishing burdensome verification barriers to public assistance and Medicaid eligibility of applicants, including homeless adults. The court granted the plaintiffs' motions for class certification and for a preliminary injunction requiring the City to help all public assistance applicants obtain verification for eligibility. The City is required to make all contacts necessary to verify eligibility as a result of this case. Further requirements of the City include posting notices advising applicants of their right to such agency assistance.[35]

Only three cases have involved onerous residence requirements for eligibility despite the fact that legislators and administrators frequently attempt to limit public assistance benefits to permanent residents of jurisdiction.

*Thrower v. Perales* challenged New York State and City policy in which single adult homeless shelter residents were considered ineligible for public assistance and Medicaid. The trial court ruled that the government's position was inconsistent with the nonpunitive and rehabilitative policy underlying New York's social welfare laws. The judge ordered the City to develop a plan to provide cash grants and Medicaid to shelter residents.

The State and City appealed the trial court decision but the plaintiffs and state defendants reached a settlement in which the State agreed to grant Medicaid eligibility to adult single homeless shelters. It was also agreed that the State would promulgate regulations providing that adult shelter residents are eligible for Home Relief grants. The State subsequently promulgated regulations providing eligible homeless persons with a $45 grant in addition to their regular grant.[36]

The state trial court in Minnesota held that a statute requiring recipients of general relief assistance to reside in the state for at least 6 months burdened the plaintiffs' fundamental right to travel. The court held that the primary objective of the regulation was to deter indigent people from traveling to Minnesota.

The court also held that the statute denied newcomers privileges that were granted to longtime residents. The defendants argued that this provision of the Minnesota Statute was necessary to promote the state's interest in removing an incentive for indigent persons to move to Minnesota and in saving money. The court ruled that the law violated the constitutional rights of the plaintiffs to travel and to equal protection of the laws under the Federal Constitution. The court did not make any determination of state constitutionality.[37]

A class-action suit filed in Superior Court in Hartford, Connecticut alleged that the City of Hartford's requirement of verification of residence before accepting or processing applications for general relief assistance (including shelter) violated state law. The court held in favor of the plaintiffs.

A review of each of the above cases indicates a clear judicial trend to rule in favor of more generous financial aid and services to public assistance recipients. Where statutes and administrative regulations governing public assistance have appeared to be inhumane or unfair, court litigation has helped remedy the inequities and hardships accorded to homeless and indigent persons.

## Notes and References

1. *In re Petitions for Rulemaking N.J.A.C. 10:82-1.2*, 117 N.J. 311, 566 A.2d 1154(1989) (Clearinghouse No. 43, 465); U.S. Senate, *National Affordable Housing Act*, Pub. L. No. 101-625, 1990, Section 558, 42. U.S.C. Section 1437f; National Housing Law Project, *Annotated Bibliography*, 39–30 (Introduction, Note 9).

2. *Burks v. Knudson*, Calif. Super. Ct., Alameda County, August 13, 1991 (Clearinghouse No. 47, 094).

3. *Emerson v. Clarke*, No. 3 Civil CO12651 (Cal. App. filed February 20, 1992) (Clearinghouse No. 47, 851).

4. *Mendly v. County of Los Angeles* (GA Grant Levels) (January 1991).

5. *Poverty Resistance Center v. Hart*, 213 Cal. App. 3d 295, 161 Cal. Rptr. 545 (Cal. App. 1989), 271 Cal. Rptr. 214, 793, P 2d 523 (1990) (Clearinghouse No. 40, 263).

6. *Boehm v. Superior Court*, 178 Cal. App. 3d 494, 223 Cal. Rptr. 716 (Cal. App. Ct., 5th Dist. 1986) (Boehm II) (Clearinghouse No. 34, 784); State of California Welfare and Institution Code, Sections 17000; 10000; *The Universal Declaration of Human Rights*, Art. 25(2), Gen. Assm. Res. 217A(III), U.N. Doc. A/810, 19 December 1948.

7. *Boehm v. County of Merced*, 163 Cal. App. 3d 447, 209 Cal. Rptr. 530 (Cal. App. Ct. 5th Dist. 1985) (Boehm I) (Clearinghouse No. 34, 784).

8. *Villa v. Arrizabalaga*, 86 Nev. 137, 466 P. 2d 663 (1970).

9. *Ventrone v. Birkel*, 54 Ohio St. 2d 461 (1978).

10. *Hughes v. Dallas County*, No. 87-2124-J (191st Judicial District Court, Dallas County, September 1990) (settlement agreement).

11.  *Heschke v. County of Sheboygan*, No. 86 CV 876 (Wis. Cir. Ct., Sheboygan County, November 7, 1988) (Clearinghouse No. 44, 211).

12.  *Johnson v. Berson*, D.Colo. C.A. No. 92-5-1129 (filed June 3, 1992) (Clearinghouse No. 45, 956); U.S. Congress, *The Family Support Act*, 42nd Cong., 2d Sess, 1991.

13.  *Quattlebaum v. Dixon*, Civ. Action No. 8207-91 (D.C. Super. Ct. April 13, 1992) (order of summary judgment) (Clearinghouse No. 46, 979).

14.  *Massachusetts Coalition for the Homeless v. Secretary of Human Services*, 400 Mass. 806, 511 N.E. 2d 603 (1987); *Massachusetts Coalition for the Homeless v. Johnston*, No. 80109 (Mass. Super. Ct., Suffolk, filed February 15, 1990) (Clearinghouse No. 40, 714).

15.  National Housing Law Project, *Annotated Bibliography*, 42 (Introduction, Note 9).

16.  *Jiggets v. Grinker*, 75 N.Y. 2d 411, 553 N.E. 2d 570 (1990), rev'g 148 A.D. 2d 1 (1st Dept. 1989) (Clearinghouse No. 43, 124).

17.  California Welfare and Institutions Code #12550; *Thornton v. Carlson*, Cal. App. (1st Dist. 1992), 92 Daily Journal D.A.R. 4107 (March 27, 1992) (Clearinghouse No. 45, 723).

18.  James F. Stephen, *A History of the Criminal Law of England* (London: Macmillan, 1883), 267.

19.  *Ibid.*

20.  *Edwards v. California*, No. 314, U.S. Sup. Ct., 162 (1941).

21.  *Shapiro v. Thompson*, No. 394, U.S. Sup. Ct., 618 (1969).

22.  Will Marshall and Elaine Ciulla Kamarck, "Replacing Welfare with Work," in Will Marshall and Martin Schram, eds., *Mandate for Change* (New York: Berkley Books, 1993), 217–236. This chapter outlines the welfare reform agenda of the Progressive Policy Institute as well as President William Clinton's general agenda on the issue.

23.  *Washington v. Board of Supervisors* of San Diego County, No. DO16346 (Cal. Ct. App. Mar. 17, 1992) (Clearinghouse No. 47, 789).

24.  *City of Los Angeles v. County of Los Angeles* (GA Sanctions) June 11, 1991.

25.  *Bannister v. Board of Supervisors of Los Angeles County*, 165 Cal. App. 3d 1083 (1985) (Clearinghouse No. 40, 916).

26.  *Jennings v. Jones*, 165 Cal. App. 3d 1983, 212 Cal. Rptr. 134 (Cal. App. Ct., 5th Dist. 1985).

27.  *Petroff v. Block*, No. 85 Civ. 7099 (GLG) (S.D.N.Y., September 5, 1985) (settlement agreement).

28.  *Franklin v. Kelly*, No. 90-3124 (D.D.C. filed December 26, 1990) (Clearinghouse No. 46, 308).

29.  *Hamilton v. Yeutter*, No. 90-16114 (9th. Cir. filed January 30, 1991) (Clearinghouse No. 43, 557); National Law Center on Homelessness and Poverty, *Annotated Docket*, 130.

30.  *Rosas v. McMahon*, 945 F.2d 1469 (9th Cir. 1991).

31.  *Pratt v. Wilson*, 770 F. Supp. 539 (E.D. Cal. 1991).

32.  *We Who Care, Inc., v. Sullivan*, 756, F. Supp. 42 (d. Me. 1991) (Clearinghouse Nos. 23, 565; 46, 026).

33. *Jackson v. Grinker*, (S.D.N.Y. January 1989) (settlement) (Clearinghouse No. 42, 988).

34. *Savage v. Aronson*, 214 Conn. 256, 571 A. 2d 696 (1990) (Clearinghouse No. 44, 743).

35. *Robinson v. Grinker*, N.Y.L.J., January 5, 1988, p. 12 (Sup. Ct., N.Y. Co.).

36. *Thrower v. Perales*, 523 N.Y.S. 2d 937 (Sup. Ct. N.Y. Co. 1987).

37. *Mitchell v. Steffen*, No. C8-91-11691 (Minn. D. Ct., January 8, 1992) (order granting summary judgment) (Clearinghouse No. 47, 194); aff'd, MN. Sup. Ct.; *State of Minnesota Statutes*, Section 256 D.O65 (Supp. 91).

# 4

## PUBLIC CHILD WELFARE

### Homeless Families in the United States

Advocates and the media frequently observe that the fastest growing group of homeless people in the United States is homeless families. This may be so but it does not support widespread concerns that most of the homeless population will be families if the current trend continues. Surveys of the gender composition of homeless samples across the United States in the 1980s consistently found that single men constitute 81% of the homeless populations studied. Furthermore, African Americans are overrepresented among all samples.[1]

These data have important policy implications about race, gender, and structural disadvantage limiting education, employment, and status opportunities for African American men. They also lead to a partial explanation for the proliferation of family homelessness during the past two decades.

As long-term joblessness began to increase for mature men between the ages of 25 and 44 in the 1970s, marriage rates declined precipitously. The number of unmarried men went from 20.3% of the total population in 1969 to 36.9% in 1989, and 23.9 to 36.6% among women.[2]

Issues of validity and reliability continue to distort research on homeless people. Conventional census and survey data produce counts of homeless people that are frequently based upon the number of people who use, or request, shelters coupled with counts of those who are visible on the streets. These data exclude people who have not requested shelter services for a variety of reasons. Nor do they include people who are precariously housed living doubled up with families and friends or on the verge of eviction.

These problems apply particularly to data about the number of homeless families and are further distorted by the fact that most shelters still do not have facilities for children. Consequently, many homeless parents tend to leave their children with others when they present for shelter. Even those shelters that accept children frequently have rules that turn away men, welcoming only women and children. Therefore, married mothers also present as single individuals.[3] All of this means that many persons in shelters are not counted as part of a family, further distorting data on the relative numbers of homeless families and individuals.

Considerations about policies, services and the law necessarily depend upon knowledge of the characteristics of the target population. Since there are very few empirical studies of homeless families, estimated at close to 30, credible findings are problematic. Accounting for any deficiencies, there is common agreement among researchers and service providers that certain modal tendencies prevail and that homeless families differ markedly from the general homeless population.

The process that produces homeless families operates selectively along race, ethnic, and gender lines reflecting the structural patterns that contribute to poverty and inequality. Demographically, the descriptive data on homeless families are similar to those of the domiciled poverty population. Female-headed single-parent families numerically dominate among homeless families. Women found on the streets or in shelter surveys are more likely to be accompanied by at least one other family member, usually their child. Those few men found in surveys of homeless families with children were twice as likely to be accompanied by a spouse.[4] The average ages for parents in homeless families ranges from 26 to 30 years, younger than the general homeless population. Large proportions had their first child as teenagers. Nearly one-half have never been married and their children are very young.

The ethnic composition of the families is dominated by African Americans at 54% nationally, 70% in Washington, D.C., and 90% in Detroit. Latinos are overrepresented nationally at 20 and 30% in New York City. The rural homeless in Ohio are the only exception to the fact that African Americans and Latinos dominate the numbers of homeless families. Nationally, white people comprise 22% of the homeless family population.

Other important characteristics that have been studied are the extent of mental illness and substance abuse, income, previous housing, and life histories.

Mental illness and substance abuse are higher among the general homeless population than among homeless families. However, substance abuse is more prominent than it is among comparable domiciled families. Homeless women with children had also spent little time in jails or prisons, unlike many single homeless people.

Most homeless families rely on AFDC or General Assistance payments. Those who receive AFDC, and related benefits, are financially better off than other homeless people, but their incomes remain below poverty levels. Homeless families also differ somewhat from other housed poor people because they have fewer social supports among family and friends who can help them. One in four to one in five had been in foster care at some time. Many of their families had also lived on public welfare. They also have fewer resources for additional income from unreported "boyfriends" or off-the-record jobs to supplement their public assistance incomes.

Inquiries about previous housing reveal a major finding about homeless families. They tend to have been precariously housed before becoming homeless. Less than half have ever been primary tenants. One in four who were primary tenants reported eviction before becoming homeless. Those who lived doubled up cite disputes with the primary tenants as the precipitating factor for their homelessness.

A final, and encouraging, set of data relates gender and the length of time homeless. Homeless women report shorter periods of homelessness than men. The average length of time homeless for men was nearly 4 years compared to just under 3 years for women. Among homeless women, those with children have been able to avoid homelessness longer with minimal resources than either single men or women.[5]

In summary, homeless families tend to be single-parent, headed by young mothers with very young children. They have few social bonds and supports, and those that they do have are also extremely poor. They are drawn primarily from minority groups associated with poverty. They rely on public assistance payments and in-kind benefits and services for income, and their housing history has been precarious, at best.[6] More homeless families resemble those who are precariously housed and live marginally as single extremely poor parents. For these housed women, the specter of homelessness for them and their children remains an imminent threat.

Finally, the combined factors of long-term joblessness, declining marriage rates, and pools of men available for marriage, and scarcity of safe, affordable housing for unemployed, and underemployed, people have contributed to the surfacing of family homelessness only in the past decade.

A seldom discussed consequence of family homelessness is that children in homeless families are regularly placed into foster care simply because parents unable to provide a home are considered unfit to care for their children. In addition, older children are often prohibited from staying with their parents in family shelters. Instead, older children, especially boys, are removed from homeless families and placed into foster care.

Notwithstanding the devastating impact these placements have on family integrity and well being, such placements are usually unsuccessful, especially among older children, since many youth would rather attempt to make it on their own than have strangers care for them. Many of these children take to the street with nowhere to go and, most often, with inadequate services available to assist them.

It is common knowledge that foster care systems across the nation are faltering under dramatically increasing case loads. The number of children placed in foster care in America rose 23% between 1985 and 1988 (340,000 children in foster care in 1988 as compared to 276,000 in 1985).[7] The nexus between the foster care services in our country and the increasing incidence of homelessness among youth is very close.

### The Policy Framework for Homeless Family Advocates

Four legislative arenas govern public child welfare policy related to the best interests of children and their families: protective services, public assistance, foster care, and adoption. Recently enacted child support payment enforcement laws enacted as part of welfare reform may also have implications for litigating on behalf of homeless mothers and children, but they have not yet been tried in any courts. Advocates for homeless families have drawn upon each of the four policy arenas in developing legal briefs representing homeless families.

The Social Security Act requires the states to develop child protective services. However, because each state is permitted to develop its own service system, there has been little uniformity across the nation. The social movement that emanated from the scandalous reports of widespread child abuse and neglect among families and public child welfare agencies in the 1960s prompted the first national uniform standard of protective services through the enactment of the Child Abuse Prevention and Treatment Act of 1974.[8]

Unfortunately, the national standards and reporting requirements led to increased reports of the number of child abuse incidents, and more disturbingly, the number of deaths from child abuse. There was sufficient blame to go around, but the public child welfare agencies responsible for enforcing the law received the harshest criticism. Child welfare workers, faced with increased demands for service and enforcement under the law, could not fulfill their responsibilities because they were given no additional resources after the passage of the law.

This led to a severe deterioration in children's services. Rather than increasing resources necessary to respond to burgeoning child abuse reports, politicians and administrators relaxed their criteria for child abuse reports that were of sufficient danger to warrant emergency intervention. Contemporary debate about the definition of child abuse is highly controversial. Many parents and educators contend that child abuse definitions are too broad and tend to interfere with traditional rights of parents, teachers, and other authority figures in the lives of children.

Different arguments emanate from more liberal people who are concerned about the imposition of middle-class values on poor people. These people contend that middle-class social workers use public child welfare services to evangelize among the poor in an effort to undermine parents and establish professional control in family matters.[9]

Children's advocates, exemplified by the Children's Defense Fund, did not leave these arguments unattended. The deterioration of public child welfare agencies, and its rationale, prompted them to launch national appeals for increased funding for children's services. They have also carefully monitored agency practices for violations of the substantive and procedural rights of children.

Foster care is the primary service for the victims of child abuse. Over one-half of children in foster care were placed there by child protective service workers. This important link between child protective services and foster care has concerned advocates for homeless families. Child welfare agencies can separate children and parents when families lose their homes and are unable to obtain, or maintain, a new home in which to adequately raise their children. They may even withhold public assistance payments until the removal of homeless children from their parents. The Mayor of New York City has recently indicated that the city will remove children from homeless parents who "refuse to sign independent living plans, or do not comply with them."[10]

The family is protected from government intervention by the Constitution and parents have a constitutional right to raise their children as they please.[11] Family privacy and parental authority can be temporarily or permanently terminated under the doctrine of *parens patriae* to protect children from abuse and neglect that threatens their well-being. This doctrine is exercised in the juvenile court system under which the courts can authorize the state to intervene in the family in four situations: (1) when a child has committed a crime, (2) when a child's behavior is judged injurious to his or her welfare, (3) when a child has been neglected or abused, and (4) when a child has no parents able to care or provide for him. The third and fourth criteria for parental termination have applied to homeless children and their parents.[12]

Foster care is relegated to the states by the Social Security Act and this system has been as varied and fragmented as protective services over its history. By the 1960s it became clear that foster care had become a long-term experience for many youngsters. One study reported that 70% of children had been in foster care for more than 1 year.[13] This study, and others, led child welfare advocates to press for more intense permanency planning and family preservation.

The ideals of permanency planning and family preservation became the central features of the Adoption Assistance and Child Welfare Act of 1980, and implementing guidelines for the states to follow. Known as the Child Welfare Act, the law was an ambitious attempt to provide comprehensive services to children and their families toward the ends of family preservation and reunification. Like most federal legislation mandating states to provide social welfare services, adequate financial resources did not follow. Moreover, the resources that were available under Title XX of the Social Security Act were cut 21% in 1981. Between 1977 and 1992, Title XX lost $3.2 billion, or 55.4% of its funding.[14]

Lack of resources, complicated by scarce quality foster care placements and inadequate family preparation, contributed to a vicious cycle in which children were repeatedly removed from their biological parents to foster placements, returned home, and removed once again. This disruptive cycle experienced by children in foster care repeated the experiences of the severe and persistently mentally ill people who go through the revolving door syndrome from hospital to community and back again.

Adoption became an essential public child welfare service under the intent of permanency planning. The Child Welfare Act provided subsidies to adoptive parents as an incentive to adopt children who had been in foster placement and had proven hard to adopt. Subsidized adoption proved to be more cost-effective than permanency planning with poorly prepared biological parents and 90% of subsidized adoptions now involve foster parents who lacked the financial resources to accept full parental responsibility for their foster children when they had formed a relationship.[15]

There have been many implementation problems associated with the Child Welfare Act, but lawyers representing homeless families have relied upon the intent and language of the law regarding family preservation in bringing lawsuits before the court to protect parents and children from temporary or permanent separation under charges of abuse, neglect, or the inability of parents to care for their children.

Finally, state welfare and social service administrative codes frequently establish standards of adequate, or minimally decent living standards. Most of these standards relate to public assistance benefit levels, but lawyers for homeless families have also applied them to destitute children who cannot be cared for in their home.

The remaining sections of this chapter identify litigation on behalf of homeless families that has been based upon the above child welfare policy arenas.

## Child Welfare Act Litigation

Legal briefs and court decisions based upon the Child Welfare Act have followed several discrete themes. The most prevalent argument has been based upon the inseverability of the parent–child bond and the intent of the law to preserve the family unit. Some cases have argued that the provision of housing is an essential requirement for family preservation. Others have focused on the provision of adequate income and benefits to keep families intact.

One of the most extensive cases using the Child Welfare Act to link housing and AFDC entitlements to homeless families was tried in a California intermediate appellate court. The court declared that "the preservation of the family unit is also an objective which courses throughout the body of laws governing the AFDC program."[16] The court determined that the combined intent of California child welfare and Emergency Assistance (EA) laws requires the State Department of Social Services to prevent the separation of families through homelessness by providing emergency shelter to keep families intact.

The Court further invalidated a state EA regulation that authorized shelter services only for children who had been removed from their parents, holding that the regulation forced parents to artificially choose between holding their families together or seeking shelter for their children. Invoking the Child Welfare Act, the court stated that the language of the law "makes evident Congressional recognition of the inseverability of child well-being from the preservation of the family unit."[17]

This decision resulted in state legislation enacting an AFDC Special Needs Program, the Homeless Assistance Program. The program provided up to 4 weeks of housing and financial assistance for costs required to obtain permanent housing, as well as immediate temporary cash assistance. An attractive feature of this program was its coordination between the housing, income, and service needs of beneficiaries. Homeless and welfare advocates alleged that 60,000 children benefited from the program in its first year of operation.[18]

A District of Columbia case, tried in the Superior Court, representing a homeless mother whose children were placed in foster care was decided upon the principle of the primacy of housing for family preservation. The family was forced out of its public housing unit by a fire and refused a replacement unit because it had an outstanding debt to the housing authority. The children were removed to foster care after 1 year when the mother could not find housing for the family.

They petitioned the court to compel the District to place them in public housing so that the family could be reunited. The Department of Human Services entered into a consent decree to pay the mother's first month rent, security deposit, and monthly rent subsidy until the public housing authority was able to place the family in subsidized housing.[19]

A class-action suit was filed in the District of Columbia in 1991 on behalf of children in foster care under the District's Department of Human Services. Children who were not yet in foster care but were known by the Department because of reported abuse and neglect were also included in the suit. The plaintiffs brought their complaint alleging that the District child welfare system was in violation of the federal Child Welfare Act, the Child Abuse Prevention and Treatment Act, and the fifth amendment of the United States Constitution. They sought injunctive relief under the provisions of these laws.

The District court held that Section 1983 of the Child Welfare Act provided a federal remedy for violation of the Act and that the Department of Human Services had deprived children of the rights conferred by the Act. The court further held that the district human service officials had deprived children in foster care of their constitutionally protected liberties.[20]

A case representing a homeless mother in Chicago alleged that the failure of the state child welfare department to provide her with greater housing assistance violated the intent of state and federal law to reunite, and preserve, families separated by a lack of housing. The court found that the family needed permanent and adequate housing and charged the child welfare department with the responsibility for assisting the family to locate such housing. The court further ordered the department of child welfare to provide cash assistance associated with finding and securing permanent housing.[21]

In *Cosentino v. Perales* (1987), Cosentino challenged the failure of New York City and State to provide preventive services in the form of emergency shelter and other housing services to curtail or avert the placement of children in voluntary foster care. The claim was based upon state statutes, under the Child Welfare Act, requiring preservation of the family unit through preventive services intended to shorten or prevent foster placement.

The court granted the plaintiffs a preliminary injunction stating that the city's failure to provide such preventive services constituted a violation of federal and state law. The city requested a court conference in which the court specified that the plan required by the injunction meant that the city had to develop a comprehensive plan to address systemic problems, and that individual approaches did not suffice under statutory obligations. The court also enjoined the state's 90-day limitation on the provision of emergency shelter as a preventive service.

Upon appeal, the Appellate division affirmed the lower court's decision. The plaintiffs then pursued enforcement of the decision and successfully negotiated with the city to provide rent subsidies to shorten or avert foster care placements.[22]

A related class action suit in New York, *Grant v. Cuomo*, sought improved protective and preventive services, including housing assistance, for families of children at risk of foster placement resulting from homelessness. The decision of the Appellate division was confirmed by the Court of Appeals. It granted substantial discretion to the city in determining which preventive services are needed.[23] This case weakened the force of the *Cosentino* decision but retained its substantive direction.

The principle of reasonable efforts to unite families, articulated in the Child Welfare Act, was invoked in Rhode Island when the Supreme Court affirmed the decisions of the Rhode Island Family Court. Both courts ordered the state Department for Children and their Families to provide rent subsidies to AFDC recipient families when it was necessary to reunite them and avoid foster placement. The courts held that the Family Court may order the child welfare department to provide housing assistance as part of its statutory duty to make reasonable efforts to reunite families. The court specified reasonable efforts to include housing assistance when homelessness is a primary factor preventing family reunification.[24]

## Litigation Based on Public Assistance and State Welfare Codes

Housing and family preservation issues have been contested on grounds other than the Child Welfare Act. Child welfare entitlement questions readily overlap with income maintenance entitlement arguments related to the definitions of adequacy and minimum standards. The premises of these cases is that the Social Security Act unequivocally protects people from institutionalization in work houses and other indoor relief requirements. Homeless welfare advocates have interpreted this to mean that people are entitled to remain with their families under the most extreme instances of destitution.

The Ventura, California Department of Social Services operated under a policy of excluding homeless AFDC-eligible children who remain with their parents from participating in the state's emergency assistance program. Individual plaintiffs filed a taxpayer's mandamus action to compel the state department to assist homeless families, arguing that the restriction irrationally induced family break-up, thereby violating the California Constitution and the state law. The trial court held that the statutes governing the state's AFDC program did not extend to finding housing for homeless families. This judgment was reversed on appeal.[25]

A case tried before the State Supreme Court of Delaware restored child custody to a homeless mother and instructed the trial courts to ensure that all concrete efforts, including housing assistance, be provided before resorting to foster placement. At the time of removal, the mother was a minor unrepresented by counsel. She claimed that she signed documents that she believed would preserve her parental rights. The court found that the department had violated her due process rights and that the sole reason for transfer of custody was that no effort had been made to assist the mother to secure shelter. This decision was based upon the fact that the state receives federal funds for its foster care program that require reasonable efforts to prevent termination of parental custody.[26]

A District of Columbia code formed the basis for a Superior Court decision compelling the District to provide a mother, who had been on the waiting list for public housing for some time, with housing suitable for her family. The decision was based upon a child welfare code that grants authority to the Department of Human Services Family Division to order any public agency in the District to provide any services that the Division determines is needed and is within such agency's legal authority.[27]

In Dade County, Florida a court action challenged the failure of the Florida Department of Health and Rehabilitative Service to prevent removal of children from their families, or to reunite families after separation when homelessness is the contributing factor to children's removal.

The plaintiff in the case was the great-aunt and temporary guardian of four children. After she was awarded temporary custody of the children, she was forced to move because her apartment was condemned. The plaintiff alleged that the Department refused to help her find suitable replacement housing and threatened to remove the children from her custody because she failed to provide a home for them. Lawyers based this contention on the state's Juvenile Justice Act, Titles IV-B and IV-E of the Social Security Act, and equal protection, family integrity, and privacy rights guaranteed by the Florida and United States Constitutions. The Department agreed to provide housing assistance for the plaintiff through vendor or third-party payments.[28]

The plaintiffs in *Norman v. Johnson* challenged the Illinois Department of Children and Family Services' failure to make reasonable efforts to assist them in securing housing. The court held that the reasonable efforts requirement of the United States Code, Section 671(a)(b) is sufficiently clear to be an enforceable right thereby requiring the Department of Children and Family Services to assist destitute parents in finding and obtaining housing so that they can be reunited with their children.[29]

The Massachusetts Coalition for the Homeless developed one of the more far reaching arguments for benefit standards sufficient to protect families from homelessness in the state's Superior Court. The plaintiffs claimed that the state benefit levels, set at 46% below the poverty line, did not comply with a 1913 state law entitling poor people to raise their children in their own home. The coalition won its claim and it was further supported on appeal to the Supreme Judicial Court, but it authorized the state legislature to set the benefit level rather than assigning it to the less political court jurisdiction. Wisely, the legislature raised the shelter allowance level to 14% of private housing and 12% in successive years.[30]

Lawyers successfully argued in *Jiggets v. Grinker*, tried in the New York Court of Appeals, that the shelter grant should be sufficient to obtain housing in New York City. The court also held that it should determine the adequacy of the benefit standard. Although this decision specifically addressed the connection between public assistance benefit levels and housing, it applies to housing for families.[31]

In Ohio, the state Department of Human Services filed a dependency complaint to secure temporary custody of a homeless AFDC recipient's children. The agency admitted that it had not referred the family to emergency shelters, did not advise the mother of its service to assist in locating housing, and did not assist her with an Emergency Assistance application. The court ordered the department to furnish an emergency housing voucher and to assist her in obtaining suitable housing within 3 days. The department also agreed to continue AFDC under the federal temporary absence provision.[32]

One major case related to welfare regulations involving housing and family preservation is pending. The Washington State Coalition for the Homeless filed a class-action suit against the Department of Health and Social Services on behalf of three homeless families with children, and an organization of shelters. The argument for the plaintiffs alleged that the department failed to provide necessary housing assistance to homeless children and their parents. They sought to represent a class of children and parents who need housing to prevent or shorten the children's foster care placement.

Their specific argument was that state and federal child welfare statutes obliged the department to provide child welfare services to homeless children, including housing assistance necessary to address their homelessness. The plaintiffs defined such necessary assistance as emergency shelter, transitional or permanent housing in the form of cash assistance for rent, deposits, or other fees, vouchers, counseling, and any other services necessary to help a family relocate itself.[33]

## Abuse and Neglect Cases

Abuse and neglect concerns may prevail over family preservation concerns and related housing requirements. They pose the most ominous threats to family preservation. Child welfare staff are responsible for assessing whether abuse and neglect are the primary problems facing parents and children. The failure to provide a suitable home may be grounds for separation and placement in foster care, but numerous courts have ruled against this, as indicated above. Nevertheless, it is incumbent upon the state to determine that homeless children would not be abused or neglected if they were in appropriate housing with their parents. This policy arena has posed greater obstacles to litigation on behalf of homeless parents and children than cases filed under the principles of family preservation.

An illustrative case was decided in Connecticut in 1986 when a mother appealed a decision of the Superior Court committing her 3-year-old child to temporary custody of the Commissioner of Department of Children and Youth Services. The court refused to continue the matter until a criminal case against the mother's male friend was resolved so that he could testify at a dispositional hearing.

A criminal case was pending against the friend alleging that he abused the child. The court further required that the trial court place the child with his paternal grandmother before continuing the hearing. The court also determined that the mother's parental rights had not been terminated by placement of the child with the grandmother.

Illinois courts have ruled that housing assistance must be provided to homeless families to avert neglect actions. The Circuit Court in Cook County, Illinois issued a similar decision. It ordered the state child welfare department to assist in locating housing and procuring cash assistance in a neglect dependency action. The children were in the custody of the welfare department and the mother lacked adequate housing for the family.[34]

Young people who become emancipated from foster care when they reach their majority age frequently face the threat of homelessness. Many actually become homeless soon after their emancipation. *Palmer v. Cuomo* addressed this problem in the state of New York. The suit was filed representing a group of homeless young people under the age of 21 seeking relief for young persons who were discharged from the foster care system to the streets. The plaintiffs sought care, education, and training necessary for independent living until they reached age 21. The court held in favor of the plaintiffs' request and the state issued new discharge planning regulations to comply with the decision.[35]

## Conclusion

The cases cited in this chapter have viewed homeless families as requiring only economic assistance to cover the costs of safe and affordable housing. Many contend that these families need more than an economic boost to prepare them for stable lives and permanent housing. Supportive housing, housing combined with service interventions, has evolved as an effective and necessary strategy for helping many homeless families. Transitional and permanent living programs that offer job training, parenting skills, education in basic literacy, money management, child care, health and mental health services, coordinated through case management planning are demonstrating that the traumas experienced by these families can be overcome. Such programs, along with an adequate economic package, have helped move families off of the streets more rapidly than the general homeless population.

## Notes and References

1.   David Snow, Leon Anderson and Paul Koegel, "Distorting Tendencies in Research on the Homeless," in Peter H. Rossi, ed., *Troubling Families: Family Homelessness in America, American Behavioral Scientist,* 37(4):478–485 (February 1994).

2.   Christopher Jencks, *The Homeless* (Cambridge, MA: Harvard University Press, 1994), 51–58.

3.   Rossi, *Troubling Families,* 357.

4.   Susan Gonzalez Baker, "Gender, Ethnicity, and Homelessness," in David A. Snow and M. Gerald Bradford, eds., *Broadening Perspectives on Homelessness, American Behavioral Scientist* 37(4):478–480 (February 1994).

5.   Baker, "Gender, Ethnicity, and Homelessness," 481.

6.   Rossi, *Troubling Families,* 363–364.

7.   Gregory Evans, Director for Youth Advocacy, National Coalition for the Homeless. Statement before the National Commission on Children Outside Their Families, Los Angeles, CA (May 31, 1990).

8.   Kathleen Faller, "Protective Services for Children," in *Encyclopedia of Social Work,* 18th ed. (Silver Spring, MD: NASW, 1987), 386.

9.   Howard J. Karger and David Stoesz. *American Social Welfare Policy: A Pluralist Approach,* 2nd. ed. (New York: Longman, 1993), 340–342.

10.   Mary Brosnahan. "The Mayor's Empty Words," *New York Times* (June 9, 1994), A19.

11.   *Parham v. J.R.,* 442 U.S. 584 (1979).

12.   Saltzman and Proch, *Law in Social Work Practice,* 157–159 (Introduction, Note 11).

13.   Theodore Stein, "Foster Care for Children," in *Encyclopedia of Social Work,* 18th ed. (Silver Spring, MD: NASW, 1987), 641–642; Karger and Stoesz, *American Social Welfare Policy,* 342–343.

14.   Karger and Stoesz, *American Social Welfare Policy,* 344.

15.   *Ibid* 345–347.

16.   *Hansen v. McMahon,* 238 Cal. Rptr. 232 (Cal. App. 2 Dist. 1987) (Clearinghouse No. 40, 807).

17.  *Ibid* 238 Cal. Rptr. at 235.

18.  Melinda Bird, Bob Newman, and Josh Bernstein, *Monitoring the New Homeless Assistance Program*, mimeographed memorandum, Los Angeles Center on Law and Poverty (February 9, 1988).

19.  *In re P., et al.*, No. 12823 (D.C. Super. Ct. filed April 12, 1982) (Clearinghouse No. 28, 858).

20.  *La Shawn A. v. Dixon*, 762 F. Supp. 959 (d.D.C. Apr. 18, 1991).

21.  *In re Annette W.*, No. 87-17975 (Ill. Cir. Aug. 26, 1988).

22.  *Cosentino v. Perales*, 138 2d 212, 524 N.Y.S. 2d 121 (N.Y. Supr. Ct., 1987), State Appeal denied, No. 1390, slip op. (N.Y. Ct. App. January 9, 1990) (Clearinghouse No. 40, 918); *Martin A.V. Gross*, 546 N.Y.S. 2d 75 (1st Dept. 1989), *aff'g* 524 N.Y.S. 2d 121 (N.Y. Sup. Ct. N.Y. Ct. App. Jan. 9, 1990) (Clearinghouse No. 40, 918); National Center on Law and Poverty, *Annotated Bibliography*, 58 (Introduction, Note 9).

23.  *Grant v. Cuomo*, 130 A.2d 154 (N.Y. App. Div. 1987), *aff'g*, 73 N.Y. 820 (1988).

24.  *In re Nicole, Peter, and Crystal G.*, 577 A.2d 248 (R.I. 1990) (Clearinghouse No. 45, 633).

25.  *Montes v. Superior Court*, No. B-012398 (Cal. Ct. App. filed July 1, 1987) (Clearinghouse No. 41, 458).

26.  *In re Derek Burns*, 519 A. 2d 638 (Del. 1986) (Clearinghouse No. 42, 330).

27.  District of Columbia Code 16-2320 (a) (5); *In re D.I.*, Nos. N-269-81, M-339-81, and N-240-81 (D.C. Super. Ct., Family Div., May 6, 1985) (Clearinghouse No. 39, 415).

28.  *Brown v. Chiles*, No. 91-54813 (28) (Fla. Cir. Ct., Dade County, filed December 23, 1991).

29.  *Norman v. Johnson*, 739 F. Supp. 1182 (N.D. Ill. 1990).

30.  Blau, *The Visible Poor*, 104–105 (Introduction, Note 5).

31.  *Jiggets v. Grinker*, 75 N.Y. 2d 414 (1990).

32.  *In re Michael L., Christopher L., and Tiffany.*, No. F89-3743 (Ohio Ct. Comm. Pleas, Hamilton Cnty., Juvenile Div.) (1990) (Clearinghouse No. 45, 670).

33.  *Washington State Coalition for the Homeless v. Department of Social and Health Services*. No. 91-2-15889-4 (Wash. Super. Ct., King County, filed July 23, 1991) (Clearinghouse No. 98, 104).

34.  *In re Kellie C.*, No. 84 J 17076 (Ill. Cir. Ct., Cook County, Juvenile Div., February 19, 1988).

35.  *Palmer v. Cuomo*, Index No. 2307/85 (Sup. Ct. N.Y. Co., 1985) (*aff'd*, 121 A.D. 2d 194, 503 N.Y. 2d 20) (1st Dep't 1986).

# 5

## MENTAL HEALTH SERVICES

### Mental Illness among Homeless People

The coexistence of homelessness and mental illness is painfully apparent, but efforts to demonstrate a causal relationship between the two remain elusive. The debate surrounding the existence of such a relationship centers on whether homeless people experience mental disorders because of their situation, or whether mentally ill people are likely to end up homeless because of their behavior and symptoms.

A second critical aspect of the debate focuses on the unintended consequences of the deinstitutionalization movement that followed the passage of the Mental Retardation Facilities and Community Mental Health Centers Construction Act of 1963. Under this law 2000 community mental health centers were to be built and operating by 1980, or one center for every 100,000 people. Only 789 were ever funded.[1] The central issues in these debates have been articulated by many researchers and policy analysts.

The United States is the only nation that attributes homelessness to mental illness. Other nations view homelessness as the inevitable result of a reduced housing supply, a restructured economy, and the retrenchment of the welfare state. Nor does the popular notion that the deinstitutionalization movement of the 1960s was a well-intentioned policy failure hold up under the scrutiny of research.[2]

Undoubtedly, homeless mentally ill people are a conspicuous group of homeless and poor people. They are also among the most pitiful and vulnerable cohort of homeless people evoking intense public responses of sympathy, revulsion, and fear. Those who discredit causality between homelessness and mental illness are frequently among those who are highly sympathetic to the plight of homeless mentally ill people. These homeless advocates generally focus on the procurement and protection of entitlements to treatment, supportive housing, and civil liberties. They also stress the value of community care approaches that offer the highest probability of treatment in the least restrictive setting, a critical objective of the deinstitutionalization agenda.

Issues of causality are inevitably linked to political perspectives. Conservative political and social activists and psychiatrists tend to inflate the percentage of mentally ill among the homeless population. More liberal homeless advocates, humanistic psychologists, and social workers emphasize a psychosocial explanation.

Some psychiatric research has estimated the number of mentally ill among homeless people to be extremely large, even as high as 96.6%.[3] Other researchers have attempted to challenge these estimates by considering the impact of social conditions upon mental health and illness. These researchers have explained that some homeless people demonstrate symptoms of severe and persistent mental illness, but every symptom seen among them does not indicate mental disorder. For example, homeless people who are withdrawn, depressed, collect garbage for food, and groom themselves inappropriately may not experience mental disorder.[4] Such symptoms and manifestations of mental disorder may, indeed reflect disabilities, but their confusion and bizarre behavior may be adaptive. They may also be a result of the conditions they must endure as street people, for example, extreme hunger, sleep deprivation, harsh weather, and fear of personal danger. Paul Koegel and others have argued that psychiatric explanations of the behavior of mentally ill homeless persons need to be combined with ethnographic approaches to gain a valid profile of this population.[5]

Among researchers who eschew any theoretical bias, general survey estimates of the number of mentally ill among homeless populations in cities across the United States hover between 30 and 35% of all homeless people. Survey data also find that more than one-half of those with a diagnosed mental disorder are also substance abusers.[6] Schutt and Garrett's survey of studies in different cities across the United States that identify rates of severe and persistent mental illness among homeless people concluded that most studies estimate that between 25 and 50% of homeless persons suffer from mental illness. About one-third have been hospitalized for psychiatric treatment at some time. However, younger mentally ill homeless persons may never have experienced long-term hospitalization because of its unavailability since deinstitutionalization.[7]

It may even be that a larger percentage of mentally ill people are found among the domiciled population. Data from the National Institute of Mental Health Epidemiologic Catchment Area Program estimated that 54% of the 22.8 million people who used ambulatory and inpatient mental health and addiction services in the United States in a 1-year period had a Diagnostic Interview Schedule mental disorder. Another 37.4% had a history of psychiatric disorder or significant psychiatric symptoms. The widespread prevalence of mental disorder and substance abuse among the general population of services users, both domiciled and homeless, further weakens any attempt to demonstrate a causal relationship between homelessness and mental illness.[8]

## The Deinstitutionalization Debate

The deinstitutionalization movement that precipitated the decline of the mental hospital census remains the most misunderstood association between homelessness and mental illness. Although the census of mental hospitals dropped 79% from its 1955 peak by 1984, this downward spiral does not explain the growth of homelessness. Sixty-five percent of the decline in the hospital census had occurred before 1975, nearly a decade before the spread of homelessness. By now, with 100,000 children reported as homeless and 40% of the homeless consisting of families, even those most committed to linking homelessness and mental illness causally must acknowledge that deinstitutionalization has played a comparatively small role.[9]

Nevertheless, a different explanation of homelessness and deinstitutionalization carries some measure of logic. It is possible to argue that the absence of institutions as havens for mentally ill people has forced many of them into the streets. Implicit in this argument is the notion that if mental hospitals were available, mentally ill people would not be homeless. Proponents of this position continue to believe in the high prevalence of mental illness among the homeless and support the goals of a growing reinstitutionalization movement. Relatives and friends of mentally ill people who refuse treatment are organizing to pressure lawmakers to relax commitment criteria. Led by the Alliance for Mentally Ill, the largest association of families of mental patients, they argue that consigning mentally ill people to live on the streets or eat out of trash cans and suffer without care or medication is a perversion of civil liberties.

Much of the impetus for reinstitutionalization and relaxed involuntary commitment laws rests upon a concerted drive to solve the problem of the mentally ill homeless population by returning people to institutions. Neighborhood groups and citizens who are frightened by, or weary of, the growing numbers of homeless people in their communities are fueling much of this effort. They contend that the balance between the rights of society and individuals is out of kilter.

One sign of the increasing public determination to resolve the problem was a recent decision by the New York state legislature to expand the state's authority to compel mentally ill people with a history of hospitalization to take medication or attend counseling on an outpatient basis. If patients refuse they may be recommitted.

Homeless advocates contend that this decision does not necessarily signify a trend or a pattern. It is more of a direct reaction to a highly publicized case involving a schizophrenic crack addict named Larry Hogue who menaced New York's upper West Side for many years. Hogue had a long history of involuntary commitments. Frequently picked up by the police and committed to hospitals, he would be released in days, or sometimes months. When discharged he would stop taking his medication, start smoking crack, and return to setting fires, grabbing passing schoolchildren, and hurling himself into traffic. One time he pushed a teenager in front of a truck. The cycle stopped when he was committed for a longer time to a state hospital on the grounds that he was likely to abuse crack and become dangerous. Exceptional cases like this tend to drive legislation.

This decision passed without any protest from civil liberties lawyers who oppose the relaxation of commitment laws and would normally be expected to challenge such an effort. Civil libertarians contended that they could not defeat the proposals and opted not to fight them. Instead, they helped draft the legislation hoping to build in sufficient patient protections and safeguards.

Clearly, attempts to reinstitutionalize do not relate only to solutions for homeless mentally ill people. They emanate more from a general frustration over the stringency of the dangerousness and disability clauses in involuntary commitment laws among psychiatrists and families of mentally ill people. Many people are convinced that concern for the rights of patients has become excessive, rendering it impossible for some people who are severely disabled to receive care. This dilemma between liberty and care has been most dramatic in those instances where homeless mentally ill people not only refuse treatment, but also refuse to enter a shelter and some eventually die of hypothermia. The saga of Rebecca Smith, who died in a cardboard box that she had outfitted as her home during the winter of 1981 in Washington, D.C., exemplifies this problem.[10] In fact, this episode drew the nation's attention to its growing problem of mass homelessness.

Over the past 25 years, involuntary outpatient commitment has been periodically proposed as a strategy of reinstitutionalization. Under this approach, patients meeting certain criteria of dangerousness or need of treatment could be compelled by the courts to take part in treatment programs in the community. Involuntary outpatient commitment would undoubtedly affect some proportion of the homeless population, but it would not substantially alleviate the public problem of homelessness because of the complex connection between mental illness and homelessness.

Statutory provisions for such a status exist in about half of the states, even though the approach is rarely used. Scant empirical research exists on the policy and opponents and proponents are sharply divided on the merits of the policy. Those who oppose the use of this strategy fear that it will promote an erosion of the civil rights of mental patients for the sake of treatment.

Supporters of involuntary outpatient commitment, on the other hand, view the issue of civil liberties from a different perspective. They accept the fact that there is a population of mentally disordered individuals who cannot function effectively in the community, or respond to treatment, without a high level of structured supervision, including a measure of coercion. Proponents view the dilemma between liberty and care as based on a negative view of liberty. Freedom can be positive only when people are in control of their own actions. This argument typically concludes that present commitment laws allow people to die with their rights on.[11]

Under pressure from the public, from relatives and friends of mental patients, and from the medical community, the strict prohibitions against involuntary commitment are being relaxed and several states have already relaxed their standards for involuntary treatment. Arizona, Oklahoma, Delaware, South Carolina, New York, and Iowa have modified involuntary commitment criteria, allowing courts to order involuntary commitment based on factors other than danger to self and others or grave disability. These include psychiatric history and potential emotional injury to a family. These new rules, in effect, permit authorities to act where the need for treatment is very clear and individuals are unable to make decisions for themselves. E. Fuller Torrey, the psychiatrist leading the movement for involuntary treatment, frequently notes that the pendulum is starting to swing back in the direction of hospitalization for people who need treatment.

Although there is no clear relationship between the failed deinstitutionalization movement and homelessness, it is far too apparent that no comprehensive system of outpatient care in the community sufficiently replaced the mental hospital. Hence, people with severe and persistent mental disorders experience many serious obstacles and barriers to the scarce care available in the public mental health delivery system. Mentally ill people are, therefore, at risk of becoming homeless because of the inadequate number of community-based inpatient or outpatient treatment facilities.

It is important to understand that such care was always scarce, but over a decade of cuts in all human services has taken a heavy toll on the mental health system. In the past three decades since the advent of deinstitutionalization, state governments responsible for mental health resources have "carved away at program element after program element."[12] Most state budgets for mental health care and prevention allot less money today than they did when they operated state hospitals. Local communities have compounded this problem by their resistance to the location of community-based facilities, even group homes for as few as six residents.

The combined factors of a deinstitutionalization movement that was never fully implemented, divergent interpretations of the relationship between homelessness and mental illness, and budget cuts at state and local government levels have set in motion new problems that tend to criminalize homeless mentally ill individuals rather than offer them care and refuge.

Los Angeles County jail is reportedly the largest mental institution in the nation, one of the few remaining places offering them shelter and a minimal level of care. Even those who are gravely disabled or sufficiently dangerous to themselves or others to be involuntarily committed are turned away from care because few acute care hospital beds or alternative sanctuaries exist.

The homeless mentally ill frequently get stuck in the criminal justice system. Panhandling, public inebriation, behaving like a "public nuisance," and sleeping on the streets are frequent examples of citable offenses.

Housing poses additional problems. Board and care homes often screen out individuals who are unable to comply with their rules, many of which are reasonable. Left to voucher hotels, mentally ill people are vulnerable to rape, violence, burglary, and assault. Various shelters exclude mentally ill people, in particular those who have dual diagnoses of substance abuse and mental illness.[13]

Advocates assert that homeless persons with severe and persistent mental illnesses have the right to live in dignity with access to treatment services and housing appropriate to their level of need in the least restrictive settings. They also maintain that those persons who meet involuntary outpatient commitment criteria of danger to self or others and grave disability must receive involuntary hospitalization.

These rights have been established in the courts since the deinstitutionalization movement began in the 1960s. The civil libertarian principles of that period began to apply to mentally ill people and spawned a nationwide movement to obtain civil rights for mentally ill people. Social workers featured prominently in that effort. Advocates and service providers for homeless mentally ill individuals have relied upon the large body of court decisions governing patient's right to secure services and resources for their clients. Several recent cases have been brought before the court to reinforce earlier decisions.

This chapter reviews those court decisions that continue to protect all mentally ill people, including those who are homeless at any time. It also reviews the few cases that have reinforced the relevance of earlier decisions for homeless people, as well as some that have endangered their interests.

The extensive body of statutes, regulations, and court opinions that has evolved during the past 30 years guarantees a wide array of rights to mental patients. These include (1) the right to treatment for involuntarily and voluntarily admitted patients, (2) the right to refuse treatment, (3) the right to humane treatment in the least restrictive manner, (4)the right to be free of restraints and seclusion, (5)protection against institutional employment requirements, (6)the right to privacy, (7)the right to personal property, (8)First Amendment rights and freedoms, and (9) the right to due process protections when transfers to other institutions occur.

Despite the breadth of this list of rights, mental patients are not well protected. Their vulnerability and dependency on caregivers mean that the quality of caregiving frequently determines the guarantee of their rights. In practice, such rights are granted only if they are respected by the institution's staff, or if patients have strong and effective advocates.[14]

## The Right to Treatment

Any analysis of a right to treatment must take into account the fact that there is no constitutional right to medical care in the United States. Hence, there is no constitutional right to voluntary admission to mental hospitals, or care in the community. Nor is there any right to treatment once they are admitted. These rights do exist, however. They are located in private accreditation or licensing requirements that govern private and public mental patient facilities.

The first precedent-setting case involving involuntarily committed mental patients, *Lake v. Cameron*, was decided in 1966. This case affirmed the right to treatment in the least restrictive environment.[15] Five years later, *Wyatt v. Stickney* established the right to adequate treatment. The case, brought to the court on behalf of patients in the State of Alabama mental institutions, initially established a constitutional right to treatment for people confined against their will in state mental institutions and retardation facilities. However, the court refused to determine the standards to be used in treatment.

Six months after the decision, no treatment plans had been developed by the mental institutions, so the court scheduled a hearing to allow the interested parties and experts to propose minimum constitutional standards for treatment. The court found none of these standards acceptable and developed its own standards. Among these were matters pertaining to patient's clothing allotments, telephone privileges, hospital and staff qualifications, number of staff required, the content of individualized treatment plans, the interval between review of treatment plans, the number of tubs and toilets per patient, and the content of patients' records. The federal court defined these rights in terms of minimum standards for therapeutic services, humane environment, and protections against misuse of hazardous, intrusive, or experimental procedures.[16]

A Florida decision reviewed by the United States Supreme Court during that period, *O'Connor v. Donaldson*, recognized the right to freedom from custodial confinement for nondangerous persons who are labeled mentally ill. That case was originally expected to establish a right of involuntarily committed patients to treatment, but the Court refused to consider the right to treatment argument presented by the lawyers for the plaintiff. Instead, the Court decided the case on the grounds that Donaldson's commitment was unjustified no matter what treatment may have been provided.

To date, no Supreme Court case has decided whether involuntarily committed mentally ill adults have a right to treatment.[17] Therefore, state court decisions, statutes, and administrative codes provide the legal structure for involuntary commitment procedures and the right to treatment, e.g., *Wyatt v. Stickney*.

In those jurisdictions where a right to treatment exists, lawyers representing mentally ill people have attempted to codify and refine those rights. *Davis v. Watkins*, tried in Ohio in 1974, established a requirement that treatment be based upon individualized plans with short-term, intermediate, and long-term goals identified, as well as a timetable for achieving the planned goals.[18]

Concern over the right to treatment has been matched by interest in protecting patients' right to refuse treatment. Medical treatment cannot be given without a signed statement of informed consent. Agreement and informed consent are more complicated for mental patients than for medical patients. The protocol of informed consent requires that a patient must consent voluntarily, with demonstrated competence and full knowledge of the risks and alternatives to treatment. This can pose problems for mental patients. The nature of involuntary commitment contradicts the principle of voluntary informed consent.

*Kaimowitz v. Department of Mental Health*, tried in the State of Michigan in 1973, held that patients involuntarily committed to a State mental hospital could not give informed consent for experimental psychosurgery.

Involuntarily confined patients cannot reason as equals with the doctors and administrators over whether they should undergo treatment. They are not able to voluntarily give informed consent because of the inherent inequality in their position.[19]

Despite their inability to give informed consent, involuntary patients may be treated. They may also be denied the right to refuse treatment.

The courts have wrestled with the issue of the right of involuntarily committed mentally ill and disabled patents to refuse treatment. The Supreme Court has refused to review any cases on the matter and has referred the question to the states. The definitive state court decision on the question was handed down in 1982. The ruling in *Mills v. Rogers* held that the right to refuse treatment may be constitutionally protected. This case, *Mills, Rogers v. Commissioner* and other state and lower Federal court decisions have recognized the right of involuntarily committed patients to refuse treatment. *Rennie v. Klein* held that the nature of confinement is limited, so that involuntarily committed patients retain a "residuum of liberty" and the right to be free from "unjustified intrusions on(his)personal security."

The same case also recognized qualifications on the right to refuse treatment. It articulated the principle that the more intrusive and experimental treatments carry the right of refusal.

In contrast, less intrusive and commonly accepted treatment forms may be administered without consent. Examples of intrusive and experimental treatments cited were electroshock therapy and mind-altering medication.[20]

More state statutes than judicial decisions recognize the right of mental patients to refuse treatment. Among these are the California Welfare and Institutions Code.[21]

A third right to treatment issue delineates the right to humane treatment in the least restrictive manner. *Dixon v. Weinberger* held that, as part of their right to treatment, patients have a right to be treated in the least restrictive setting. The court ordered the creation of community-based services for patients who do not need to remain in a mental institution.[22]

This principle was upheld by the Supreme Court in 1982 when it issued its first rulings on the rights of mentally disabled people. *Youngsberg v. Romeo* granted the right to protection from harm for a mentally retarded institutionalized resident. The Court held that a mentally retarded patient had the right to be free of restraints. However, the Court did not prohibit the use of all restraints, only those that could not be substantiated as compelling, relying on a standard of professional judgment.[23]

The right of involuntarily confined mental patients to refuse forced administration of psychotropic drugs was established in *Mills v. Rogers*.

*Dixon v. Weinberger*, originally tried in the District of Columbia in 1975, established the right of Washington, D.C. residents with severe and persistent mental illness to appropriate treatment in the least restrictive setting possible. The original decision mandated the development of a comprehensive system of community-based mental health care.

In January 1992, the judge in that jurisdiction signed a consent order to address the treatment and housing needs of targeted groups of Dixon class members, including 2500 homeless mentally ill people. The decree mandated a 5-year Service Development Plan requiring the development of new and expanded treatment, residential, rehabilitation, and support services, and special services for class members who are homeless. All of these services are to be delivered in the least restrictive settings, ranging from shelters, soup-kitchens, individual apartments, group homes, and transitional residential beds.[24]

One California decision proved to be a major setback to homeless mentally ill people in the state. Brought by the Mental Health Association, the plaintiffs/appellants sought declaratory and injunctive relief to compel state and local government officials to create and fund community-based mental health residential and rehabilitative programs. The court found against the plaintiffs, stating that it was the responsibility of the legislative and executive branches to set up a bureaucracy to supervise and deliver mental health services. The judge argued that the state's involuntary commitment laws established a preference for the least restrictive treatment but did not establish a right to this. This case held that the courts did not have the authority to prescribe the structure of the mental health delivery system.

The court also held that the State Legislative scheme concerning treatment of "gravely disabled" persons under involuntary commitment laws provides adequate due process. The appellants had characterized "gravely disabled" persons as "hard core," "revolving door" patients who had no recourse to hospitals since the closure of state mental hospitals. The absence of this option constituted due process in the appellants arguments. The trial court judge and the appellate courts followed the "professional judgment standard" explicated in *Youngsblood v. Romero*.

This decision has held in California and a strong coalition of mental health advocates is attempting to reverse it with a more common sense plan.[25]

This survey of court decisions governing treatment pertains to patients who are either in inpatient or outpatient settings. Issues related to the commitment process itself fall under a separate category of mentally disordered people's civil rights and will be discussed later in this chapter.

## Housing for Mentally Ill People

Major studies have demonstrated that mentally ill people are primarily concerned with their lack of material resources, employment opportunities, privacy, and personal and physical protection. The most frequently and intensely expressed need of mental health consumers is housing. Studies by the Rand Corporation, Ball and Havassy, and Lipton, Nutt, and Sabatini support the argument that permanent and affordable housing, and accompanying resources, carry the same value and primacy among mentally ill homeless people as they do among homeless people who have no diagnosable mental disorder and domiciled people.

A review of the State of California's Homeless Mentally Disabled program begun in 1987 by the Rand Corporation found that few placements in independent or other types of housing could be provided. Reasons given were lack of low-income housing and the need for additional long-term beds.[26]

Ball and Havassy conducted a unique study of self-identified mentally ill homeless recidivists in San Francisco 10 years ago. Their study found that the respondents were more concerned with a lack of material resources than social services and psychiatric care. Housing was their most frequently expressed need.[27]

Lipton et al. completed a study in 1987 that further corroborated the primacy of housing for mentally ill people. In that experimental study, one group of mentally ill people was placed in a residential treatment program following discharge from a psychiatric hospital. The control group received standard postdischarge care. All of those who were offered treatment in the residential facility accepted the option. At the end of 1 year 69% of the subjects were in permanent housing. Compared with the control group, those in the residential facility spent more nights in adequate shelter, fewer nights in hospitals or homeless, and were generally satisfied with their living arrangements.[28] Service and shelter opportunities for homeless mentally ill people have expanded during the past decade. Foremost among these is the Department of Housing and Urban Development (HUD) Transitional Living Program. This program offers up to 2 years of supportive housing for homeless mentally ill people. Its objective is the preparation for independent living at the conclusion of the 2-year residential program.

Five major lawsuits have addressed housing entitlements of homeless mentally ill people. Each case has linked appropriate housing to psychiatric treatment and care.

An Arizona decision ordered broad revisions of state and county mental health services on behalf of deinstitutionalized mentally ill persons, some of whom were homeless because of inadequate services. The court ordered a continuum of residential services, including group homes with 24-hour supervision, apartments with health professionals on site, and independent living facilities with outreach and supportive services. This decision was confirmed by the state supreme court.[29]

A case in the Massachusetts Superior Court raised the most extensive issues relating housing, mental illness, and homelessness. Brought as a class-action suit but certified as a test case by the court, *Williams et al. v. Forsberg et al.* challenged the Massachusetts Department of Mental Health (DMH) service protocols for homeless people with mental disabilities. The plaintiffs alleged that homeless people who are admitted to DMH inpatient facilities are regularly discharged back to singles shelters or the streets. The plaintiffs also complained that the defendants discriminated against those who are dually diagnosed for alcoholism and mental disability.

Plaintiffs requested that the defendants be required to operate a housing subsidy program for those people ready for discharge from inpatient facilities who have no place to live. The request further sought sufficient case managers and services to ensure that those discharged actually find a place to live and obtain the support necessary to remain there.

*Williams* utilized many courses of action, including federal and state due process clauses and provisions of the state mental health statute. However, the claims with the greatest applicability to all states and local jurisdictions fell under the Americans with Disabilities Act (ADA) and the Fair Housing Amendments Act (FHAA), as well as common law tort of wrongful discharge.

The central argument under the ADA was that the defendants' segregated housing system for those with mental disabilities violated the intent of the 42nd United States Code, which provides

> INTEGRATED SETTINGS. Goods, services, privileges advantages, and accommodations shall be afforded to an individual with a disability in the most integrated setting appropriate to the needs of the individual.

Plaintiffs produced evidence that 65% of the stock utilized by DMH to house its clients in the community required people to live in buildings where every tenant was mentally disabled. One-third of the tenants were forced to share rooms and other facilities with persons who are not of their choosing. Perhaps the most compelling aspect of this argument lay in its observation that the system is so rigid that people have nowhere to go when they are "too well" to live in a residential treatment facility. This backs up the inpatient and supportive housing systems and results in unnecessary retention of people in inpatient units because there is no place in the community.

Lawyers for the plaintiffs presented testimony describing supportive community housing models as "not the most integrated . . . and appropriate for people with mental disabilities." Therefore, the DMH would have to justify continuing the existence of segregated services as "necessary to provide the (disabled) individual or class of individuals with a good service, privilege, advantage, or accommodation that is as effective as that provided to others." Because the ADA specifically subjects segregated housing and facilities to the strictest scrutiny, this would have been extremely difficult for the DMH to justify.

The provisions of the ADA mandate that a mental health system must house mentally disabled people in the most integrated settings possible in the community. Segregated services must be clinically recommended and allow clients to refuse those settings in favor of integrated housing facilities.

In challenging the DMH practice of discharging patients to the streets or emergency shelters, lawyers for the plaintiffs argued that one who takes charge of another who is incapacitated has a duty not only to act reasonably while the person is in custody, but also to act reasonably in the manner and place in which the person is discharged from custody.

This key concept of reasonable discharge has been recognized in numerous other states, including Massachusetts, New York, Indiana, Kentucky, Kansas, Alabama, and North Dakota. In many instances, the negligent discharge refers to discharge of an intoxicated railroad passenger who has been let off at a train station or near railroad tracks. The concept has been equally applied to patients discharged from hospital and from police custody. Plaintiffs in these instances have acquired expert testimony pertaining to the foreseeable harm that such discharge is likely to subject a person to, especially those with mental disabilities who are forced to stay in the streets or open-barracks type of shelters all day. Foremost among such harm is the foreseeable risk of readmission to the hospital with a recurrence of the destabilization that placed him or her there initially.

Finally, the plaintiffs challenged the DMH practice of refusing to refer dual diagnosed patients to independent apartments if the client had been actively involved with alcohol abuse within the past 6 months. The DMH would make such a referral only if the client gave informed consent and permission to the DMH to reveal that the client is an alcoholic.

Such practice is a violation of the FHAA regulations, 24 C.F.R. #100.1 et. seq. Section 100.70(a) that provides

> It shall be unlawful, because of . . . handicap . . . , to restrict or attempt to resist the choices of a person by word or conduct in connection with seeking, negotiating for, . . . or renting a dwelling so as to . . . discourage or obstruct choices in a community, neighborhood or development.

In addition, Section #100.201(a)(2) of these regulations states that alcoholism, whether active or inactive, is a handicap for purposes of the FHAA.[30]

In *Heard v. Cuomo*, tried by the Coalition for the Homeless, a New York State appellate court addressed the issue of housing for discharged psychiatric patients. The ruling affirmed a trial court decision that the New York City Health and Hospitals Corporation is obligated to ensure that persons discharged from psychiatric hospitals operated by the Department obtain adequate and appropriate housing. The State of New York agreed with the plaintiffs that public shelters are not appropriate places for discharged psychiatric patients.

However, the court recognized that no adequate supply of appropriate housing for mentally disordered people existed and did not hold the State subject to an "obey the law" injunction. Instead, the court approved an agreement entered into by the City and the State to create 5225 beds for homeless mentally ill individuals over a period of 2 years, from 1990 to 1992. Plaintiffs contended that this number created only one-half of the necessary beds. Nor did it ensure that funds would be appropriated to implement the agreement.[31] The court's response was that the judgment would provide for implementation over a period of time.

A pending class action suit for mentally disabled adults in New York City contends that a place to live is a component of appropriate mental health care. The suit argues that community care, acute hospitalization, or residential treatment must be provided. It further argues that referral to an emergency shelter, even combined with outpatient care, is inappropriate.[32]

These five cases have established sound legal precedents supporting the principle that appropriate care and treatment for mentally disabled adults should incorporate adequate residential provisions. The legal basis in the cases has rested upon general applications of equal protection and due process. The nondiscriminatory intent of the Americans with Disabilities Act has formed an equally convincing argument not only for housing mentally disabled persons, but also for seeking integrated housing wherever and whenever possible.

## Civil Liberties

Most civil liberty protections for homeless mentally disabled persons have been well established by the strong involuntary commitment laws operating in every state. Other aspects of civil rights fall under more general considerations of the rights of homeless people to constitutional protections of free speech, travel, use of public spaces, and shelter.

Public officials and service providers face frequent frustration over the rigidity of involuntary commitment laws that prevent them from forcing mentally ill homeless people to accept care, or shelter, against their will. Much of this contention is echoed in the debate on involuntary outpatient commitment.

The saga of Rebecca Smith's choice to freeze to death in her cardboard box home, despite intense efforts to induce her to accept shelter during the winter of 1981 in Washington, D.C., dramatized the complexity surrounding the civil rights of homeless mentally ill people. For Rebecca Smith, life in the box was preferable to her previous experiences with treatment for schizophrenia.[33]

Some cities have set up programs to remove mentally ill homeless people from the streets. New York City established such a program and it was challenged in a highly publicized case in 1987 when a New York State appellate court barred the release of a woman found by a state judge to have been inappropriately hospitalized. This case became the test case for New York's program, as well as those in other cities. It established how far the City could go in involuntarily hospitalizing homeless people for their own good.

The Appellate Division ordered that Joyce Brown, a.k.a. Billie Boggs and Ann Smith, who lived on a hot air vent in Manhattan, be held and treated for at least 2 weeks in Bellevue Hospital Center. New York's program used a broad definition of the State Mental Hygiene Law to involuntarily hospitalize homeless people who are deemed to be in need of treatment and likely to endanger themselves on the streets in the foreseeable future.

Patients taken off the streets were given high priority for placement in scarce acute care beds at psychiatric hospitals, community residences for the mentally ill, nursing homes, and single-room-occupancy hotels.

The Joyce Brown case was noteworthy for the conflicting psychiatric diagnoses of grave disability that were presented. One team of city psychiatrists had conceded that she had been able to successfully keep warm in the winter, feed herself, and stay in good health while living on the sidewalk for nearly 1 year. They admitted that she defecated in the street and tore up money, but alleged that she used the streets because she had no bathroom, and tore up the money because people threw it at her when she did not want it. In other words, her behavior was rational and adaptive for her circumstances.

A second team of city psychiatrists diagnosed her as suffering from severe mental illness. They also reported that she defecated in the street and in her clothing, shouted abuse at passers-by, ran in front of traffic, and cut up money in neat piles and urinated on it.

A State Supreme Court judge, in a separate hearing, ruled to discount expert testimony because the psychiatric assessments were so diametrically opposed. Eventually the court held that individuals swept up from city streets and confined in city mental hospitals without a showing of dangerousness were to be released. This decision was based upon three important principles. The first is that loitering on the street is not against the law. Second, the dangerousness clause protecting people from involuntary commitment must be honored. Finally, the city health code identifies public urination or defecation as a misdemeanor punishable by a fine of up to 15 days in jail. Moreover, most police officers do not view such acts as serious offenses and few give them high priority in comparison with more serious offenses.[34]

This case attracted worldwide attention in the media making Joyce Brown an overnight celebrity for several weeks. Its importance lies in the final decision that city laws relating to protection of homeless mentally ill people cannot override state involuntary commitment protections. This legal principle is now applied across the United States.

### Unresolved Issues for Advocates

The homeless mentally ill population remains one of the lowest priorities when state and local governments determine their annual budgets. Without the militia of mental health advocacy organizations like the Mental Health Association, coalitions of mental health service providers, and lawyers, homeless mentally ill people would have little or no public voice. Even the courts are reluctant to take positions that challenge the legislative and executive branches holding that the protections established in involuntary commitment laws and codes provide sufficient due process and access to care.

Mental health practitioners have even been reluctant to work with severe and persistently mentally ill patients, homeless or domiciled. Some report frustration and "burn out" when working with them over time. Others are highly committed to working with them but resist the cumbersome and too frequently discouraging bureaucratic barriers encountered in the public mental health service delivery system. Finally, all report occasional despair over the scarcity of resources for severe and persistently mentally ill persons.

This weak political climate compels vigilant oversight and persistent advocacy on behalf of one of the most vulnerable groups of people in the nation.

## Notes and References

1. U.S. Congress, *Mental Retardation Facilities and Community Mental Health Centers Act*; E. Fuller Torrey, *Nowhere to Go: The Tragic Odyssey of the Homeless Mentally Ill* (New York: Harper & Row, 1988), 145–146.

2. Madeleine R. Stoner, *Inventing a Non-Homeless Future: A Public Policy Agenda for Preventing Homelessness* (New York: Peter Lang, 1989).

3. Frank R. Lipton, Albert Sabatini, and Steven E. Katz, "Down and Out in the City," *Hospital and Community Psychiatry* 34(9):817–821 (1988); Ellen Bassuk, "The Homelessness Problem," *Scientific American* 251(1):40–45 (1984); A. Anthony Arce, Marilyn Tadlock, Michael Vergare, and Stuart Shapiro, "A Psychiatric Profile of Street People Admitted to an Emergency Shelter," *Hospital and Community Psychiatry* 34(9):812–816 (1984).

4. Leona Bachrach, "The Homeless Mentally Ill and Mental Health Services: An Analytic Review of the Literature," Alcohol, Drug Abuse, and Mental Health Administration, U.S. Department of Health and Human Services, 1984, and "Interpreting Research on the Homeless Mentally Ill: Some Caveats," *Hospital and Community Psychiatry* 35(9):914–916 (1984); Irene Shifren Levine and James Stockdill, "Mentally Ill and Homeless: A National Problem," in Billy E. Jones, ed., *Treating the Homeless: Urban Psychiatry's Challenge* (Washington, D.C.: American Psychiatric Press, 1986).

5. Paul Koegel, Audrey M. Burnam, and Roger K. Farr, "Subsistence Adaptation Among Homeless Adults in the Inner City of Los Angeles," *Journal of Social Issues*, 46:83–107 (1990).

6. George Vernez et al., *Review of California's Program for the Homeless Mentally Disabled* (Santa Monica: Rand Corporation, 1988); The Chicago Coalition for the Homeless, *When You Don't Have Anything: A Survey of Homeless People in Chicago* (Chicago, IL: The Coalition, 1983); Robert W. Surber, et al., "Medical and Psychiatric Needs of the Homeless: A Preliminary Response," *Social Work*, 33:(2) (March–April, 1988); U.S. Conference of Mayors, *Mentally Ill and Homeless: A 22-City Survey* (Washington, D.C., 1991).

7. Russell K. Schutt and Gerald R. Garrett, *Responding to the Homeless: Policy and Practice* (New York: Plenum, 1992), 14–15.

8. William, E. Narrow, Daniel A Regier, Donald S. Rae, Ronald W. Manderscheid, and Ben Z. Locke, "Use of Services by Persons with Mental and Addictive Disorders: Findings from the National Institute of Mental Health Epidemiologic Catchment Area Program," *Archives of General Psychiatry*, 50:95–107 (February 1993).

9. Blau, *The Visible Poor*, 84–85 (Introduction, Note 5).

10. Madeleine R. Stoner, "The Plight of Homeless Women," *Social Service Review*, 37(4):565–581 (19??).

11. Edward P. Mulvey, Jeffrey L. Geller and Loren H. Roth, "The Promise and Peril of Involuntary Outpatient Commitment," *American Psychologist*, 42(6):571–584 (1987); Richard Lamb, "Deinstitutionalization and the Homeless Mentally Ill," *Hospital and Community Psychiatry*, 37:899–907 (1987).

12. Coates, *A Street Is Not a Home*, 300 (Introduction, Note 22).

13. The Santa Monica Task Force on Homelessness, *A Call to Action* (City of Santa Monica, Community Development Department, 1991), 30–31.

14. Saltzman and Proch, *Law in Social Work Practice*, 358–360 (Introduction, Note 11).

15. Cited in 42 U.S.C. 6009 (2).

16. *Wyatt v. Stickney* 325 F. Supp. 781 (M.D. Ala. 1971); 334 F. Supp. 1341, 1972.

17. *O.Connor v. Donaldson*, 422 U.S. 563, 1975; Saltzman and Proch, *Law in Social Work Practice*, 360–361 (Introduction, Note 11).

18. *Davis v. Watkins*, 384 F. Supp. 1196 (N.D. Ohio, 1974).

19. *Kaimowitz v. Department of Mental Health*, Mich. Wayne County Cir. Ct., 1973 C.A. No. 73-19434-AW; discussed in Saltzman and Proch, *Law in Social Work Practice*, 365 (Introduction, Note 11).

20. *Mills v. Rogers*, 457, U.S. 291, 1982; *Mills, Rogers v. Commissioner*, 390 Mass. 489, 458 N.E. 2d 308, 1983; *Rennie v. Klein*, 654, F. 2d 836 (3d Cir. 1981).

21. *California Welfare and Institutions Code* #5325(f),(g), and 5326.2.

22. *Dixon v. Weinberger*, 405 F. Supp. 974 (D.D.C., 1975).

23. *Youngsberg v. Romeo*, 457 U.S. 307, 1982.

24. *Dixon v. Weinberger*, 405 F. Supp. 974 (D.D.C. 1975), *sub nom; Dixon v. Kelly*, C.A. No. 74-285 (D.D.C. Consent Order January 28, 1992) (Clearinghouse No. 17, 175); summarized in National Law Center on Homelessness and Poverty, *Annotated Bibliography*, 62–63 (Introduction, Note 9).

25. *Mental Health Association v. Deukmejian*, 233 Cal. Rptr. 130 (Ct. App., 2d Dist. 1986), *depublished by the California Supreme Court when denying review*, March 5, 1987; Coates, *A House Is Not a Home*, 301–302 (Introduction, Note 22).

26. George Vernez, M. Audrey Burnam, Elizabeth McGlynn, Sally Trude, and Brian S. Mittman, *Review of California's Program for the Homeless Mentally Disturbed* (Santa Monica: Rand Corporation, 1988).

27. F. L. Jessica Ball and Barbara Havassy, "A Survey of the Problems and Needs of Homeless Consumers of Acute Psychiatric Services," *Hospital and Community Psychiatry*, 35(9):917–921 (September 1984).

28. Frank R. Lipton, Suzanne Nutt, and Albert Sabatini, "Housing the Homeless Mentally Ill: A Longitudinal Study of a Treatment Approach," *Hospital and Community Psychiatry*, 39(1):40–45 (January 1988). This study was extensively described in Stoner, *Inventing a Non-Homeless Future*, 205–212.

29. *Arnold v. Department of Mental Health Services* 775 p. 2d 521 (Ariz. 1989) (Clearinghouse No. 40, 117).

30. *Williams et al. v. Forsberg et al.*, C.A. No. 91-3835, Super. Ct., Suffolk

County; summarized in National Center on Homelessness and Poverty, *Annotated Bibliography,* 63–66 (Introduction, Note 9).

31. *Heard v. Coumo,* No. 44429 (N.Y. Sup. Ct., App. Div., January 14, 1992) (Lexis 171), *aff.g* No. M-3009 (N.Y. App. Div. July 2, 1991) (Lexis 10023).

32. *Love v. Koch,* No. 4514/88 (N.Y. Sup. Ct.) (1984).

33. Stoner, "The Plight of Homeless Women," 563.

34. *Boggs v. New York City Health and Hospital Corporation,* 132 A.D. 2d 340, 523 N.Y.S. 71 (1987).

# 6

# EVICTIONS

## Homelessness, Housing, and Evictions

Poverty and a lack of affordable housing are at the critical center of homelessness. The nationwide imbalance between the number of households requiring low-income housing units and the number of such available units reflects the growing gap of affordable housing and the increase in poor households. This imbalance leads extremely poor families and individuals to live in the most precarious housing, doubled up with family or friends, in more formal rental arrangements between strangers, or in the most substandard housing.

One consequence of doubling up so that families can live in affordable quarters is overcrowding, defined by the Department of Housing and Urban Development (HUD) as having more than one person per room. Poor, minority households are more likely to live in overcrowded dwellings than are white households, even though they are not at a special disadvantage regarding rent.[1] The stress of overcrowded living conditions frequently breaks down such arrangements and forces individuals and families into the streets.

The concentration of minority group members in inadequate and overcrowded housing is associated with several factors. Among these is the density of the supply of low-income housing in inner cities and rural areas. It is even more attributable to generational patterns of racial discrimination in the housing market, even among very poor people. This is an important consideration because it helps to explain further the predominance of minority groups among homeless populations.

Government actions have also contributed to an increase in poverty between 1979 and 1980, thus contributing to the equation of poverty, housing, and homelessness. Erosion of benefits and the tightening of eligibility requirements in public assistance programs were the largest contributors to poverty increases for single-headed families, 43%. Social insurance changes, particularly disability requirements, increased the married and "other" poverty categories by one-third. Social Security

Disability Insurance drastically reduced the number of eligible recipients in 1981 leaving many more of those disabled by mental illness with insufficient incomes to secure housing. The United States Congress reversed these changes in 1983, but their destructive efforts remain evident. The combined effect of reductions in social insurance and public welfare programs accounted for 45% of the increase in poverty between 1979 and 1990.[2]

One cannot establish a direct association between extreme poverty and homelessness without explanations of who becomes homeless, or is at a very high risk of homelessness. Burt (1992) analyzed variations in the rates of homelessness in 147 cities with populations over 100,000 across the United States. He found that the rates of homelessness were positively associated with unemployment, employment in low paying services rather than retail or manufacturing sectors, and the percentage of one-person households. These are the individuals who are inclined to rely on the low-income housing market, and are frequently the single-room-occupancy tenants (SRO). They are also the people who are most likely to become homeless.

General assistance benefits also affect this population. Their availability keeps people in low-income housing and, conversely, their reduction or removal spells homelessness for many tenants. Studies in two states demonstrate that many people who lost their General Assistance because of state cutbacks also lost their housing.[3]

For all of these extremely poor at-risk people, eviction is identifiable as the singular point in time at which they either become homeless, or are at the greatest danger of becoming homeless. Many families have no place to go after losing their homes from eviction.

In 1988, four Coro Foundation Fellows in Public Affairs in San Francisco spent 6 weeks studying the question of how intervention through eviction could be prevented in that city. They interviewed legal aid attorneys, social workers, shelter directors, and homeless families. They also studied court records documenting the legal eviction process and problems associated with it. It is reasonable to expect that findings for an urban area with a high rate of homelessness would correspond to similar areas in the nation. It is also reasonable to conclude that the legal processes involved in eviction would minimally differ from those in other cities with similar demographic characteristics.

During a 2-week period, the Fellows formally interviewed a sample consisting of 28 homeless families and learned that 57% had been evicted from a house or an apartment. There are too few studies of eviction, but this figure corresponds to the data found in them.

A major study of homelessness in Chicago found that 30% of those interviewed said that eviction caused them to seek emergency shelter or other forms of temporary housing.[4] The Report of the New York City Commission on the Homeless identified persons facing eviction as a large and identifiable serviceable group.[5]

An earlier study in New York City also found that 30% of the respondents had become homeless because of eviction.


## The Eviction Process


The Coro Fellows identified 13 "just cause" eviction actions that can be brought in San Francisco. But they found that most occur because of problems with payment of rent. Eighty-nine percent of those interviewed were evicted for this reason. An earlier study found that 90% of eviction cases stemmed from nonpayment of rent.

Although nonpayment of rent is a "just cause" for eviction, there are several steps in the process that can impose unrealistic demands on people who are threatened with eviction. These are the points at which intervention to prevent homelessness can occur.

In the San Francisco survey of municipal court records, over 4300 people were served with Unlawful Detainer (UD) actions. These are a landlord's first step in the legal eviction process. The Coro analysis of the data from a random sample of lawsuits involving UD actions showed that over 75% of them were filed because of nonpayment of rent.

The findings of the Coro Fellows and earlier surveys indicate that a large number of people are evicted from their homes every year, and many have no other place to go. Eviction, for many, is the last step before homelessness.

Eviction is a formal "Summary Legal Process." A tenant has only 5 days—including weekends and holidays—to file a formal "Answer," or written response to the charges. All other civil suits provide a period of 30 days. If the "Answer" is not filed within the 5-day period, the landlord can request that a default judgment be entered in the court. The landlord then regains possession of the property after a second 5-day waiting period.

Whether some defendants in default judgments could avoid eviction with a longer period is hard to predict. However, of the San Francisco sample, only four people filed written responses within the legal 5-day period. The rest could have been evicted immediately if the landlord filed a default judgment. On the average, only 32 days elapsed between the filing of the UD action and the default decision to evict. Evicted tenants had only 1 month to raise the money necessary to cover the cost of moving and to find another home.

These data raise concerns about the summary nature of eviction and its bias against tenants. They also suggest possible strategies for reducing the risk of homelessness from eviction. Clearly, a 5-day response period, or any similarly brief time allocated in other cities (3 days in Los Angeles), is inadequate protection of tenants and almost certainly guarantees eviction. It simply does not allow sufficient time to hire a lawyer and prepare a written response. A limited response period is a strong predictor of homelessness because of the brief period available to locate and secure replacement housing.

All laws and public policies reflect the weighing of competing dilemmas and priorities. Landlords have a perfectly justifiable right to protect their rental property and income from it. On the other hand, tenants should have equal rights to due process. In the interest of equitable public policy that could prevent homelessness for many, tenants should be granted more protected eviction-prevention efforts, in particular more time to respond to notices.

Revised eviction laws offer a relatively simple intervention point for the prevention of homelessness compared to the many structural and institutional problems associated with homelessness.[6] Homeless advocates have not yet drawn upon this issue as a litigation strategy.


## Eviction Litigation


The docket of court actions on eviction covers shelters, SROs, hotels, motels, and boarding houses. These housing accommodations are extremely vulnerable to eviction because they are less subject to codes governing tenants rights in long-term housing. Rental terms are generally set on a weekly or bimonthly basis. Even monthly rents are let on a month-by-month basis rather than the annual agreements found in permanent housing. These units comprise the lowest cost housing stock in the nation thereby attracting many transient people and those who lack the financial stability to secure permanent housing.

In most situations, residents of these accommodations do not carry the status of "tenancy" and are considered transients who are not entitled to the same protections as tenants. For many, however, these units *are* permanent housing. This has been the basis for numerous court actions and, in most instances, residents have been accorded eviction rights as though they were tenants.

Cases brought for tenants of these facilities generally draw upon state and municipal welfare codes, the authorized level of housing benefits for public assistance recipients being based on equal protection under the Fourteenth Amendment of the United States Constitution.

A larger body of law governing landlord–tenant relations and rights was developed in the post-World War II era when cities began to adopt rent control ordinances. During the 1960s, a broad-based tenant's rights movement, along with the many other civil rights efforts, expanded this law, but, as indicated above, the balance of equity continues to lean toward landlords.

Homeless advocates have generally not brought court actions on behalf of people threatened with eviction from general residential facilities, e.g., rental housing and apartments. This would be a fruitful direction for new impact litigation, given the logic of homeless prevention, and a suitable case will probably be presented to the court in the near future.

## Eviction from Hotels

A 1990 case filed in the District of Columbia involved a plaintiff who had fallen into arrears on his rental payment and was given a written request to pay the delinquent charges within 3 days. When he ignored the request the defendant (landlord) changed the locks on the plaintiff's room thereby evicting him.

The plaintiff argued that the district's Rental Housing Act of 1985 defined him as a tenant, even though he entered into only an oral agreement to rent his hotel room. As a "tenant" he would be entitled to protection from self-eviction. The defendant argued that the plaintiff was a roomer, not a tenant, and was not entitled to protection under the Rental Housing Act.

The court granted the plaintiff's motion for a summary judgment holding that the plaintiff was entitled to a judgment on the issue of his claim for wrongful eviction because the defendant resorted to self-help to evict the plaintiff, as opposed to resorting to the legal process. The court noted that the forcible entry and detainer act was restricted to use against tenants only up until 1953, but after that it was amended to apply to "any person."[7]

A similar hotel eviction case in New Jersey raised the issue of tenancy rights for hotel residents. In *Williams v. Alexander Hamilton Hotel*, the plaintiff and his family were forced to live in a room at the Alexander Hamilton Hotel for more than 2 years. They were locked out of their room when they accumulated a back-rent debt and the plaintiff brought an action alleging that the Anti-Eviction Act prevented him from being dispossessed without due process actions. He sought repossession of the room and damages.

In testifying, Williams stated that he would return to work when permitted, and that he would want to find a more suitable home at that time. The trial court held that the plaintiff and his family were transient guests and therefore not entitled to protection under the Anti-Eviction Act.

The Appellate Division reversed the decision of the lower court noting that the plaintiff and his family had lived in the hotel room for more than 2 years, that his children attended school in that neighborhood, and that his wife was registered to vote on the basis of her residence at the hotel. The court held that the case involved actual residence for over 2 years and an intention to remain there for an indefinite period, thus justifying the status of a "tenancy" at the time of the lock-out. As a "tenant," the plaintiff and his family were entitled to protection under the Anti-Eviction Act.

The case, *Lacko v. City of Chicago*, representing 300 men who were involuntarily displaced from two residential hotels in a federally funded urban renewal project area and denied any relocation assistance, established a clear precedent for the right to be protected against homelessness under such conditions. The city paid each resident only $10 in relocation fees and, then, only if the resident could show that another unit had been leased. The plaintiffs claimed that each resident was entitled to $4000 plus moving expenses under the federal Uniform Relocation Act (URA) because the project area in which they were located was funded by the Community Development Block Grant program.[8]

Many of the residents were rendered homeless by this action. The plaintiffs also argued that safe, decent, sanitary and affordable units were unavailable in Chicago and that the city was responsible for the creation of replacement housing, or resources, under the "last resort" provisions of the URA.

The case was settled outside of court in a consent decree. Approximately 140 class members displaced from a hotel demolished by the city received $3121.42 each. The city relocated 23 other class members who were paid $225 each and will receive $4000 when the city vacates and demolishes their current homes.

The consent decree also required the city to conduct a study of housing opportunities for low-income single people and to document the number and location of residential units demolished or converted to other uses by the city or the private sector during the preceding 10 years. The study found that 7000 SRO units had been demolished over the preceding 14-year period in that relocation area. The city was also directed to provide data on the number of SRO units remaining with accompanying data on their code compliance, vacancy rates, and rents. Finally, the study was required to include a report on proposals for preserving the remaining SRO stock.[9]

In San Francisco, an appellate court upheld the constitutionality of a municipal ordinance requiring permits for SRO conversions conditioned on a one-for-one replacement at affordable levels and provision of relocation benefits. The hotel owner claimed that the ordinance constituted a taking, but the court held that it did not deprive the owner of all reasonable use because the owner could always sell.

Contrary to the owner's claim, the court stated that there was no fundamental right to go out of business. The court suggested, but did not decide, that the ordinance did not violate recently enacted California legislation that prohibits municipalities from enacting laws requiring landlords to continue to offer their property for rent.[10]

Limits on stays under AFDC emergency assistance provisions were challenged in *Vingara v. Borough of Wrightstown* in 1987. The plaintiffs challenged a municipal zoning ordinance that limits occupancy in motels to 30 days. They had received emergency AFDC assistance and were placed in the motel. The zoning ordinance was also used to prevent homeless children living in the motel from attending borough schools. Vingara argued that implementation of the ordinance conflicted with state AFDC requirements, state and federal constitutional protection guarantees, and state land use law prohibiting exclusionary practices. The court granted a temporary restraining order (TRO).[11]

In Westchester County, New York, a motel owner brought suit to recover possession of one of the units from the defendant, a homeless person who was placed there by the Department of Social Services (*Universal Motor Lodges, Inc. v. Seignious*). The plaintiff argued that the defendant was a mere "transient" or licensee subject to a 10-day notice to quit under the Real Property Actions and Proceedings Law (RPAPL).

The Justice Court held that the defendant was a monthly tenant, entitled to the rights of a tenant, whose occupancy could be terminated only by a 30-day notice to vacate, and not a mere transient subject to a 10-day notice. In the decision, the court noted that the defendant had occupied the room at the motel for more than 2 years and was clearly not a transient because this was her only home.[12]

The same chain of motels, Universal Motor Lodges, was challenged for bringing summary proceedings against three tenants of the motel. The court consolidated this case with the *Seignious* case cited above and held that the eviction notices they served were defective because they did not cite which of the motel house rules the tenants had violated, even though the court agreed that the residents were licensees and not tenants.

The defendants brought a new action alleging that two of the tenants violated rules by cooking in their rooms, and that the third tenant had been involved in disturbing altercations with other guests. The court found that these were sufficient reasons for the tenants to defend themselves at a trial. This case established certain rights of homeless people who are placed in motels paid for by the Department of Social Services. [13] Eviction issues frequently arise when hotel and SRO owners are involved in bankruptcy proceedings. Problems also arise when they seek to convert their rental properties to more profitable residential uses. Two bankruptcy cases, tried in New York City, have set precedents protecting residents.

The Court intervened in the bankruptcy case filed by the Holland Hotel requesting that representation be provided to tenant homeless families. The Court denied requests by the hotel owners to summarily remove homeless families from the hotel and appointed a series of trustees to operate the hotel. Subsequently, the Court denied a request by one of the trustees to obtain rental payments directly from the City. This would have prevented the residents from withholding their rent.

The Court denied this request based upon a state landlord–tenant law and a consent judgment in *Montes v. Krauskopf* that prohibits the City from implementing rent restrictions without a finding of mismanagement, prior notice, and an opportunity for a prerestriction hearing. After a lengthy evidentiary hearing, the Court permitted New York City to purchase the hotel from the trustees because the City had agreed to relocate the homeless families in the hotel to permanent housing. The City also intended to renovate the hotel for use as temporary housing for homeless adults. [14]

The Court also provided representation to homeless families placed at the Times Square Motor Inn when it was undergoing bankruptcy proceedings. The hotel had appointed a notoriously exploitive hotel operator to manage the hotel during the proceedings and the City joined the tenant's opposition to the appointment of criminal contempt for failing to make court-ordered repairs to another hotel he owned. In that proceeding, the hotel owner was found to have engaged in a pattern of illegal evictions of tenants from a third hotel that he owned.

After another extensive evidentiary hearing, the Court appointed an examiner to oversee the daily operations of the hotel. The City finally took over operation of the hotel when the examiner resigned 1 year after the evidentiary hearing. It took this action based in part on the examiner's findings of mismanagement and the plaintiffs' efforts in *McCain* to prohibit further placement of homeless families at the Times Square Motor Inn because the operators failed to correct lead hazards. The examiner resigned to forestall enforcement proceedings in *McCain*. The City also agreed to relocate homeless families to permanent housing, and this effort was completed by the end of 3 months.[15]

In 1984 an SRO property owner sought a preliminary injunction against the application of an ordinance that restricted conversion of SRO dwellings to more profitable residential uses where harassment and displacement of those units had occurred. New York City Local Law 19 (1983) governs the renovation and demolition of SROs and requires certification that no harassment had occurred during a 3-year period of inquiry pending application for a plan approval or permits for demolition or renovation. A waiver of the certification requirement may be granted for SROs purchased prior to the date on which the law was approved by the legislative committee.

The property owner had not recorded his contract for purchase prior to the cut-off date and was denied the waiver. The owner was also denied certification based on the findings of a hearing officer that harassment had occurred. The lower court, and the appellate court, rejected the owner's claim that the ordinance constituted a taking without just compensation in violation of the Fifth and Fourteenth Amendments.[16]

Although not strictly hotels, tenancy rights of rooming and boarding houses have been challenged. The Appellate Division of the Superior Court of New Jersey granted a motion to withdraw a lower court opinion holding that a week-to-week resident in a furnished, rented room did not have the procedural and substantive rights of a tenant under state law. On appeal, the Department of Public Advocate sought to intervene arguing that the lower court erred in concluding that a rooming and boarding house is not a hotel, motel or guest house, and that a resident of a rooming house is not a transient guest. The intervenor also argued that a regulation issued by the State Department of Community Affairs established residents of rooming and boarding houses as tenants for purposes of the antieviction statute.[17]

## Eviction from Shelters

Public and private emergency shelters generally operate under extremely circumscribed rules and regulations governing the terms and conditions of shelter occupancy, including the length of stay. Although many of these rules have been criticized as too harsh, such as those requiring shelter guests to vacate premises at dawn or to attend prayers sessions, other codes exist to comply with municipal health and safety codes. More recently, shelter operators have been attempting to apply "tough love" criteria for shelter occupancy requiring participation in counseling and job training programs as a condition of residency.

In what may be the most extreme "tough love" approach, the Giuliani mayoral administration in New York City introduced a plan that requires homeless people to commit themselves to rehabilitation and sign an individual treatment plan for addiction, mental illness, or job training before being given shelter in a community-based rehabilitation program. Those who refuse would be asked to contribute a small sum toward their upkeep, scaled to government benefits or other income. Homeless families would be required to agree to learn living skills such as budgeting, housekeeping, and maintenance before being placed in permanent housing.[18]

Homeless advocates have charged that there are not enough service and treatment programs to meet the needs of the large homeless population and that this proposal is a smokescreen used by the Mayor to bypass the city's requirement to shelter all homeless people. It is anticipated that litigation will challenge this proposal based upon the *Callahan* consent decree.[19] However, a similar policy has been considered successful in Philadelphia and it has not been the subject of any litigation.

Shelter operators have generally attempted to apply health and safety rules when evicting guests. Frequently they have disguised their complaints in safety and health codes authorizing eviction citing danger to other guests. New "tough love" policies arising in cities across the country will undoubtedly offer other acceptable criteria for eviction from shelters.

The Massachusetts Coalition for the Homeless sought a preliminary injunction prohibiting the State Department of Public Welfare from evicting people from temporary shelter after 90 days. The court held that the department's Emergency Assistance rule limiting such stays to 90 days was inconsistent with state law. The court also denied three other claims for preliminary relief.[20]

A 1988 Baltimore case resulted in a consent order prohibiting termination of shelter assistance without due process. The shelter operator (defendant) was required to establish rules for eligibility and termination.[21]

One of the most extensive shelter eviction precedent setting cases took place in Massachusetts. The plaintiff was a blind woman with mental problems who resided in the Parker Street Shelter run by the State Department of Mental Health. She allegedly attempted to strike a staff member who tried to awaken her. The shelter director then barred the plaintiff from the shelter alleging that she posed an immediate danger and risk of harm to other guests and staff. The plaintiff received no hearing or opportunity to contest, despite the procedures outlined in the shelter's written standards governing the operation of the shelter providing such a hearing.

The standards forbade violence or the threats of violence. They also describe a "bar" from the shelter as having occurred when a guest is denied access between the hours of 3:00 P.M. to 9:30 P.M. and specified that the duration of the bar depended upon the seriousness of the violation. To protect guests, the standards state that no guest can be barred unless the shelter operator believes in good faith that the action is a reasonable and necessary protection against a danger to community health and safety. The standards also provided for different procedures depending on the severity of the exclusion.

The plaintiff filed suit against the Massachusetts Mental Health Center and the Massachusetts Department of Mental Health for violations of the Fourteenth Amendment and the United States Code Section 1983. The defendants testified that the bar imposed on the plaintiff was "provisional" and of uncertain duration and that a hearing was not held because the incident prompting the bar involved sufficient violence that it was believed that her continued presence was a threat to the health and safety of staff and guests.

The State District Court found that the standards created an entitlement to the plaintiff's continued residence at the shelter, that she had a "property interest" in same, and was entitled to a due process protection. The court recognized the defendant's interest in protecting the staff and guests, but concluded that the "high risk of erroneous deprivation" had not been considered when she did not have access to a hearing or challenge to the bar.

The Court further stated that "in emergency situations, especially those involving violence . . . a prompt posttermination hearing would have been sufficient to satisfy the requirements of due process." It also argued that the plaintiff was likely to succeed on her claim that the defendants had violated her Fourteenth Amendment rights by failing to provide any due process protections, and recommended that the defendants be enjoined from barring the woman until they followed the procedures outlined in the standards. More specifically, the court ordered that the plaintiff be given a written statement detailing the facts and circumstances of the decision to bar her, a justification for the action, and daily monitoring of the decision to bar by the shelter operator. However, the court did note that if an "emergency situation" arose, requiring immediate action, the defendants could bar the plaintiff before a hearing.[22]

Not all shelter eviction cases have been decided in favor of homeless plaintiffs. Some courts have held that shelter residency does not carry the rights of tenancy guaranteed by municipal codes and the federal Fair Housing Act.

A group of homeless men and women in New York City challenged the city's practice of ejecting residents from municipal shelters without set guidelines or procedures. The plaintiffs sought to require the city to adhere to some standards of who is to be disciplined and a process for having such decisions reviewed. The plaintiffs claimed that some alternative care was required under law even for those lawfully ejected. The District Court found that the plaintiffs lacked standing and abstained on the question of whether their due process rights were violated because the issue of a right to housing was unclear and about to be decided by a state appellate court.

*Johnson v. Dixon,* brought before court in the District of Columbia, challenged the District's closing of two shelters for homeless men. The court denied an application for a temporary restraining order and the shelters were closed. The plaintiffs next sought a preliminary injunction requiring that the District provide at least equivalent shelter opportunities and services. The court denied this motion holding that the plaintiffs were unlikely to succeed on their claims under the federal Fair Housing Act or the due process clause of the Fourteenth Amendment.

In this case, the court moved against the *Williams v. Barry* decision granting entitlement to overnight shelter.[23] It argued that changes in local law eliminated this entitlement. The plaintiffs then challenged the pertinence of the changes in local law that had developed between 1980 and 1983.

Their second substantive claim, based on the Fair Housing Act, was also denied even though the court accepted the plaintiffs' evidence that a substantial proportion of the population of both shelters was mentally ill and that others had chronic illnesses or infirmities that would be regarded as handicapping under the Fair Housing Act. The court argued that this provision did not apply to shelters. It also rejected the claim that the closing of the two shelters discriminated against handicapped former residents and that the District had not made reasonable accommodations for them holding that all of the plaintiffs had been accommodated in other shelters.[24]

An appellate court in the District affirmed the district court's ruling that shelters may be closed because adequate alternative facilities existed. This case involved a General Services Authority building used as a shelter that precipitated the nationally watched hunger strike of Mitch Snyder, the director of the Community for Creative Non-Violence (CCNV). When federal funding for renovations was denied by the Department of Health and Human Services (DHSS), President Reagan requested the Department to transform the shelter into a model shelter for homeless people.

When the proposed renovations were judged to be inadequate, Snyder and the Community sued and DHSS decided that it would permanently close the shelter. A temporary restraining order was issued, requiring public notice, comment, and a reasonable analysis by DHSS for its decision. DHSS claimed that adequate facilities existed to rehouse the shelter's homeless population in two other facilities. The court found, on appeal, that the agency's action was neither arbitrary nor capricious.[25]

Five other suits to prevent the closing of shelters were decided on similar grounds. Four were in the District of Columbia and one was in Brookhaven, New York.[26]

There is some room for speculation that the preponderance of such actions in the District was a direct response to the confrontation strategies employed by Mitch Snyder and the Community for Creative Non-Violence. Snyder's strategy was to bring many shelter eviction cases to litigation in the District, and he did this more than advocates in other cities. Moreover, these cases tended to use the same legal bases for their arguments.

One favorable action was attributed to the Community for Creative Non-Violence in a suit that sought to prevent the District of Columbia from closing its only full-time drop-in center for homeless people, a place where during the day street people could eat a hot meal, shower and launder their clothes, read, and generally come in from the streets. The facility was owned by the District and leased to the Community for this purpose.

The federal court action was filed a few days before the District initiated a state court eviction action against CCNV. The plaintiffs claimed that the District's threatened closing was a taking of their property without due process of law and without just compensation in violation of the Fifth Amendment, that it was a breach of contract, and a violation of a section of the urban renewal statute and Title VI of the Civil Rights Act of 1964. The federal government agreed to house the drop-in center at a vacant city college facility. The plaintiffs therefore dismissed their suit.[27]

## Eviction from Housing Programs

Transitional housing programs for people who are involved in efforts to prepare for permanent housing are subject to more rules and regulations than shelters. The very nature of their service requires resident's commitments to participate in a semicontractual relationship. These rules are a condition of acceptance into a transitional facility. Any one of a variety of violations can result in eviction, e.g., drug use, failure to manage money, unsanitary and unkempt maintenance of self and accommodations, as well as violence or threats of same.

Four cases have been argued on behalf of transitional housing occupants.

A 1990 case in Massachusetts was brought against the Friends of the Homeless by a plaintiff who was accepted for occupancy in one of its transitional housing programs, Worthington House. This program is funded by the Executive Office of Communities and Development under the state's rental assistance program, and is therefore governed by the state's laws and regulations governing that program.

The plaintiff signed an occupancy agreement specifying his monthly rental amount and other terms and conditions of his occupancy. He was not provided with a copy of the Occupancy Agreement in accordance with the Worthington House policy. He was expected to participate in a vocational rehabilitation program and he enrolled at the Massachusetts Career Development Institute (MCDI), which receives most of its funding from state agencies and programs. The plaintiff was asked to leave the premises after he had a series of disagreements with his job counselor.

Following his dismissal, the Program Manager of Worthington House ordered him to leave immediately. The director gave as reason the fact that he did not believe the plaintiff was ready for single-room-occupancy independent housing. At the suggestion of his welfare caseworker, the plaintiff demanded a written statement of the reasons for his ouster. The director wrote the letter in the form of a release of information authorizing her to communicate to a third person regarding the situation. The plaintiff advised her that the letter was unsatisfactory and repeated his request for a written notice specifying the reason for his eviction. That request was refused.

The plaintiff was not even allowed access to his room to pack his belongings. Instead, two Worthington Staff were instructed to pack up the contents of the plaintiff's room and put them on the curb. When the plaintiff tried to gain access to the temporary shelter located in the same building, he was denied. He also tried to obtain food from the soup kitchen located there but was denied admittance.

The plaintiff brought a suit against the Friends of the Homeless and the Director of Worthington House, alleging that they had violated Massachusetts General Law by depriving him of advance written notice of the reason for his eviction, a pretermination hearing, and his property without due process, in violation of the Fourteenth Amendment and

Article XII of the Declaration of Rights of the Massachusetts Constitution. The plaintive sought injunctive and compensatory relief.

The plaintiff argued that he was a tenant, and the defendants argued that he was a licensee of the premises. They explained that they orally revoked his license, and were thereafter entitled to use self-help to remove him.

The trial court entered a temporary restraining order restoring the plaintiff to the possession of his room. This order was continued on a preliminary injunction. The court ruled that the plaintiffs' occupancy could be terminated only according to the procedures of the public housing and lodging statutes, thereby granting him tenancy status. These procedures were to include written notice of the grounds of termination, and appropriate administrative determination of the justification for the termination.[28]

Abused women in a YWCA transitional living program in Massachusetts brought action as plaintiffs in a case in which they refused to participate in required counseling. The YWCA gave them 30-day notices to leave. The plaintiffs refused to do so and the YWCA changed the locks on their doors.

The plaintiffs initiated their suit against the YWCA and the trial court granted the defendant's motion to dismiss the case. The court held that the plaintiffs were not statutorily protected from self-help eviction because their relationship to the YWCA was that of "voluntary social service clients and not tenants."

The Massachusetts Appeals Court reversed the decision, holding that even if the plaintiffs were not tenants, self-help eviction would breach the covenant of quiet enjoyment under the statute. The court said that pretermination denial to program participants may "only perpetuate the cycle of temporary shelter and dislocation."[29]

A denial of pretermination from a transitional housing facility was also contested in Loudon County, Virginia. The plaintiff, a mother and two children, resided in a facility that receives funds under the Department of Housing and Urban Development's Supportive Housing Demonstration Program.

Federal regulations permit the execution of contracts between facility operators and residents. The plaintiff had signed a "Client Handbook" that, among other things, prohibited occupants from using any physical force, but did not define the term. The handbook also stated that the use of physical force, or even the thought of causing harm against a person or object, was grounds for immediate removal from the program.

The plaintiff was accused of using physical force and denied the accusation. The program operators, the Volunteers of America and the County, maintained that the plaintiff's recourse was the grievance procedure detailed in the handbook for persons who allege that they have been treated badly. The procedure did not offer any pretermination relief or elementary components of due process such as the right to confrontation, representation, or an impartial arbiter.

The court held that the plaintiff was entitled to be protected in her residency pending provision of a due process hearing, or a reversal of the court after considering the full merits of the case. The court found it likely that the plaintiff would prevail under *Goldberg v. Kelly*, which entitled her to a pretermination hearing, arguing that the plaintiff and her children might suffer irreparable harm if they were required to leave the shelter and that there was no evidence that she constituted a threat to others.[30]

A group of recovering addicts sought to share a single-family house in Plainfield, New Jersey. Neighbors protested and the City sued in state court, securing an interlocutory order that limited occupancy of the house to six persons pending resolution of the City's claim that the operation was forbidden in a single-family home.

Oxford House, Inc. (OHI), the organization that had established the house, was the defendant in the state court proceeding. It argued that the house was financially feasible only with an occupancy of nine, but the court continued to limit occupancy to six. OHI appealed the six-person limit without success, claiming violations of the federal Fair Housing Act as well as state land use law. The United States Department of Justice signed on in an *amicus curae* brief on behalf of the plaintiffs.

The federal district court granted preliminary relief from the limit and rejected abstention holding that the plaintiffs were likely to succeed on Fair Housing Act claims. The parties then settled the case, agreeing that up to 12 persons could reside at the house. The city also paid $62,000 to the plaintiffs.[31]

## Squatters Rights

Poor people needing housing have taken to "squatting" in abandoned properties and rehabilitating them with their own labor. This form of sweat equity expanded during the decade of the 1980s when homelessness increased, and affordable housing decreased.

Federal law authorized urban homesteading activities as early as 1974 by authorizing the Federal Homesteading Demonstration Program of the Community and Redevelopment Act. The law was amended in 1983 and the program targets participation to low-income families who live in substandard dwellings and pay more than 30% of their income for shelter.

Organized homesteading campaigns have been launched in eight cities. The most notable was ACORN, the Kensington Joint Action Council, in Philadelphia.[32] The most recent urban homesteading initiatives have occurred in Los Angeles since the 1994 earthquake. "Squatters" are taking over condemned properties that tenants have been required to vacate.

Urban homesteading is not popular among housed residents and merchants, but it does carry the force of federal law so local opponents have been reluctant to initiate legal actions to expel squatters. Two court cases, however, have found against homeless squatters.

Homeless residents of Portland, Oregon occupied a vacant HUD-owned single-family dwelling, as part of a nationwide protest against homelessness. HUD sued in the federal district court to force the defendants to leave the property. The defendants argued that HUD had acted counter to its statutory duty to pursue an adequate inventory of single-family units to house homeless individuals. The court granted HUD's motion for a summary judgment and ordered the plaintiffs to vacate the building.[33]

A more unusual case involved a homeless squatter who built a makeshift shelter on private property in Rhode Island. When the city condemned the structure, the owner evicted the squatter. The defendant unsuccessfully pled necessity and upheld the eviction order.[34]

Despite these setbacks in court, most squatters have not been evicted because of federal homesteading provisions. They experience harassment and organized antisquatting attempts by neighbors instead.

## Conclusion

The eviction cases surveyed in this chapter indicate the general tendency of courts to grant occupants of shelters, hotels, motels, and transitional living facilities the same rights of tenants in more permanent rental housing. Most of these rights are articulated in the Fair Housing Act and local government municipal codes. This has proven to be a critical safety valve for homeless people who rely upon temporary shelter arrangements.

Current efforts to apply "tougher" standards of behavior for admission to shelters, such as enrollment in a job training program, will raise new legal issues related to eviction from emergency shelter. This will undoubtedly become a subject of litigation relying upon equal protection criteria and tenants rights law.

## Notes and References

1. E.B. Lazere, P.A. Leonard, C. Dolbeare, and B. Zigas, *A Place to Call Home: The Low-Income Housing Crisis Continues* (Washington, D.C.: Center on Budget and Policy Priorities and Low Income Housing Information Service, 1991).

2. Marybeth Shinn and Colleen Gillespie, "The Roles of Housing and Poverty in the Origins of Homelessness," in David A. Snow and M. Gerald Bradford, eds., *Broadening Perspectives on Homelessness, American Behavioral Scientist*, 37(4):516–517 (February 1994).

3. *Ibid.*, 517–518.

4. Michael R. Sosin, Paul Colson, and Susan Grossman, *Homelessness in Chicago: Poverty and Pathology, Social Institutions and Social Change*, School of Social Service Administration, The University of Chicago (Chicago: The Chicago Community Trust, June 1988).

5. The New York City Commission on the Homeless, *The Way Home: A New Direction in Social Policy* (New York: February 1992), 97.

6. Shelter Partnership, "Prevent Evictions to Prevent Homelessness: A Home Base Work in Progress," *Homeless Reporter* (Los Angeles CA), 7–8 (May 1989).

7. *Samuel v. King*, No. 89-11788 (D.C. Super. Ct. Nov. 9, 1990) (order for partial summary judgment), 118 Daily Wash. L. Rptr. 2758 (Dec. 18, 1990) (Clearinghouse No. 46, 351).

8. Uniform Relocation Act. 42 U.S.C.; 5301 et. seq.

9. *Lacko v. City of Chicago*, No. 82-C-5031 (E.D. Ill. June 12, 1984) (consent decree) (Clearinghouse No. 32, 995).

10. *Terminal Plaza Corp. v. City and County of San Francisco*, 177 Cal. App. 3d 892, 223 Cal. Rptr. 379 (Cal. Ct. App. 1986).

11. *Vingara v. Borough of Wrightstown*, No. C-7545-87 (N.J. Super. Ct. Sept. 29. 1987) (Consent order of dismissal was entered after the Borough of Wrightstown voluntarily agreed to rescind its model occupancy limit.) (Clearinghouse No. 42, 795).

12. *Universal Motor Lodge, Inc. v. Seignious*, 550 N.Y.S. 2d 800 (Justice Ct. 1990).

13. *Universal Motor Lodge v. Holt*, No. 0999/89 (White Plains, N.Y., City Ct. Apr. 4, 1990) (Clearinghouse No. 45, 661).

14. *In re Chadbourne Industries, Ltd./In re Pan Trading Corp.* (U.S. Bankruptcy Court, S.D.N.Y., Abram, J.), cited in National Housing Law Project, *Annotated Bibliography*, 87 (Introduction, Note 9).

15. *McCain v. Koch* (Chapter 2, Note 9); *In re New York International Hostel, Inc.* (U.S. Bankruptcy Court, S.D.N.Y., Brozman, J.) (1990).

16. *New York City Local Law 19, Act of May 31, 1983; Sadowsky v. City of New York*, 578 F. Supp. 1577 (S.D.N.Y. 1984) aff'd, 732 F. 2d 312 (2d Cir. 1984) (Clearinghouse No. 38, 571).

17. *Syria v. Lichtenstein*, No. 5579-89T3 (N.J. Super. Ct., App. Div., Aug. 6 1991) (Clearinghouse No. 47, 116).

18. Heather MacDonald, "Hope for the Homeless?: Common Sense From Giuliani." *New York Times* (June 9, 1994), A19.

19. *Callahan v. Carey* (Introduction, Note 4).

20. *Massachusetts Coalition for the Homeless v. Johnston*, No. 80109 (Super. Ct. Suffolk County, Feb. 28, 1990) (Clearinghouse No. 40, 714), *supra*.

21. *Parker v. Baltimore County Department of Social Services*, No. 47/88 LSP 3315 (Md. Cir. Ct. Oct 1, 1988) (Clearinghouse No. 43, 991).

22. *Olson v. Massachusetts Department of Mental Health*, No. 86-3136-T (D. Mass. Oct. 21, 1987) (order granting preliminary injunction).

23. *Williams v. Barry*, 490 F. Supp. 941 (D.D.C. 1980) 798 F. 2d 789 (D.C. Cir. 1983).

24. *Johnson v. Dixon*, Civ. Action No. 91-1979 (D.D.C. Sept. 5, 1991) (Clearinghouse No. 47, 048).

25. *Robbins v. Reagan*, 780 F. 2d 37 (D.C. Cir. 1985) (per curiam) (Clearinghouse No. 39, 614).

26. *Williams v. Barry*, 708 F. 2d 789 (D.C. Cir. 1983) (Clearinghouse NO. 29, 265); *Community for Creative Non-Violence v. Barry* (D.D.C. filed Aug. 13, 1983) (Clearinghouse No. 35, 031); *Caton v. Barry*, 500 F. Supp. 45 (D.D.C. 1980) (Clearinghouse No. 29, 655); *Manhold v. Bowen*, No. 86-1296 (D.C. Super. Ct. 1986); *Town of Brookhaven v. Marlan Chun Enterprises*, 528 N.Y.S. 2d 822 (1988) (Clearinghouse No. 43, 639).

27. *Community for Creative Non-Violence v. Barry* (D.D.C. filed Aug. 13, 1983) (Clearinghouse No. 35, 031).

28. *Carr v. Friends of the Homeless, Inc.*, No. 89-LE-3492-S (Hampden, Mass., Hous. Ct. April 3, 1990) (Abrashkin, J.) (Clearinghouse No. 45, 664).

29. *Serreze v. YWCA of Western Massachusetts, Inc.*, 572 N.E. 2d 581 (Mass. App. 1991).

30. *Goldberg v. Kelly* (Introduction, Note 1); *Bosse v. Duvall*, No. 10476 (Cir. Ct. Loudon Cnty. Jan. 21, 1992) (order granting temporary injunction) (Clearinghouse No. 47, 977).

31. *Oxford House-Evergreen v. City of Plainfield*, 769 F. Supp. 1329 (C.D.N.J. 1991) (Clearinghouse No. 47, 047).

32. Stoner, *Inventing a Non-Homeless Future*, 348 (Chapter 5, Note 2).

33. *United States v. Martin*, No. 88-848-MA (Or. Dist. Ct. filed July 18, 1988) (Clearinghouse No. 43, 735).

34. *Driscoll v. Philip*, No. 86-1223 (R.I. Dist. Ct. answer filed May 23, 1986).

# 7

# VOTING RIGHTS

## The Significance of Voting for Homeless Americans

American history is replete with struggles of minority group populations to overcome disenfranchisement. The most dramatic historic events associated with gaining the right to vote are those of women and African Americans. The women's movement relied on the amendment process as a strategy, whereas the pervasive resistance to equal voting rights for African Americans compelled a broader strategy that focused on legislation, litigation, and enforcement of both by the United States Department of Justice and the Federal Bureau of Investigation (FBI).

Clinical and policy practitioners in most human service arenas acknowledge that the paradigm of personal and political empowerment defines the critical imperative for social equity and justice. The rights of citizenship are empty without such power and the vote represents the most fundamental right in a democracy. Although the right to vote does not guarantee political power, let alone registration and voting, its absence spells a clear violation of democratic participatory principles.

After the National Association for the Advancement of Colored People had won its major challenges to exclusions of African Americans from voting in the 1950s and 1960s, there were few changes in the voting patterns in the Southern part of the United States. The exclusion of African Americans from the franchise in the South rested on deeper institutions of racism, as well as entrenched resistance to federal invasion of local statutes imposing qualifications to vote such as literacy. Thurgood Marshall concluded that litigation was but one strategy and that all court victories on voting rights in the South required enforcement by the FBI and the Department of Justice.[1]

Similarly, it took many years for women to independently exercise their vote. Women either did not vote, or voted the way their husbands, or husband's employers, directed them. The "year of the woman" occurred only in 1992, decades after women won the franchise.

Homeless advocates understand that homeless Americans need a political voice in order to challenge the existence and consequences of homelessness. Few efforts to politically organize homeless people have succeeded, however, because their lives mitigate against the organization and support necessary for political influence. Although the ballot may not effectively achieve this, its absence is a harsh denial of their worth as citizens in their own country. For homeless people, the right to vote may be more important than for other groups because they have no financial resources that can translate into political power.

Other more powerful groups have not attained measurable advances after winning their franchise and it would be highly improbable that homeless Americans would experience different results. Nevertheless, large blocs of registered homeless voters could carry some potential for impact on elected officials and citizens. Some homeless advocates cynically allege that voter registration campaigns among homeless people will result only in increasing the number of "wrong" votes that are manipulated and ill-informed. Nevertheless, the right to vote is intrinsic in any democracy. While it may be only a symbolic value initially, secure enfranchisement may be a harbinger of a greater political voice in the fullness of time.

The possession of voter registration cards can serve tangible ends other than political influence. They can be used to establish identity at public welfare benefits offices and hospitals, sparing the embarrassment and prolonged search for identity proof through birth, military discharge, or social security records, as well as drivers' licenses that so many homeless people experience. Their establishment as registered voters, despite a lack of private addresses, can elevate their status as more than mere "transients," thereby reducing some of the negative stereotypes that sanction indignities against them by public officials and private citizens.[2]

The fundamental right of homeless Americans to retain their franchise regardless of their residential status need not be justified on the basis of any political or social goals. Democratic morality and faith rest upon the principle of franchise rights for all citizens.

## Voting Rights Litigation

Just as the lack of a bona fide mailing address provided cause to refuse public welfare benefits to homeless people, it has been the basis for denying homeless people registration to vote in seven states and the District of Columbia.[3] Homeless advocates and service providers recognized the injustice of this position and organized a campaign to reverse this. They combined organizing strategies of impact litigation with appeals to the media and local government officials, as well as efforts to organize homeless people around their disenfranchisement.

All litigation on behalf of the right of homeless persons to vote has focused on the reconstruction of the definition of residence. Each legal brief has referred to equal protection rights.

Justice Thurgood Marshall was among the first to perceive the injustice of disenfranchising homeless people. He argued that the homeless need political power if they are to attain and preserve civil liberties. He registered this dissenting opinion in *Clark v. Community for Creative Non-Violence*.[4]

This case did not involve homeless people themselves. It related to the First Amendment rights of political protesters planning to stage a sleep-in demonstration in support of homeless people. Justice Marshall raised the issue of political power and the vote in his dissent stating,

> Though numerically significant, the homeless are politically powerless inasmuch as they lack the financial resources necessary to obtain access to many of the most effective means of persuasion. Moreover, homeless persons are likely to be denied access to the vote since the lack of a mailing address or other proof of residence within a State disqualifies an otherwise eligible citizen from registering to vote.[5]

The Committee for Dignity and Fairness for the Homeless brought the first legal challenge to homeless disenfranchisement in 1984 in Pennsylvania. The plaintiffs alleged that homeless people were being denied the vote in violation of the First Amendment and the state voting statute because they lacked an address.

The court denied a preliminary injunction citing a failure to show that irreparable harm had occurred because homeless people were not allowed to register. The case was settled during the hearing on a permanent injunction and the judge issued a decree designating homeless people as residents of the Commonwealth of Pennsylvania. Such status was considered sufficient to allow them to vote by designating a shelter for mailing purposes, even if they do not live there. Most states have followed this pattern since the decision.[6]

A second precedent setting challenge to the disenfranchisement of homeless people was brought in the 1984 case of *Pitts v. Black* in New York City. This case was certified as a class action representing 150,000 homeless people in the state of New York. It was brought by a man who claimed that he lost his job and had been living in a New York City park for 3 years.

The challenge to disenfranchisement was brought under the Equal Protection Clause of the Fourteenth Amendment, the New York Constitution, and state voting laws. The federal district court dismissed the claims brought under the state constitution and voting law. However, the defendants conceded that persons living in emergency shelters and welfare hotels are legally entitled to register to vote, but not other homeless people without such accommodations.

One month later, the district court ruled in the plaintiffs' favor, stating that the strict scrutiny test applied because the state had placed restrictions on the fundamental right to vote. The court applied the strict scrutiny standard relying upon the voting plans of Philadelphia, Pennsylvania and the District of Columbia, which define the traditional concept of residency to include homeless persons. The court found that New York State had failed to establish a sufficiently broad definition of residence.

The district court formulated a less restrictive residency test based upon state common law. It suggested a new "home base" definition that permits homeless persons to identify a specific location within a political community as their residence. "Home base" was designated as a location to which people return regularly, demonstrate an intent to remain for the present, and a place where they can receive messages and be contacted.[7]

This case established the precedent used by homeless advocates elsewhere to secure voting rights for homeless people.

Although not a law suit per se, a proceeding in the District of Columbia occurred close to the time that *Pitts v. Black* was being tried. It interpreted the residence requirement for voting to include homeless persons by allowing designation of any location as a home, with an accompanying effective local mailing address. This challenge took place when homeless advocates attempted to register homeless voters so that they would be eligible to sign and circulate petitions to place a right-to-shelter initiative on the ballot.

The District of Columbia Board of Elections and Ethics reversed its earlier position on the right of homeless people to register and vote. Homeless people have been permitted to designate a shelter for mailing purposes as a condition of registering to vote, regardless of whether they are actually residing at a shelter.[8]

In 1985 *Collier v. Menzel* was brought to court in Santa Barbara, California representing three homeless Santa Barbara resident plaintiffs who submitted voter registration applications identifying public parks as their residence. The court held that city parks qualify as a place of habitation for voting purposes, stating that denial of the vote to homeless persons is an equal protection violation.

Initially, the Santa Barbara County Registrar of Voters rejected the applications of park residents to vote based on insufficient residence address. The trial court also denied the petition. These decisions were reversed on appeal. Lawyers for the plaintiffs successfully argued their compliance with statutory requirements for voter registration alleging that failure to process the applications violated the constitutional right to equal protection.

The court found that the park residents satisfied statutory requirements of a fixed habitation and an intention of remaining at that place or returning to it after temporary absences. It held that access to vote for homeless persons was a fundamental right in a democratic society, ensuring them the same rights as domiciled persons. The court also stated that its position imparted a sense of responsibility to homeless people by giving them a political stake in their future and the community.[9]

A Connecticut case tried by Neighborhood Legal Services resulted in a court ruling based upon *Pitts*. The Secretary of State ruled that a homeless person may be a bona fide resident by identifying a specific location to which she or he returns regularly, including a shelter or a park bench, and intends to remain there. The court also ruled that a homeless person may be required to maintain a separate mailing address to enable the registrar to canvas voters regularly.[10]

Three other cases directed County Boards of Elections to register homeless persons to vote, even if they live on the street. A Chicago case, filed by the Chicago/Gary Area Union of the Homeless, authorized homeless people to present two pieces of identification providing an address or location description sufficiently precise to enable assignment to a voting precinct or ward.[11]

In 1991 the advocacy organization, Voter Registration of Homeless Persons, campaigned to register homeless persons in New Jersey. The Attorney General of the state issued a formal opinion directing county Boards of Elections to register homeless persons, even if they live on the street. The Attorney General issued this order in correspondence to the presiding Judge.[12]

An earlier New Jersey case was settled out of court in response to a complaint regarding an ordinance that denied the right to vote to persons living in a campground. The ordinance was deleted in the settlement.[13]

## Conclusion

This litigation docket has been recommended as a prototype for establishing the entitlement of homeless persons to register to vote throughout the United States. Courts and administrative agencies have concluded that residency requirements mandating domicile in a traditional home violate the Equal Protection clause of the Constitution and that an intention to remain at a specific location and provision of an address at which one may receive mail, whether a shelter or Post Office box, sufficiently meets residence requirements. These decisions have effectively balanced the right of homeless persons to vote with the legitimate right of states to regulate the voting process.

Policy advocates and organizers played key roles in bringing these cases to litigation. It is noteworthy that four of the legal challenges were brought by homeless advocacy organizations. The favorable decisions demonstrate the power of single interest organizations, as well as coalitions, to achieve their ends through the courts. They also indicate the efficacy of partnerships between policy practitioners, citizen advocates, and lawyers.

There is no clear evidence that any of these cases have translated into visible political power on the issue of homelessness, or other aspects of extreme poverty and human services. Nor are there any available data on how many homeless people actually use their voter registration cards for identification. The absence of data, however, does not obviate the value of preserving the right of homeless persons to vote. Enfranchisement is far more than a token symbol in a democracy.

It protects the integrity of the ballot box.

## Notes and References

1. Tushnet, *Making Civil Rights Law*, 115 (Chapter 1, Note 3).
2. Coates, *A Street Is Not a Home*, 292–294
3. California, Connecticut, Delaware, District of Columbia, Illinois, New Jersey, New York, and, Pennsylvania.
4. 468 U.S. 288 (1984); discussed in Coates, *A Street Is Not a Home*, 293 (Introduction, Note 22).
5. *Ibid.* brief for National Coalition for the Homeless as *amicus curae.*
6. *Committee for Dignity and Fairness for the Homeless v. Tartiaglinoe*, No. 84-3447 (E.D. Pa. Sept. 14, 1984) (order and decree) (Clearinghouse No. 40, 030).
7. *Pitts v. Black*, 608 F. Supp. 696 (S.D.N.Y., 1984) (Clearinghouse No. 38, 514); National Housing Law Project. *Annotated Bibliography*, 125–126.
8. *In re Applications for Voter Registration of Willie Jenkins, et al. Before the D.C. Board of Elections and Ethics* (June 7, 1984) (Clearinghouse No. 40, 029).
9. *Collier v. Menzel*, 176 Cal. App. 3d 24, 221 Cal. Rptr. 110 (1985) (Clearinghouse No. 40, 884).
10. *Letter from Secretary of State to Shirley Bergert, Esq., Neighborhood Legal Services, Hartford, Connecticut* (July 28, 1986) (Clearinghouse No. 40, 943),

11. *Board of Elections Commission v. Chicago/Gary Union of the Homeless*, No. 86-29 (Ill. Cir. Ct. Sept. 26, 1986) (Clearinghouse No. 41, 666).

12. *Voter Registration of Homeless Persons*, Formal Opinion No. 2 (Op. N.J. Att'y Gen., April 17, 1991).

13. *Asher et al. v. Township of Middle et al.*, No. 90-4091 (SSB) (D.N.J., filed October 11, 1990).

# 8

## EDUCATION

### Discrimination in Schools

Before considering the issue of education for homeless children, it is important to note that education is the only area of human service law in which local government prevails. Public, primary, and secondary schools are created, financed, and operated by local school districts in every state except Hawaii. State governments may provide some funds to local school districts. They may also regulate some aspects of the school's operation, but local school districts, administered by elected school boards, prevail.

This norm of local control has historically constrained state and federal intent to intervene, but the federal government also provides some funds to local school districts and conditions receipt of these on compliance with designated federal laws. The United States Supreme Court has also been reluctant to overrule local school boards. A 1973 decision demonstrates this. The court refused to rule that discrimination in education on the basis of wealth may not be a violation of the Fourteenth Amendment in San Antonio, Texas.[1] That same decision stated that education is neither an explicit nor implicit fundamental right protected by the Constitution. However, either the Constitution or separate statutes in each state, except Mississippi, guarantee a free public education requiring children within certain ages to attend school and imposing civil and criminal penalties on parents who fail to comply with the law by educating their children.

A significant federal inroad to local jurisdiction occurred in 1975, when the Supreme Court held that if a state offers free public education to all children and requires attendance, it creates a property right protected by the Fourteenth Amendment. Under this property right, a child cannot be suspended or expelled from school unless certain protection is offered. *Goss v. Lopez* defined the protection as a right to notice and a minimum right to be heard. State and local statutes generally provide more procedural protections.[2]

The Supreme Court has prevailed in issues of discrimination in schools based on race, gender, or disability. *Brown v. Board of Education* overruled the "separate but equal" doctrine of *Plessy v. Ferguson* that it had upheld since 1899, effectively prohibiting racial discrimination in public schools.[3] Legislative law protects gender discrimination. Title IX of the Education Amendments of 1972, as amended by the Civil Rights Restoration Act of 1987, forbids discrimination on the basis of sex in any school that receives federal funds. This pertains to virtually every primary and secondary school.[4] State constitutions and statutes also prohibit discrimination on this basis.

The Supreme Court has also aggressively overturned local school district policies pertaining to the children of undocumented immigrants. In *Plyler v. Doe,* the court denounced the unfairness of punishing children for circumstances beyond their control. The injustice of such policies led to the court's decision that depriving undocumented children of free access to public schools violated their right to equal protection of the laws guaranteed by the Constitution.[5] This decision is clearly relevant for homeless children.

Two lower federal courts ruled that disabled children could not be excluded from the schools in 1971 and 1972. These decisions extended the equal opportunity rights of *Brown v. Board of Education* and they led to the enactment of the Education for All Handicapped Children Act, which forbids discrimination against handicapped students by federally assisted facilities. Because of this law, it is no longer possible to deny children an education on the basis of mental or physical disability. It is not yet resolved whether this Act can be applied to children because of the possibility of contagion under the law. Asymptomatic children with AIDS are, however, covered by Section 504 of the Rehabilitation Act. In *The School Board of Nassau County v. Arline,* the Court held that when Congress passed Section 504 to prohibit discrimination against those who were impaired, it also applied to those who were thought to be impaired by contagiousness. The case was brought against a teacher, not a student, on the basis of tuberculosis not AIDS, but the precedent pertains to students and teachers with AIDS, as well.[6]

This combination of federal antidiscrimination judicial decisions and legislation provided the legal precedent for the mandate of the Stewart B. McKinney Homeless Assistance Act that states not discriminate against homeless children. The Act provides funds for the creation of state programs to ensure access to schools by homeless children. Signed into law by President Ronald Reagan in 1987, the Act was one of the few pieces of legislation in the 1980s to authorize services and expenditures for homeless people. The original intent of the legislation was to focus on short-term solutions to alleviate the immediate problems of homeless people. It includes more than 20 programs and provides funds for homeless prevention, emergency food and shelter, health care, transitional housing, mental health services, job training, and education.[7]

The Congress amended the Act in 1990 to remove barriers that prevented homeless children from attending school. Some of these barriers were required proof of immunization, former school records, and proof of residence.[8] The amendments tightened monitoring regulations, mandated the provision of technical assistance, and permitted the use of McKinney Act funds for direct educational services. The amendments also tightened requirements that states eliminate all barriers to education, including a lack of transportation, and mandated coordination with other social service programs.

Although these amendments were a significant foreword step, Congress never appropriated the full amount of authorized money. In the worst instance, only $7.2 million was appropriated of the $50 million authorized in FY 1991. Additional implementation problems resulted from Department of Education (DOE) monitoring and guidance of state's activities. The Government Accounting Office (GAO) found that the DOE had not monitored any states during the first year of the program. In many cases, states submitted plans to meet the educational needs of homeless children and youth but never implemented them. Even where access to schools was provided, other programs necessary to bolster homeless students were not provided. The Los Angeles Unified School District, which operates one of the most extensive programs under the 1990 McKinney Act Amendments, relies on volunteer tutors to provide most of these needed special services.

New leadership at the federal level has remedied many of these noncompliance issues, but it remains clear that all homeless children and youth do not have access to education. Many shelters remain without transportation. Advocates report that up to 50% of all homeless children are not attending school.[9]

## The Problems of Homeless Children in Attending School

The DOE estimates that 450,000 children are homeless in the United States. DOE estimates allege that 28% of these children are denied access to public education. Residency requirements, inability to obtain school records, and lack of transportation keep these children out of public schools.[10] In the long run, this lack of access to an education dooms homeless children to failure and emotional traumas and precludes even the most limited opportunities to obtain the skills necessary for productive work and citizenship.

Homeless children experience acute problems because of being homeless. A seminal study conducted in a Boston shelter by Ellen Bassuk found that 47% of the children had at least one developmental lag; one-third had difficulty with language skills, fine and gross motor coordination, and social and personal development; almost half were clinically depressed; 43% had failed a grade, 24% were in special education classes, and nearly half were failing or doing below average work in school. Many of these findings were corroborated by the St. Louis Health Care for the Homeless Coalition that added health indicators to its survey. The coalition found that among 360 homeless school children physically examined in a shelter, over 32% suffered from respiratory upper infections, 25% had incomplete immunizations, more than 14% suffered from skin disorders and infestations, and almost 9% had poor dentition.[11]

School districts, spurred on by community residents, have contended that these developmental, psychological, and physical disabilities render homeless children unsuitable for attendance at schools with housed children who do not suffer from such conditions. Parents and school officials are frequently concerned that the presence of disease among homeless children will be contagious and/or infectious, and that problems associated with developmental lag will slow the learning progress of their children. In the 1980s, these sentiments prevailed and formed the basis for public opposition to inclusion of homeless children in many schools, until the McKinney Act prohibited such discrimination against homeless children. Moreover, many large urban school districts have established special programs for homeless children with McKinney Act education funds.

The protections of the McKinney Act have provided legal assurances of schooling for homeless children. Local governments have performed unevenly, so that some school districts have literally ignored the law. In contrast, others have established extensive programs in compliance with the law.

Only eight cases have been brought to litigation. The general theme of these cases has related to the location of the school that homeless children are entitled to attend. Some cases have argued that children should be allowed to continue attendance at their home district school if they have been forced to move because of homelessness. Others have argued the opposite, seeking attendance rights in schools where shelters and transitional housing facilities are located. Advocates for both positions have expressed concern for continuity in children's schooling seeking not to force further disruption beyond the loss of a home. One case sought to compel compliance with the McKinney Act.

## Litigation

Immediately after the McKinney Act was passed, the National Coalition for the Homeless brought a suit against the United States Department of Education. This action sought to require the Department of Education to implement the McKinney Act mandate that states not discriminate against homeless children, as well as the creation of state programs funded by the Act to ensure homeless children access to schools. Under the pressure of the plaintiffs' pending motion for a preliminary injunction, the Department of Education agreed to set a deadline for implementation of the McKinney Act program and to monitor states' participation in it.[12]

This litigation strategy of forcing compliance in the face of resistance to a law, or laggard implementation, has proven necessary and critical to the enforcement of many laws. During the era of civil rights legislation, in the 1950s and 1960s, lawyers repeatedly returned to court to press for compliance or challenge organized resistance.

Three suits sought to permit homeless children to attend their "home" school after they moved away. One suit, tried in Chicago, forced the city and state to allow homeless children to attend the school that they attended prior to becoming homeless. Is also sought the provision of transportation. The court found in favor of the plaintiff thereby allowing children to remain in their "home" school.[13]

*Fulton v. Krauskopf*, tried in New York City in 1986, challenged the City's failure to provide homeless children and their parents with transportation grants to permit them to travel to school from distant emergency housing locations. The claims were based on provisions in New York State regulations and federal law that designated "a single State agency" with education responsibilities. The Appellate Division enjoined the City to provide school transportation grants to homeless families and denied leave to appeal.[14]

A homeless parent in Freeport, New York sought to enroll her five school-aged children in their prior school district while they were shuttled from one district to another in search of permanent housing. The trial judge ruled that residency, for the purpose of school enrollment, is determined by the physical location of the child and refused the plaintiffs' request.[15]

In New Jersey, the Department of the Public Advocate opposed the transfer of a homeless family from one shelter to another contending that the transfer would disrupt the special education of the children. The case was settled after briefing and acceded to the opposition of the Public Advocate.[16]

One case arose in New York because neither the school district in which the family temporarily resided nor the school district in which they hoped to obtain permanent residence would admit children residing in emergency housing. The court ordered the school district in which the family temporarily resided to admit the children, pending a decision on the merits of the family's constitutional challenge of the residency requirement.

In a related case, the district court allowed a claim for damages against the Commissioner of Education. In this case, the plaintiff sought declaratory and injunctive relief for damages and due process violations because she was given no notice and hearing regarding school decisions to deny her admittance.[17]

School attendance has also proven to be grounds for continued residence at shelters, transitional living facilities, and hotels. *Vingara v. Borough of Wrightstown* granted tenant's rights to a family living in a transitional housing facility on the grounds that the children had established residency in that district by their attendance at the local school.[18]

The most recent case representing homeless children was filed in the District of Columbia in 1992. It was dismissed for lack of a cause for action. The plaintiffs sued to enforce the McKinney Act contending that the District of Columbia (1) had failed to consider the best interests of homeless children by placing them in public schools, (2) failed to ensure transportation to the schools that are in the best interests of the children to attend, (3) failed to coordinate social services and public education for homeless children, and to ensure access to comparable educational services and school meal programs, (4) failed to ensure access to free, appropriate public education for homeless children, and (5) denied them equal protection of the laws by providing transportation assistance to handicapped children while denying it to the homeless children.

This case, *Lampkin v. District of Columbia,* was overturned in the appeals court in July 1994. The court ruled that the McKinney Act requires the District to ensure that homeless children have an enforceable right to education. The court held that the McKinney Act requires the District to guarantee homeless children access to public schools. It also found that the McKinney Act mandates are not advisory, but create enforceable rights for homeless children. This ruling has important implications for homeless children across the United States.[19]

## Conclusion

The combination of McKinney Act mandates prohibiting discrimination against homeless school children and its categorical funding for school districts is slowly resolving access problems and barriers for this vulnerable population. Protections against discrimination of homeless children were safeguarded, for the most part, when the Act became law. It is encouraging to note that numerous large school districts have established special programs coordinating educational provisions for homeless children. On the other hand, reports and observations of advocates noting that one-half of homeless children are still without access to school are not only discouraging, they are harsh reminders of the fact that the best intended legislation can falter at the implementation level.

Because parents and local community leaders persist in their opposition to accepting homeless people in their midst, organized opposition to having these children attend school with housed children continues to be a problem. Most opponents concede that homeless children are entitled to attend school, but the controversy focuses on *where* and *which* school. Typically, the NIMBY (not in my backyard) syndrome manifests itself when homeless parents attempt to enroll their children in schools. This explains why the central question raised in litigation has been about whether children should attend their home school or the school where they are temporarily residing.

The docket of cases cited in this chapter has set fundamental precedents to ensure that homeless children can attend school in either place. They have also attached residency rights to attendance at schools as in *Vingara*. These judicial decisions have forcefully applied strategies to ensure homeless children continuity in their education. They have addressed the problems of weak implementation of the 1990 McKinney Act Amendments and added the power of the courts to that of the legislature.

## Notes and References

1. *San Antonio School District v. Rodriguez*, 411 U.S. 1 (1973).
2. *Goss v. Lopez*, 419 U.S. 565 (1975).
3. Tushnet, *Making Civil Rights Law*, 168–231 (Chapter 1, Note 3).
4. Education Amendments of 1972, Title IX, 20 U.S.C. #1681; Civil Rights Restoration Act of 1987, P.L. 100-259.
5. Howard F. Chang. "Shame on Them, Picking on Children," *Los Angeles Times* (September 6, 1994), B5.

6.  Saltzman and Proch, *Law in Social Work Practice*, 223 (Introduction, Note 11).

7.  U.S. Congress. Stewart B. McKinney, *Homeless Assistance Act*, H.R. 4352 99th. Cong., 1st. sess.; U.S. Congress, *Urgent Relief for Homeless Act*, Public Law 100-77, 100th. Cong., 1st. sess.

8.  Karger and Stoesz, *American Social Welfare Policy*, 373 (Chapter 4, Note 9); National Low Income Housing Coalition, *Advocate's Resource Book* (Washington, D.C.: National Low Income Housing Coalition, 1992).

9.  Child Welfare League of America, *Homeless Children and Their Families: A Preliminary Study* (1987), 2.

10. *1989 Report on Department of Education Activities* [Section 724(b)(2) of P.L. 100-77]; *1989 Status Report on Education of Homeless Children and Youth from State Coordinators* [Section 724(b)(3) of P.L. 100-77] (March 1990).

11. Ellen Bassuk, "Homeless Families: Single Mothers and Their Families in Boston Shelters," in Ellen Bassuk, ed., *The Mental Health Needs of Homeless Persons* (San Francisco: Jossey-Bass, 1987); Health Care for the Homeless Coalition of Greater St. Louis, "Progress Report" (St. Louis, Missouri, 1987); Karger and Stoesz, *American Social Welfare Policy*, 372n373 (Chapter 4, Note 9).

12. *National Coalition for the Homeless v. Department of Education*, No. 87-3512 (D.D.C. Jan. 21, 1988).

13. *Salazar v. Edwards*, 92 CH 5703 (1988).

14. *Fulton v. Krauskopf*, 117 A.D. 2d 198, 502 N.Y.S. 2d 720 (1986).

15. *Mason v. Freeport Union School District*, No. 2865/87 (N.Y. Sup. Ct. April 22, 1987) (Clearinghouse No. 42, 819).

16. *In re Linda Beggess*, N.J. OAL (Office of Administrative Law) Dkt. No. HPW 9037, 1988.

17. *Orozco ex rel. Arroyo v. Sobel*, 674 F. Supp. 125 (S.D.N.Y. 1987) (Goettel, J.) *dismissed in part*, *Orozco v. Sobel*, 703 F. Supp. 1113 (S.D.N.Y. 1989) (Clearinghouse No. 43, 336).

18. *Vingara v. Borough of Wrightstown* (Chapter 6, Note 11).

19. Shelter Partnership, "Overcoming Barriers to Education for Homeless Children," *Homeless Reporter*, 10:30, 8.

# II

# THE CRIMINALIZATION OF
# HOMELESS PEOPLE

A disturbing backlash against homeless people has emerged in cities across the United States in the past 2 years. Cities that have a record of providing generous services and supports to homeless people are becoming increasingly hostile to them. Pressured by small groups of anti-homeless business people and residents, even many liberal people who formerly expressed sympathy for the plight of the homeless are now proclaiming their "compassion fatigue." They feel justified that their former compassion has given way to impatience, frustration, and even anger toward homeless people.

Some who once volunteered in soup kitchens and shelters are now engaged in campaigns to restrict service provisions and prohibit begging and the use of public spaces by homeless people. Service providers report a sharp drop in volunteers and donations for all programs that serve homeless people.

This growing antihomeless vehemence has resulted in a rash of local ordinances intended to criminalize homeless people by sweeping them off the streets or public parks, prohibiting begging, sleeping, sitting, or loitering in public places. Local governments and citizen groups have also attempted to reduce or eliminate services to the homeless. Overwhelmed and angry at the growing numbers of homeless people, they are trying to address the problem by criminalizing the condition rather than addressing its causes.

The National Law Center on Homelessness and Poverty conducted a survey of antihomeless actions in 16 cities and found that 80 laws had been passed against begging, sleeping, camping, loitering, destruction of property, vagrancy, and unequal enforcement. Restrictions on services also featured among these.[1]

Some of this backlash can be explained in terms of traditional and historic mean-spirited responses to the "unworthy poor." But today's antihomeless backlash must also be understood as part of larger concerns for public safety and fear of crime manifesting themselves across the United States. Proponents of "tough-love" solutions fear that their neighborhoods are in danger of crime and disease emanating from amassed groups of homeless people. They contend that the rights of the community must take precedence over the rights of individuals and that lawmakers must strike a better balance between rights to public safety and health and the civil rights of homeless people.

Although this analysis of contemporary attitudes toward the criminalization of homeless people is valid, it should not obscure they many constructive alternative responses to the problems of homelessness. Service providers and advocates are engaged in dialogues with local governments, business leaders, and community organizations intended to counteract antihomeless sentiment. Some local ordinances have positively responded to concerns about begging, use of public places, and sanitation. The City of Berkeley has operated an effective voucher program for panhandlers for several years. Community policing programs have emphasized sensitivity to the needs of homeless people and referral to service agencies. People are setting up job referral services with information banks of available jobs. The California state legislature is considering a bill that would establish model procedures for local agencies concerning the removal and protection of personal property left by homeless people. Dade County, Florida Commissioners passed an ordinance to charge a 1% tax on restaurant meals. The revenue from this new tax is earmarked for housing and social service for homeless persons.

Finally, advocates have won legal victories against antihomeless actions on the grounds that they are unconstitutional denials of protected rights that may not be denied or infringed. These victories, along with examples of constructive alternatives to antihomeless actions, are positive trends in the struggle for the civil rights of homeless persons.

This section addresses the recent homeless backlash by reviewing and analyzing antihomeless legislation prohibiting or curtailing begging, loitering, sleeping, camping, and arrests or property seizures authorized under such laws. It describes the legal challenges against these bans that have been brought by coalitions of concerned citizens, service providers, and lawyers. Many of the challenges that have been filed in the courts are pending final decision. It is likely that such decisions will continue to be delayed as long as possible under the current avalanche of antihomeless sentiment.

### Note

1.   National Law Center on Homelessness and Poverty, *The Right to Remain Nowhere: A report on Anti-Homeless Litigation in 16 United States Cities* (Washington, D.C., December 1993), Table II, Anti-Homeless Actions, by City.

# 9

# FREE SPEECH AND BEGGING

## Concerns about Begging

Begging has had a resurgence over the past 5 years. Although people have grown accustomed to the increasing numbers of homeless people in their neighborhoods, many are frightened and disturbed by their appearance. Public perceptions of imminent danger, whether substantiated or imagined, have compelled people to avoid frequenting neighborhoods populated by beggars, or panhandlers, as they are currently labeled. Businesses fear a loss of activity. Residents feel threatened for their safety. More compassionate people experience discomfort at the sight of too many panhandlers. Many who want to assist panhandlers feel overwhelmed by the numbers complaining that they simply cannot afford to give to so many people.

Forms of panhandling may be legal or illegal in different states. However, the free speech provisions of the United States Constitution dictate that only certain forms of panhandling are illegal. Aggressive panhandling, defined as the use of force or threats, has been declared illegal. In contrast, nonaggressive requests for help remain protected as free speech entitlements. The distinction between these two forms of begging is frequently blurred by subjective perceptions of aggression, so that many people have begun to support laws that would make all panhandling illegal.

Numerous community groups have developed alternative plans for directly giving money to panhandlers. Spurred by stereotypes that panhandlers use their money only to purchase liquor or drugs, or are actually earning very good income, campaigns are encouraging alternatives to giving money. These include giving service referral cards instead of money, voucher programs for food and services, and direct contributions to agencies or pooled community funds for homeless people.

Other communities have ignored alternative schemes in favor of "just say no to panhandlers" campaigns. Some of these campaigns have developed euphemisms for just saying no. In West Hollywood, California the term used is "Do the right thing." Homeless advocates and homeless people in these communities contend that alternative plans will not achieve their agenda of forcing homeless people out of the community.

The issue of panhandling has immobilized communities, and the nation, from considering broader solutions to address the problems of homelessness and poverty. Although the hardships of the business community and concern for public safety are valid, "just say no to panhandlers" campaigns do not solve any problem. Instead, they serve only to push homeless people from one community to the next.

Many organizations of homeless advocates and service providers are attempting to change public opinion about "just say no" campaigns. They emphasize that people have a legal right to ask for money, calling attention to the blatant unfairness of differentiating between a homeless person and a Girl Scout asking for change.

Referring to "just say no" campaigns as the "big lie," they explain that alternatives to panhandling in the form of referral cards and contributions to agencies are unsatisfactory solutions. Referral cards are unnecessary because homeless people generally know where services are. The problem is not the location of services but the need for money to make telephone calls and pay for transportation to services. Moreover, the need for service far outstrips service capacity in any city. For example, high estimates of the number of homeless people in Los Angeles County are 60,000 and there are less than 8500 shelter beds and only 34 drug treatment centers.

Giving money to agencies rather than people is equally unsatisfactory because social service agencies have reported neither increases in requests for services nor increased donations. On the contrary, they are reporting fewer donations. Results of the first 3 months of the Dolphin campaign in Santa Monica have netted $12,000 in contributions. In this campaign, people were advised to contribute money to a container in a public monument shaped like a dolphin instead of giving to panhandlers. Advocates note that the sole beneficiaries of these campaigns are the businesses that push people from one community to the next under the guise of charity. This, too, is short-sighted, because it ignores the probability that businesses are faltering because of a failing economy rather than aggressive panhandling.

The most profound argument against "just say no to panhandler" campaigns rests upon a belief that all people should be treated with dignity and respect, not out of anger or the fears perpetuated by stereotypes. Communities must go beyond blaming and punishing the victims and begin to address the long-term solution to panhandling-ending homelessness.[1]

## Antibegging Ordinances

As local governments launch efforts to "crack down" on the homeless, their first priority is frequently the prohibition or regulation of begging. Some have passed ordinances against aggressive panhandling in an effort to regulate the manner of begging. Advocates contend that these ordinances are unnecessary because they duplicate existing laws against threatening behavior. They simply reflect efforts to harass and criminalize homeless people. Homeless service providers and homeless persons report that many cities are using antibegging ordinances to authorize excessive police actions against homeless persons.

The National Law Center on Homelessness and Poverty survey of antihomeless actions in 16 cities identified prohibitions against begging in 10 cities. This section documents these ordinances, and several others.

The City Council of Atlanta passed a restrictive antibegging ordinance prohibiting "aggressive begging" as part of a larger effort to combat nuisances in the form of loitering or sleeping in abandoned buildings and entering or remaining on a parking lot unless the person doing so has a parked car there. Subsequently, the Atlanta City Council passed an ordinance prohibiting the washing of car windows on public streets. The ordinances passed by appealing to community fears about public safety and crime, but their primary target was homeless people.

The Mayor originally proposed that all beggars obtain a license, but this idea was rejected because many believed that it would encourage, rather than discourage, beggars. It is noteworthy that these ordinances were passed immediately after Atlanta received its contract to host the next summer Olympics.[2]

In San Francisco, thousands of homeless people were arrested for begging. This was authorized under the California Penal Code prohibiting accosting other persons for the purpose of begging.[3] The City also passed Proposition J in 1992. This referendum stated that "aggressive solicitation for money directed at residents, visitors and tourists in areas of the City open to the public imperils their safety and welfare." The referendum also noted that aggressive panhandlers harm the city's economy by turning away shoppers and tourists.[4]

Proposition J defined aggressive panhandling as harassment or hounding by

> Closely following another and requesting money or a thing of value after that person has expressly or *implicitly* made it known to the solicitor that the person does not want to give money or other things of value to the solicitor.[5]

Violations of Proposition J can result in up to 6 months imprisonment or fines of up to $500.

This proposition had a ripple effect in neighboring communities where similar ordinances were passed prohibiting panhandling that involved intimidating behavior.

Four cities in Southern California have passed antibegging ordinances. San Diego passed an "aggressive solicitation" law prohibiting individuals from "coercing, threatening, hounding, harassing or intimidating another person for the purpose of soliciting money or goods."[6]

In Anaheim, panhandlers are barred from using physical threats, blocking a person's path, interfering with traffic, or continuing to pester someone who has said no. A companion measure prohibits beggars from washing car windshields without permission, soliciting people entering or leaving a car and standing on a curb or in the street to beg from passing vehicles.[7]

Beverly Hills has banned coercive, threatening, or intimidating behavior.[8] The City of West Hollywood, which has a large network of homeless services, passed a similar ordinance banning threatening or coercive behavior.

The City Council of Memphis recently passed an ordinance that is believed to be the first, and one of the harshest, of its kind in the nation. It requires all beggars to obtain a free city permit. Begging without the permit is grounds for arrest. Under the law, panhandlers must not only obtain a permit to beg in public places such as the library and the airport, but they are banned from begging on buses, at trolley stops, and after sunset or before sunrise.

Panhandlers in Memphis can also be charged if they use profane or abusive language, work in groups of two or more, and intimidate pedestrians. Violators can be charged with a misdemeanor or fined $50. This measure is one of the most restrictive in use in the nation. Moreover, it was cleverly drafted to target behavior rather than completely banning solicitation to avoid legal challenges on the grounds that begging is protected by free speech.[9]

Chicago police are authorized to harass homeless people by using the City Code, which prohibits "begging or soliciting funds on public ways." This code is frequently cited as the basis for periodic police sweeps of homeless people in Chicago.[10]

An ordinance in Cincinnati, Ohio makes it a misdemeanor to interfere with pedestrian or vehicle traffic and defines interference as "requesting money in a way that would alarm, intimidate, threaten, menace or coerce a reasonable person." It also defines interference as repeated requests after the denial of money.[11] This ordinance implicitly defines aggressive panhandling to include speech as well as behavior.

A similarly broad antibegging ordinance was passed in Dallas in 1991. It provides that those who engage in begging can be arrested if their behavior can reasonably be interpreted as threatening or coercive. Business leaders have pressured the police in Dallas to aggressively enforce this law against homeless people as a way of pressuring them to leave the downtown business area.[12]

A recent ordinance in the state of Nevada authorizes local governments to enact ordinances regulating the time, place, or manner in which people may beg in public places. To date, no city has enacted implementing ordinances.[13]

New York City has addressed begging in the New York City Transit Authority. It prohibits begging and sleeping in subway stations, subway cars, and railroad stations. Violation of these rules is grounds for arrest or ejection from Transit Authority property. This even applies to beggars who silently carry or extend a cup.

In sharp contrast, the regulations permit organized charities, artistic performers, and political groups to continue to solicit donations in the subways. New York's regulation clearly targeted the removal of homeless people from Transit Authority property permitting solicitation by any other person or group who is not homeless.[14]

The City of Seattle has defined begging as pedestrian interference. Its antibegging ordinance interprets aggressive begging with sufficient latitude to include walking, sitting, lying, or being situated in any way that would interfere with pedestrian passage. As in other ordinances, this one avoids prohibitions of speech to block First Amendment legal challenges.[15]

The District of Columbia repealed its earlier general antibegging ordinance in favor of a far more restrictive ordinance that prohibits aggressive asking, begging, or soliciting money and other valuable items in any public place. The new law, passed in 1993, is among the toughest in the nation. It offers latitude for a subjective interpretation of aggressive begging by people who are solicited and perceive a threat of bodily harm. The ordinance also prohibits begging within 10 feet of automatic teller machines, at bus, subway, or train stops, and washing cars for money. Violation may result in fines up to $300 or 90 day imprisonment.[16]

This trend prohibiting begging in public places is growing and some city leaders are even attempting to promulgate stricter ordinances than those that currently exist. Some cities that have not issued bans on begging are considering stronger measures than those passed by other cities. For example, the City of Santa Monica passed a law prohibiting aggressive panhandling, but two members of the City Council are pressing for tougher steps that would ban all forms of begging, aggressive or otherwise.

These and future laws are all part of larger efforts to restrict the rights of homeless people in the face of growing complaints by residents and businesses in local communities. Although they do nothing to provide solutions to the problem of homelessness, they have become a dangerous rallying point for many who are wrestling with the problem and want "to do something about the homeless." Service providers and homeless advocates report that they are spending inordinate amounts of time and energy in efforts to combat such laws and the public sentiment that has inspired them, efforts that divert them from service delivery.

## Legal Challenges to Antibegging Ordinances

Some general themes have emerged in recent court challenges to antibegging ordinances. Courts that have upheld the free speech rights of beggars under the First Amendment have also found that limits and regulations on such activity are not unconstitutional on this basis. Other courts have disagreed with this position holding that restrictions on begging cannot be separated from its expression.

In general, limited bans on begging may be upheld as constitutional, but broader-based bans could infringe on the First Amendment. It may, however, become less possible to distinguish between limits on conduct and limits on speech. This would mean that it could be unconstitutional to pass antibegging ordinances that allow overly broad or subjective interpretations of aggressive panhandling. Instead, only narrow ordinances that define specific behaviors such as physical assault or clear blockage of pedestrian passage may prove to be constitutional. This offers the possibility that most bans on aggressive panhandling may be unconstitutional.

The distinction between aggressive begging and free speech First Amendment rights predates the recent growth of homelessness and related activities. In 1976, an individual convicted under the California antibegging law filed an action in Oakland.[17] The code states that one is guilty of disorderly conduct when he or she accosts another person in public for the purpose of begging or soliciting.

The suit challenged the state's code on federal and state constitutional grounds. The court held that the First Amendment rights are not invalidated by the law because it prohibits certain conduct rather than speech. However, the decision encouraged ambiguity in the interpretation of "certain conduct" by arguing that begging may not be protected by the First Amendment. The judge stated, "Begging and soliciting for alms do not necessarily involve the communication of information or opinion;

therefore approaching individuals for that purpose is not protected by the First Amendment."[18]

The federal court declared California's antibegging law unconstitutional. The 1991 ruling, *Blair v. Shanahan*, defined begging as protected free speech under the First Amendment and found that the state's interest in avoiding "annoyance" was not sufficiently compelling to justify a restraint on the exercise of the right to free speech. The court further held that there can be no distinction between the right of a homeless person to solicit money and that of a charity.[19]

This decision, important in its own right, had broader implications. It rejected the antibegging argument of the Second Circuit Court of Appeals in New York, which held that begging was not a form of free speech protected by the First Amendment. In 1990 the United States Court of Appeals for the Second Circuit upheld the New York City regulation of begging in subways. *Young v. New York City Transit Authority* challenged the Transit Authority prohibitions against begging as an unconstitutional restriction on the free speech rights of homeless persons.

The majority of the Court held that the regulation was directed at the conduct of beggars not their speech, and therefore did not violate their First Amendment protections. The court further held that the Transit Authority had a compelling interest in prohibiting begging, the protection of its patrons from being accosted.[20]

The judge who wrote the opinion for the majority directly attacked begging in stating

> Whether with or without words the object of begging is the transfer of money. Speech simply is not inherent to the act: it is not the essence of the conduct.

Despite the *Blair* ruling that repealed California's antibegging ordinance, police in San Francisco still apply the antibegging law to harass homeless people. The decision has been appealed and a ruling is expected soon.

More recently, a superior court appellate judge refused to follow the opinion of *Blair v. Shanahan* holding that a state aggressive panhandling statute did not limit speech under the First Amendment, but only conduct. *People v. Zimmerman* reversed a lower court decision to dismiss a misdemeanor complaint against a man who was begging in Beverly Hills. The judge rejected the lower court's ruling that California Penal Code prohibits accosting "other persons in any public place for the purpose of begging or soliciting alms." The court also held that the word "accost" in the Penal Code could be interpreted as narrowly as walking up to or approaching a person.[21]

The different interpretations of the First Amendment in *Blair* and *Zimmerman* demonstrate the ambiguity in legal deliberations of the right of people to beg. They also call attention to the need for further challenges in the courts and in communities.

Another New York City opinion, delivered in the Second Circuit Court in 1993, disagreed with *Young*. The court upheld a federal district court ruling that a New York State law prohibiting begging on city streets was unconstitutional. The case was filed against the New York City Police Department to challenge police harassment of beggars. In this case, *Loper v. New York City Police Department*, the court argued that the state's prohibition against begging on streets and sidewalks must be supported by evidence of a "compelling" state interest in regulating communication and expressions in traditionally public fora. The state failed to meet the test of compelling interest because the begging prohibition was not sufficiently written to prevent only those "evils" associated with begging without infringing on constitutionally protected speech.

The judge agreed with the *Young* decision distinguishing between begging on public streets and subways, alleging that such activity in the confinement of the subways is potentially dangerous. It can block people's passage, startle them, and stimulate mass danger. However, the judge disagreed with *Young* in its prohibition of extending a cup for donations and also noted that the conduct that *Young* intended to regulate was already covered by laws prohibiting fraud, intimidation, harassment, and assault.

Perhaps the greatest force of the *Loper* decision lay in its interpretation of begging as nonverbal speech, or communication, and not conduct, and that begging is equivalent to other forms of charitable solicitation that receive full protection under the First Amendment.

Another important early case that overturned a prohibition against all forms of begging was filed in Jacksonville, Florida in 1984. The plaintiff challenged the state's ban and the appellate court held that the ordinance was unconstitutionally overbroad. The decision stated, "protecting citizens from mere annoyance is not a sufficient compelling reason to absolutely deprive one of a First Amendment right."[22]

The Greater Cincinnati Coalition for the Homeless filed a legal challenge to the city's aggressive panhandling ordinance on the grounds that it violates the First Amendment because it regulates begging, or speech, on public streets or sidewalks. The Coalition also argued that the ordinance is too vague and broad leading to unequal enforcement against homeless persons. This violates the Fourteenth Amendment's guarantees of equal protection under the law.

The U.S. District Court dismissed this complaint, holding that the plaintiffs failed to show that they "had suffered a past or future injury sufficient to confer standing." The ruling has been appealed and settlement negotiations are in process.[23]

In Nevada, the American Civil Liberties Union (ACLU) raised a constitutional challenge to the state's loitering with intent to beg statute. The ACLU argued that the statute is unconstitutionally vague and broad restraining First Amendment rights to freedom of speech and expressive conduct in public fora. This case is pending in the federal district court.[24]

In November 1993 homeless advocates in Seattle filed suit challenging the city's amended aggressive begging ordinance and prohibition against sitting or lying down in public places. The complaint alleges violations of constitutional rights of free speech, due process of law, equal protection under the law, and the right to travel. A decision is pending.[25]

The significance of this suit lies in the fact that it challenges a 1990 decision delivered in the Supreme Court of Washington that rejected a challenge to the constitutionality of Seattle's "pedestrian interference" ordinance. The case involved a man who had been arrested for "stopping pedestrians on the sidewalk, blocking their path, sticking his hand out and asking for spare change."[26]

The court held that the city's ordinance did not violate the First Amendment, relying upon conduct as well as intent in its conclusion. The court also held that the "specific intent" aspect of the ordinance passed constitutional muster in the due process challenge. Nor did the court find that the ordinance violated equal protection rights of homeless people because it did not discriminate against them, but applied to all who might block a pedestrian's path.[27]

The Community for Creative Non-Violence in Washington, D.C. successfully challenged a Washington Metropolitan Area Transit Authority regulation that required permits for "certain free speech activities," clearly targeted at beggars. In addition to the permit requirement, the regulation allowed for suspension of permits in case of emergency, restricted the number of persons allowed to engage in free speech activities at the station, and mandated that all activities occur in a "conversational tone."

The permit requirement and other parts of the regulation were removed as unconstitutional after the United States Court of Appeals found that they were prior restraints on free speech in violation of the First Amendment.[28]

The Community for Creative Non-Violence used a confrontational strategy to force this case. Its members organized a demonstration to protest the regulation, and were arrested and prosecuted during the demonstration. Their next step was filing the successful law suit.

### The Current State of Antibegging Law and Public Opinion

Citizens and local governments are continuing to respond to the problem of homelessness out of frustration and anger, rather than sympathy. This frustration has focused largely on panhandling, which regularly brings people into the most direct contact with homeless persons. Some communities that have taken a hard line have become even tougher.

The City of Beverly Hills in California passed a law prohibiting "aggressive solicitation, drinking in public, and sitting or lying, or leaving personal property in the public ways."[29] There are no official data on the number of homeless people in Beverly Hills, but several have responded to this inquiry by estimating that there are 50 to 100 people in the community in response to inquiries. These numbers clearly do not justify such a harsh ruling.

Even social service providers among homeless agencies disagree about efforts to prohibit begging. Many who work with substance abusing homeless people agree that giving money simply enables people to engage in defeating behavior such as drug and alcohol abuse. Others contend that panhandling is a direct consequence of Reagan–Bush era budget cuts in the social safety net and that prohibition of begging cannot solve such a weighty problem. They view panhandlers as desperate people who beg as a form of survival. All agree, however, that it will take more than tougher proposals to effectively deal with pan—handling.

Court decisions have set clear precedents indicating that anyone who tries to prohibit begging would face a vigorous legal challenge. The courts have generally held that panhandling is a protected form of free speech under the First Amendment, although local governments may designate limited exceptions. However, they have allowed cities to regulate where, when, or how panhandling can take place.

Nevertheless, there is sufficient ambiguity over interpretations of aggressive conduct in the court decisions to encourage antihomeless groups to attempt to more restrictively regulate panhandling.

One benefit of threatened, or actual, legal challenges to proposed bans on begging lies in the fact that any new law cannot be enforced until it passes constitutional muster in the court. All of the earlier court decisions ruling that antibegging ordinances violate First Amendment protections of free speech serve as precedents for any new suits. They may even withstand further assaults on begging.

## Notes and References

1.  Los Angeles Coalition to End Homelessness, *Principles on Panhandling* (June 6, 1993), Draft Mimeograph.
2.  City of Atlanta, *Code of Ordinances, Amendment to Part 17*, Chs. 1 and 3, July 17, 1991; National Law Center on Homelessness and Poverty, *The Right to Remain Nowhere*, 29 (Part II, Note 1).
3.  National Law Center on Homelessness and Poverty, *The Right to Remain Nowhere*, 39–40 (Part II, Note 1).
4.  *San Francisco Municipal Code*, Part II, Chapter 8 (Police Code), Section 120-1.
5.  *Ibid.*
6.  *Ibid.*
7.  Jonathan Volzke and Teri Sforza, "Putting Curbs on Street Begging," *Orange County Register* (October 28, 1993), 1.
8.  *Beverly Hills Municipal Code*, Sec. 5-6. 1301.
9.  Lynda Nataly, "Memphis Turns Up Heat on Its Downtown Pan-handlers," *Los Angeles Times* (February 16, 1994), A5.
10. National Law Center oh Homelessness and Poverty, *The Right to Remain Nowhere*, 63–64 (Part II, Note 1).
11. *City of Cincinnati Municipal Code*, Sec. 910-13.
12. *Ibid.*, 70–71.
13. *Ibid.*, 89.
14. Calvin Sims, "Transit Police Intend to Remove All Subway Pan-handlers," *New York Times* (May 31, 1990).
15. National Law Center on Homelessness and Poverty, *The Right to Remain Nowhere*, 108 (Part II, Note 1).
16. *Panhandling Control Act of 1993*, D.C. Act 10-98, Section 22-3306, August 4, 1993.
17. California Penal Code, 647(c).
18. *Ulmer v. Municipal Court for Oakland-Piedmont, J.D.*, 127 Cal. Rptr. 445 (Cal. App. 1976).
19. *Blair v. Shanahan*, 775 F. Supp. 1315 (N.D. Ca. 1991).
20. *Young v. New York City Transit Authority*, 903 F. 2d 146 (1990) *cert. denied*, U.S. 984 (1990).
21. California Penal Code, Section 647(c); *People v. Zimmerman*, 19 Cal. Rptr. 2d 486, 489 (Sup. Ct. App. Div. 1993).
22. *C.C.B. v. State of Florida* (Fla. App. 1984).
23. *Greater Cincinnati Coalition for the Homeless v. City of Cincinnati*, No. 1-92-733 (S.D. Ohio 1992), Plaintiff's Memorandum in Support of their Motion for Preliminary and Permanent Injunction and Declaratory Relief, September 16, 1992; No. C-1-92-733 (S.D. Ohio) Court Order, July 23, 1993.

24.  *Heathcott v. Las Vegas Metropolitan Police Department et al.*, Case No. 93-S-45-LDG-RJJ, Amended Complaint. (D. Nev. March 11, 1993).

25.  *Roulette et al. v. City of Seattle et al.*, Civil Action No. C93-1554, Complaint, U.S.D.C. (W.D. Washington), November 10, 1993.

26.  *City of Seattle v. Webster*, 802 P. 2d 1333 (Wash. 1990).

27.  National Law Center on Homelessness and Poverty, *The Right to Remain Nowhere*, 113–114 (Part II, Note 1).

28.  *Community for Creative Non-Violence v. Turner*, 893 F. 2d. 1387 (D.C. Cir. 1990).

29.  *Beverly Hills Municipal Code* Sec. 5-6.1301.

# 10

## LOITERING AND SLEEPING IN PUBLIC

### Public Encampment Issues

Many federal and local officials, and citizen groups, agree that the problem of homelessness has grown so huge that the patchwork of shelters and soup kitchens is more inadequate than ever. While there are many excellent programs and services, the demand far exceeds the supply everywhere. The shelter system falls so far short of need that people have no other choice but to live in the streets and parks.

Some communities are attempting to deal with this through "tough love" approaches. Others are merely being tough. The National Law Center on Homelessness and Poverty 16-city survey of antihomeless actions has identified 25 local ordinances prohibiting sleeping, camping, loitering, sitting, or vagrancy.[1]

People differ in their explanations of these harsh actions against homeless people. Some explain the proliferation of hostile government actions as a sign of decreased public sympathy for homeless persons. Others describe the frustration and "compassion fatigue" that has set in among those who remain sympathetic. A third explanation is that antihomeless actions have resulted from increased pressure from an increasingly vocal minority of residents and business leaders who promote stereotypical attitudes about the dangers to public health and safety imposed by homeless people. Whatever the reasons, it is clear that the same system that forces people to live in the streets is now arresting or harassing them when they get there.

Across the nation, people have had their fill of parks and sidewalks turned into campsites by homeless people. They are pressing for action, not only to help homeless people, but to get them off of their streets and out of their parks. Homeless advocates frequently observe that people are tired of the problem of homelessness and just want it to disappear. Marcia Martin, Director of the Interagency Council on the Homeless, has said, "We are at a point in this nation where we can't afford the homeless crisis anymore. It's affecting who we are and how we look—and we look terrible."[2] In response, most local governments are initiating laws targeting loitering in public places. Others are adopting strategies to get homeless people out of public encampments and into alternative settings. Miami, Orlando, and Dallas have erected outdoor facilities for homeless people. The City of Santa Monica has built a 100-bed shelter to be used in enforcing a law to expel people from its parks at night. Because Santa Monica has a credible record of generosity to homeless persons (some believe that the city spends more per capita than any other city on its homeless residents) this measure indicates just how extensive the outrage against homeless people has grown. These "pods" or "pavilions" are located in remote sections of the city. Homeless persons who refuse to go to these facilities may be arrested.

While this alternative repeats the historic patterns of institutionalizing people with problems "out of sight and out of mind," it also includes some constructive approaches to service provision for homeless people. The City of Miami has accompanied its plan to house 250 to 300 people each for 7 to 30 days with social services. During this period, caseworkers will evaluate and counsel residents and send them to treatment centers for substance abuse, or mental illness, if needed, or to transitional housing and jobs. Dade County intends to fund this program through a 1% sales tax on food and beverages at large restaurants.

Another Florida city, Orlando, has constructed a campus for the homeless. As many as 500 people a day stay in the pavilion, which has been minimally constructed to house so many people. The city opened a more comfortable 180 person facility, with barracks-like accommodations for women and single rooms for families.

The City of Dallas has built pavilions outside of its downtown business district, funded by donations from private merchants. The "pods," as they are called in Dallas, will sleep approximately 240 people on the floor, which is heated in the winter. Homeless persons are allowed to stay in the pods from 4:00 P.M. to 9:00 A.M., a schedule that resembles shelter regulations. As in Miami. people who refuse to go to the pods may be arrested.

The concept of these pavilions is based upon the Miami federal district court ruling that ordered the city to create two "safe zones" where homeless persons can go without fear of arrest or harassment.[3]

Some homeless advocates and public officials are critical of this strategy. They argue that large shelters are less effective than smaller facilities and spend too much for shelters rather than treatment programs and transitional housing. Critics point to the debacle of the large public shelter system in New York City decrying efforts to repeat that mistaken policy. They are even more exorcised over the use of pavilions to forcibly expel homeless persons from other public places.

Officials in the three cities that have built pavilions contend that their plan is the only affordable way to reach all of the homeless people who need help. Caseworkers also perceive it as the most humane solution to aid homeless people. While conceding that smaller shelters are more humane and satisfactory, they view minimal shelter as a safety net for people who either do not want to help themselves or whom society does not want to help.

Other cities are considering the adoption of this strategy, but many are simply passing laws to evict homeless persons from public places with no place to send them. San Francisco is a leading example. The city has issued thousands of citations since August 1993 when its Mayor instituted the Matrix Program directing police to arrest and issue $76 tickets to people for sleeping, camping, or urinating in public or otherwise disturbing the quality of life.

Official efforts to harass, punish, or restrict transient people who use public space are repeating six centuries of antivagrancy and loitering lawmaking. Enforcement of such laws against homeless persons may abridge their constitutional rights to freedom of movement. They may also violate constitutional prohibitions against cruel and unusual punishment and equal protection guarantees.[4]

The problem of the use of public parks and streets by homeless persons involves a complex set of conflicting interests and policies and raises a series of ethical dilemmas. The presence of large numbers of homeless people in public places presents both a misperceived threat, and a real threat, to other persons who wish to use public places. A number of academic critics have defended "street justice" as a means of keeping homeless and other disorderly people in line. James Wilson and George Kelling, noted criminologists, argued that the arrest of a single drunk may seem unfair on its own merits, but failing to do so may destroy an entire community by encouraging public inebriation.[5] These concerns about public health and safety must be addressed while protecting the civil rights of homeless persons to use the same public space as domiciled persons.

Merchants and business leaders also pose a valid argument that the presence of so many homeless persons where they conduct their businesses has a strong negative impact. This is not a false perception and it demonstrates the importance of balancing the rights of homeless individuals and groups with those of property owners and business people. Neighborhood groups contend that they are asserting their property and protest rights. They also express what they believe to be a legitimate fear of an influx of troubled people.

When there is no other place for homeless people to stay, it is difficult to justify any municipal ordinance prohibiting encampments in public places. The only grounds for prohibiting use of public spaces should be the commission of a violent crime, illegal sale or use of drugs, public inebriation, and public health violations.

On the other hand, there is some merit to the argument that it is unfair for people with homes to be deprived of the use of public places. This position leads people to argue that it is possible that ordinances prohibiting permanent and semipermanent encampments in public parks would protect access to public lands for everyone.

All of these problems, and solutions, concerning the use of public places by homeless persons fall on the same continuum of antihomeless actions as begging. Any definition of the homeless problem in terms of threats to public health and safety obscures more fundamental explanations of the problem and rationalizes false solutions that are too frequently inhumane.

## Restrictions on the Use of Public Places

Restrictions on use and access to public places have targeted loitering, sleeping, camping, and the use of transit systems. Some cities have imposed curfews in parks. Others have issued outright bans on loitering or sleeping. A few have simply made their public places less attractive to homeless people by building "bum benches" that prevent homeless people from sleeping on them. This section describes such restrictions.

In Atlanta, the same ordinance that prohibited aggressive begging, banned loitering or sleeping in abandoned buildings without permission of the owner.

Eight cities in Southern California have issued ordinances that prohibit sleeping or camping in public places. All were adopted within a brief period between 1992 and 1993. This suggests a domino-effect in which neighboring communities copy each other. One motive for imitation is the prevention of the ancient practice of sending undesirable people from one community to the next. A second motive lies in common perceptions of the problem and proposed solutions.

These municipalities have all attempted to define "camping" with sufficient specificity to avoid court challenges. The City of West Hollywood prohibition against camping in public parks and recreation areas defined camping as follows:

> residing in or using a park for living accommodation purposes as exemplified by remaining for prolonged or repetitious periods of time not associated with ordinary recreational use of a park with one's personal possessions . . . sleeping or making preparations to sleep, storing personal belongings . . . regularly cooking or consuming meals, or living in a parked vehicle.[6]

This definition became the model for other Southern California municipalities.

Long Beach, Santa Monica, Fullerton, Santa Ana, the City of Orange, Santa Barbara, and Beverly Hills passed similar ordinances with slight variations. Some cities designate only parks and recreation areas. Fullerton, Beverly Hills, Santa Ana, and the City of Orange make it illegal to camp anywhere. The City of Santa Monica ordinance does not clarify the extent of its prohibition against the use of public space.[7] The California Supreme Court has begun a review of the Santa Ana city ordinance. Whether the regulations in other cities will be allowed depends on the decision in this case. Legal advocates suggest that this case could prompt the United States Supreme Court to help resolve the issue of antihomeless ordinances.

In addition to San Francisco's Matrix Program, the city continues to enforce an earlier code that prohibits camping and imposes a 10:00 P.M. curfew for city parks. Police use this code more frequently to harass homeless people than to arrest them. Another San Francisco Police Code prohibits anyone from obstructing the free passage of any person on the street, sidewalk, passageway, or public place.[8] This section of the code is rarely used because it is so broad that obstruction is difficult to prove.

They also use a state law prohibiting lodging in public to harass homeless people.[9] California state law also makes loitering at public transportation stops illegal.

The City of Dallas has begun to enforce a long-standing ordinance which prohibits sleeping in public. It also passed the resolution to relocate homeless persons to pavilions.[10]

A Key West, Florida antilodging in public ordinance has been enforced against homeless people for sleeping on public beaches at night. The law orders the closing of all public beaches and parks at 11:00 P.M. Because there are no shelters in Key West this is an extremely harsh law.

Before the City of Miami developed its pavilion strategy, it was illegal to obstruct free passage on any street or sidewalk. Homeless people who sleep on the sidewalks or streets are also subject to arrest in violation of that law. The City Code also includes specific language prohibiting loitering, stating that "any person shall be deemed guilty of disorderly conduct who . . . is idle, loitering, and sleeping in public."[11] Police have regularly used these laws to arrest homeless people.

Homeless people in Las Vegas and Reno, Nevada were routinely arrested for violating the city's loitering, trespassing, and public nuisance statutes since the early 1980s. The Las Vegas law and a companion provision at the state level have been declared unconstitutional.[12]

In addition to antihomeless actions in the New York City Transit Authority, the New York City Parks and Recreation Department has promulgated regulations that prohibit sleeping in parks, leaving personal possessions unattended, and building unlicensed structures, or encampments. The regulations also include bans on begging.[13] City laws also prohibit loitering and sleeping in public places, but they are rarely enforced. However, the city's new get tough on the homeless" sentiments, reflected in statements by Mayor Giuliani, may change the enforcement climate.

Seattle has installed a battery of bans on the use of public venues. It probably has more antihomeless actions on its books than any other city in the nation.

The City Council has recently added harsher amendments to its extensive body of antihomeless laws. These amendments provide that any persons sitting or lying in any public street or sidewalk in downtown or neighboring districts between the hours of 7:00 A.M. and 9:00 P.M. are committing a criminal offense. Public urination after the second citation is also a criminal misdemeanor.[14] This law blatantly criminalizes homeless people who have nowhere to go and forces them to be constantly moving.

Seattle also restricts access to its parks at night. The Parks Department attempted to remove benches from downtown parks where homeless people congregate. It succeeded in removing some before homeless advocates forced a halt in the action.

Merchants in Seattle have initiated a "No Loitering Program," which is operated by the Seattle police department. The program uses private security forces to patrol the shopping district. Although they have no legal authority, the security patrols harass homeless people, force them to leave the area, and intimidate them by masquerading as police.

Under the "No Loitering Program," Seattle police have also organized a campaign to prevent loitering through enforcement of the state's trespassing laws. The police have entered into an agreement with local business merchants to arrest individuals in privately owned semipublic areas such as alleys and doorways. Merchants merely complete a form authorizing police to request unauthorized persons to leave their premises and post signs prohibiting criminal trespass or loitering. A person can be arrested after one warning.[15]

Seattle's police also use the state's trespassing laws to arrest homeless persons who loiter at bus shelters. The transit authority has posted no trespassing signs at these shelters.

In the nation's capitol, park police patrol the mall and adjacent areas that include the national monuments. They also patrol other parks in the District. The police rigorously enforce federal regulations against public sleeping, begging, and the erection of unlicensed structures in the District.[16] These regulations allow any national park superintendent to impose conditions on sleeping, camping, or storing personal possessions in the park area. They were promulgated as a direct assault against homeless people as recently as 1992.

The list of these vagrancy and loitering laws has changed only in form, not substance, since the earliest recorded efforts in Elizabethan England to control homeless people. The intent of these laws reflects a historical continuum that began with the enactment of the Statutes of Labourers in the fourteenth century, the Poor Laws of colonial America, and the antivagrancy measures of the eighteenth and nineteenth centuries in the United States, and other nations, and the Great Depression. Fortunately, they never went unchallenged and today's challenges are stemming the tide of antihomeless prohibitions on the use of public spaces.

## Legal Challenges to Restrictions on the Use of Public Places

The courts have overturned vagrancy laws on several grounds. They have held that vagrancy laws punish status or condition, which amounts to cruel and unusual punishment. They have also viewed the laws as impermissible restrictions on the right to travel. A benchmark case tried as early as 1971 overturned a vagrancy law on due process grounds because it was too vague and therefore failed to give fair notice of the prohibitions on specific conduct.[17]

This last case, *Papachristou v. City of Jacksonville*, was tried in the United States Supreme Court. Eight persons were arrested under the city of Jacksonville's vagrancy ordinance. Among the charges were lack of identification, thievery based upon their reputation as thieves rather than any specific act of theft, and loitering by standing in a driveway. The plaintiffs challenged the constitutionality of the ordinance on the grounds that it was too vague and did not give fair notice of what was considered vagrancy.

The Florida Circuit Court upheld the convictions and the District Court of Miami denied certiorari, request for review. However, the U.S. Supreme Court granted the petition to review the ordinance. Writing for the unanimous court, Justice William Douglas stated that the ordinance was void for vagueness and failed to give fair notice of prohibited conduct. Justice Douglas also emphasized that the indefiniteness of the ordinance encouraged arbitrary arrests and convictions noting that Jacksonville's ordinance was archaic and criminalized activities that are entirely innocent by modern standards. Finally, the Supreme Court rejected the justification for vagrancy laws on the basis that they prevent future criminal behavior and, as such, were consistent with the Fourth Amendment that guarantees arrest upon probable cause.

Another profound conclusion in the *Papachristou* decision was that vagrancy laws target the poor and other undesirable people tipping the "scales of justice" against minorities and the poor.[18]

Police continued to arrest people for loitering after the *Papachristou* decision and state courts upheld the arrests arguing that the police needed such power to prevent future criminal activity. This changed after 1983 when *Kolender v. Lawson* was heard in the Supreme Court.

In *Kolender*, The Supreme Court struck down a California loitering statute that punished failure by any person walking the street to produce credible identification upon request by a police officer. Agreeing with *Papachristou*, the Court held that the statute was too vague to fulfill due process requirements. This reinforced the earlier decision and has become a critical principle in assessing the constitutionality of anti-vagrancy ordinances.[19]

Challenges to prohibitions against sleeping, camping or lodging on public grounds have met with less success in the courts than those dealing with loitering. Numerous cases have been tried since 1970. Litigants have attempted to use the earlier successful arguments against loitering, but their contention that prohibitions against sleeping or camping are too vague or overbroad has met with only limited success. A few courts have agreed that the laws are vague and overbroad, but the general theme in the courts has been that prohibitions against sleeping and camping sufficiently identify specificity of conduct to meet the requirements of fair notice and due process. This specificity has meant that the constitutionality of bans on sleeping, camping, and lodging in public places as they apply to homeless persons remains unsettled.

Although the *Papachristou* and *Kolender* decisions clearly state a set of principles that would prohibit all vagrancy laws, nine other cases demonstrate the reluctance of the lower courts to overturn vagrancy ordinances. Three cases have overturned such laws, three have upheld them, and four decisions remain pending. One of the pending decisions was filed as long as 5 years ago.

The Nevada Supreme Court delivered the broadest victory against vagrancy laws in 1991. In *Richard v. State of Nevada*, the court held that the Nevada antiloitering statute and related ordinances in the Municipal Code were too vague, and therefore unconstitutional and violated the Fourteenth Amendment Due Process Clause.

The precipitating events of the *Richards* case exemplify many activities that lead to arrests elsewhere on loitering and vagrancy charges. A group of Catholic clergy, volunteers, and four homeless persons were arrested in Las Vegas for loitering and vagrancy. The church had obtained a permit to occupy city property for the purpose of serving breakfast to homeless people. After some of the homeless people moved to a nearby lot to eat their meal, the police arrested them. The clergy protested that this was a violation of the Las Vegas Municipal Code.

They subsequently filed an action stating that the Municipal Code and state statutes were unconstitutionally vague. The court found that the Fourteenth Amendment invalidated the state antivagrancy statute but upheld the municipal antiloitering code. In its decision, the court stated that the federal court was the inappropriate jurisdiction to rule on a municipal code. The antiloitering statutes were returned to the Nevada Supreme Court and are still pending.[20]

The United States District Court of California preliminarily enjoined the City of Santa Monica from enforcing provisions of a city ordinance regulating the use of public parks by requiring groups of 35 or more to obtain a permit before using any park. The plaintiffs in the case were homeless activists who charged that the ordinance was directed at them and authorized grounds for denial or revocation of permits on grounds that represent typical behavior and conduct of homeless people.

The American Civil Liberties Union, acting for the plaintiffs, based their brief on First Amendment rights and vagueness. The City defendants countered that the ordinance passed constitutional muster because it applied the First Amendment "exception" by being content-neutral, leaving open ample alternatives for communication.

The decision to enjoin the permit requirement was a substantial victory for homeless people on its own merit. The judge went beyond the specific ordinance and stated that

> While the Court is not unsympathetic to the administrative, managerial and fiscal problems which the City of Santa Monica surely faces, these concerns simply cannot outweigh the potential deprivation of the First Amendment rights of Plaintiffs.[21]

The force of this statement lay in its assertive approach to balancing public and private rights.

An earlier legal victory overturning a vagrancy ordinance occurred in Carmel, California in 1971. An ordinance had been enacted in 1968 to prohibit "hippies" from sitting on sidewalks, or steps, and sitting or lying on lawns. However, a public meeting was held to protest the 1968 ordinance.

A case was also brought to the Municipal Court on behalf of a plaintiff who had been arrested for sitting on the park lawn. The plaintiff argued that the ordinance violated the Fourteenth Amendment by discriminating against "hippies" because of their status. The Court of Appeals agreed with the plaintiffs and reversed a previous ruling, thereby striking down the ordinance. The Court decision held that "the discriminatory impact is achieved by the hostile tone and the critical description directed to one segment of society."[22]

A 1984 court decision in Pompano Beach, Florida invalidated anti-sleeping ordinances as impermissibly overbroad, basing its opinion on lower court decisions that viewed vagrancy and loitering laws as punishment of "essentially innocent conduct."[23]

Courts that have upheld vagrancy and loitering ordinances have decided that laws are unconstitutionally overbroad only if they reach a substantial amount of constitutionally protected conduct. They have determined that sleeping, sitting, or lying in public places does not comprise a large enough body of conduct.

In Phoenix, plaintiffs challenged a city code that prohibited lying, sleeping, or sitting on a public right of way on the grounds that it was overbroad and too vague. They also argued that the code violated the right to travel and equal protection.

The case was brought after the plaintiffs were arrested, and sentenced for 60 to 90 days in jail, for sitting on a public sidewalk. The lower court upheld the ordinance and the Court of Appeals affirmed the decision because it did not recognize any constitutional prohibitions against the specific conduct of sleeping, sitting, or lying in public rights of way.[24]

The circuit court in San Francisco rejected First and Fourth Amendment claims in a civil suit challenging the arrest and dispossession of a homeless man and a spokesperson for other homeless people who had been displaced from a city park in which they lived.[25]

A similar ordinance was overturned in Santa Barbara, California in 1985. In that case, plaintiffs protested the convictions of a number of homeless persons for violating an ordinance banning sleeping in public. The Superior Court in Santa Barbara held that the public ordinance against sleeping was overbroad. The City of Santa Barbara appealed the decision where it was held that the ordinance was not void for vagueness. The court held that "The sleeping ordinance is clear of discernment to both enforcer and violator."[26] One year later the National Coalition for the Homeless requested the United States Supreme Court to review these convictions. The Court denied the request.

The cases that remain pending pose arguments that are more complex than considerations of vagueness and unequal protection. They have commingled concerns about the use of public space with requirements for alternative living provisions.

The San Francisco Coalition on Homelessness sued the city to enjoin a prohibition against sleeping in public parks and the Civic Center pending resolution of the claim that the city must provide homeless people with adequate shelter. The intermediate appellate court affirmed the trial court's denial of a preliminary injunction relying on a balance-ofhardship analysis. The Court held that "while the plight of the homeless would be eased a bit if they were permitted to camp in public parks the City presented compelling evidencethat prior camping caused even greater harm to the City by resulting in the profound deterioration of the parks, particularly Civic Center Plaza and Golden Gate Park."[27]

Two pending cases have used similar arguments on behalf of the plaintiffs, one in Reno, Nevada and the other in Miami, Florida. The Reno suit, *Benavidez v. City of Reno, Nev.* alleges that city ordinances against sleeping and loitering in public places discriminate against homeless people. The plaintiffs are claiming cruel and unusual punishment, malicious abuse, unlawful search and seizure, invasion of privacy, violation of equal protection, vagueness, overbreadth, and infringement of the right to travel. All of these charges have been brought under the federal and state constitutions.[28] *Pottinger v. City of Miami* is challenging the City's right to prevent homeless people from living on public property on the same grounds.[29]

### Legal Uncertainty about Public Access

The range of court decisions about rights of access and use of public space by homeless persons reflects widespread ambiguity about the constitutionality of laws regulating these rights. Even though the U.S. Supreme Court has overturned bans on homeless people using public spaces, lower courts have rejected even the simplest challenges based on overbreadth and vagueness. Nevertheless, advocates must look to those court decisions that have overturned bans and other antihomeless actions for precedents and future litigation. Citizen groups must also continue to strategically apply political and public pressure to garner support for the rights of homeless persons to use the same public spaces as domiciled persons. Eventually, the enforcement of so many homeless bans may prompt a backlash as sympathetic people witness the humiliation of unequal protection wielded against homeless persons.

### Notes and References

1. National Law Center on Homelessness and Poverty, *The Right to Remain Nowhere*, Table II (Part II, Note 1).

2. Elizabeth Shogren, "Cities Seek Solution to Dilemma of Homelessness," *Los Angeles Times* (February 7, 1994), A1,10.

3. *Pottinger v. City of Miami*, 810 F Supp. 1551, 1559 (S.D. Fla. 1992).

4.  Simon, "Towns without Pity," 664 (Introduction, Note 7).

5.  James Q. Wilson and George L. Kelling, "Broken Windows," *Atlantic Monthly*, 29, 35 (March 1982).

6.  *West Hollywood Municipal Code* Sec. 4801(8)(a), January 16, 1992.

7.  *Beverly Hills Municipal Code*,93-0-2165, Article 13, Section 5-6. 1302, March 23, 1993; Fullerton Municipal Ordinance 2808, May 5, 1992; Long Beach Ordinance No. C-6984, March 24, 1882; Orance Municipal Ordinance 10-92, May 26, 1992; Santa Ana Ordinance NS-2106, August 3, 1992; Santa Monica Municipal Ordinance No. 1620, April 14, 1992; Shelter Partnership, *Homeless Reporter*, 9 (April 1993).

8.  *San Francisco Police Code*, Section 22.

9.  *California Penal Code*, Section 647(i).

10.  Supra, Note 3.

11.  *Miami City Code*, Sections 37–63, 37–17.

12.  National Law Center on Homelessness and Poverty, *The Right to Remain Nowhere*, 88 (Part II, Note 1).

13.  City of New York Parks and Recreation, *Rules*, 19–22.

14.  Amendment to *Seattle Municipal Code* Section 12.A.10.100 (A).

15.  Seattle Police Department, Directive D89-35, May 8, 1989.

16.  *Code of Federal Regulations*, 36 Section 2.10(a)(b), Section 7.96(i) (1992).

17.  Simon, "Towns without Pity," supra. 643.

18.  *Papachristou et al. v. City of Jacksonville*, 405, U.S. 156 (1973); *Ibid.*, 66.

19.  *Ibid.*,644–45.

20.  *Richard v. Sate of Nevada*, No. CV-S-51 (U.S. Dist. Ct. November 1991); National Law Center, 116.

21.  *Rubin et al. v. City of Santa Monica*, CV 93–1255 LGB (U.S. Dist. Ct.) (1993).

22.  *Parr v. Municipal Court for Monterey-Carmel, J.D.*, 479 P.2d 353 (1971).

23.  *City of Pompano Beach v. Capalbo*, 455 So. 2d 468, 469–70 (Fla. Dist. Ct. App. 1984); Simon, "Towns without Pity," 664 (Introduction, Note 6).

24.  *Seeley v. State of Arizona*, 655 P.2d 803 (1982).

25.  *Stone v. Agnos*, F.2d (9th Cir. 1992) (92 Daily Journal D.A.R. 4525) (No. 91-15206, April 3, 1992).

26.  *People v. Davenport*, 222 Cal. Rptr. 736 (Sup. Ct. App. Div. 1985), *cert. denied*, 475 U.S. 1141 (1986).

27.  *San Francisco Coalition on Homelessness v. City of San Francisco*, No. A052918, Ct. App. 1st. Dist. (February 20, 1992).

28.  *Benavidas v. City of Reno, Nev.*, MN92–25, filed July 28, 1992.

29.  *Pottinger v. City of Miami*, 720 F. Supp. 955 (S.D. Fla. 1989).

# 11

## HOMELESS ARREST CAMPAIGNS

### Street Justice or Holocaust?

The backlash against homeless people is manifested at its cruelest in homeless arrest campaigns. Homeless sweeps are even more common and equally inhumane. These occur when the police raid areas inhabited by homeless persons and force them to leave. Seizure and destruction of personal property frequently accompany these neighborhood sweeps.

Arrest campaigns are the ultimate outcomes of antibegging, loitering, camping, and sleeping laws. The presence of such laws authorizes police and local officials to enforce them by expelling noncompliant homeless people from public spaces.

More recently, homeless people may even be arrested for scavenging trash. Local governments have begun to disguise antihomeless campaigns as a concern for public sanitation and recycling efforts. Scavenging has emerged as a serious issue in Southern California where residents report that it has become an organized business.

The images of homeless sweeps are reminiscent of holocaust round-ups in Nazi Germany. To dramatize the message that homeless people are not welcome, police officers frequently conduct large-scale campaigns in which they arrest homeless people, handcuff them, mark their arms with identification numbers, drive them to the police station where they await formal charges for hours without food and water, and finally drive them to the edge of town after detention, drop them off, and tell them not to return.

This scenario is not invented, it happens frequently. The City of Santa Ana arrested 64 homeless persons in the civic center area in just this way.

Not all homeless sweeps end up as arrests or detention. Frequently, police use antihomeless ordinances to harass homeless people and force them to move elsewhere. Even these seemingly harmless official acts threaten and humiliate people who have committed no offense except having no known address.

Homeless sweeps are often timed to "clean up" special areas of a city just before the arrival of conventions or national sporting events, or at other periods that attract large numbers of tourists and visitors. As the sight of mass homelessness becomes more embarrassing and uncomfortable, cities and neighborhoods are stepping up their efforts to push the problem out of sight and mind by hiding it.

Justification for arrest campaigns follows the same line of reasoning applied to antibegging, loitering, and camping actions. Community activists, and local officials, appeal to concerns for public health and safety. The general theme of such arguments appeals to fear of unsanitary conditions and personal assaults.

Whether such fears are grounded in any discernible patterns of trouble is considered less important than the possibility of such occurrences. Some homeless advocates contend that homeless persons are being blamed for many social problems, even the economy. There is some truth to their contention that homeless bashers are creating a climate of fear through rumors, misrepresentations of homeless people, and general fear mongering.

Proponents of homeless sweeps argue that the arrests of large groups of homeless people prevent the occurrence of more explosive conflict and confrontations. This approach to street justice rationalizes the arrest of people for innocent behavior on the grounds that relatively minor offenses have the potential to escalate into more serious crimes.

People pressing for the arrest of homeless people reflect no single ideological or political perspective. They may be liberal on most others issues, but do not apologize for their tough stance on homelessness. They are part of a wave of resentment that has developed across the United States replacing earlier sympathy or compassion. New images of homeless people as pathological predators dominate the media and public forums. They now tend to dismiss views of homeless people as the unfortunate deserving poor as naive or foolish.

These unsympathetic images have even been reinforced by recent scholarly analyses of homeless populations. Baum and Burns present data claiming that 85% of all homeless people are drug and/or alcohol abusers, as well as mentally ill. Their data contradict all earlier reports that fewer homeless people are so afflicted and that most are extremely unfortunate, or the poorest of the poor. The authors have lodged their data in a sophisticated argument for addressing the underlying problems of homelessness.[1] However, their critics contend that the book further stigmatizes homeless persons, driving a deeper wedge in the antihomeless backlash and contributing to the tendency to blame the homeless for every problem, including trash recycling.

The surge in homeless arrests for camping, loitering, begging, and scavenging raises critical questions about freedom and equality. It is reasonable to accept limitations on personal freedom in the service of collective needs as moral and ethical. Therefore, those who argue that freedom for homeless people conflicts with the freedom of the non-homeless community do so with some merit. The converse of this argument may be equally true.

What is less morally and ethically clear is whether homeless people are being arrested because they have less equal rights to use public space than domiciled people. Homeless service providers and advocates in most cities allege that a pattern of unequal enforcement of city laws against the homeless prevails. The arrests of homeless people who do not commit serious crimes, and are themselves vulnerable to being victimized by criminal behavior does not ensure that public safety is available for everybody. If this is so, than communities across the nation are participating in a holocaust in the name of street justice.

## Homeless Arrests

The Atlanta Homeless Task Force reported that over 225 people were arrested for panhandling in a 3-month period in 1993. During the months of May and June at least 625 different persons were arrested within 4 days of a convention, or during a convention. The Task Force estimates that the City of Atlanta spends between $300,000 and $500,000 a year to incarcerate homeless people.

Before the City enacted its new antihomeless ordinances, the Police Department conducted periodic sweeps of certain neighborhoods to rid them of homeless people. One homeless advocate in Atlanta claimed that the police arrest homeless people for no reason, and then decide what to do with them.[2]

San Francisco's Matrix program, launched in 1993, took more than 3200 actions during its first 3 months. These initially centered on the area surrounding the Civic Center, but rapidly spread to residential districts. One of the expressed goals of the Matrix arrest program is to assert that homeless people are unwelcome in San Francisco. By demonstrating zero tolerance for criminal activity by homeless people, the city has classified innocent homeless behavior as criminal activity. Media investigations of the Matrix program found that only 145 people charged with nuisance crimes under the program were actually found guilty of any offense. Of the 3200 arrests 800 were simply referred to municipal traffic court.

The Matrix program has effectively banished many homeless people from San Francisco. Nearby cities of Oakland and Berkeley reported an influx of homeless persons who had either been expelled from San Francisco or were afraid of arrest.[3]

The arrest of 64 homeless persons in Santa Ana, California was but one in a series of incidents directed against homeless people in that city. In that incident, 28 people were charged with littering, 18 with jaywalking, 7 with urinating in public, 2 with destroying vegetation, 2 with obstructing doorways in violation of fire codes, 2 with riding bicycles on sidewalks, 2 with drinking in public, 1 with removing trash from a bin, and 1 with the possession of glue with an intent to inhale it.[4]

During the 1992 Los Angeles civil uprising, homeless persons were arresting for violating the curfew imposed on all domiciled people in the city. In 1987, 40 police officers swept through the city's skid row area forcing homeless people to abandon and destroy their self-constructed shelters and tossing their personal belongings into the street. Many were arrested. These periodic sweeps continue where tent cities or other homeless encampments develop.

Chicago police use municipal codes against homeless people to harass and convince them to move elsewhere. In most homeless sweeps, Chicago police usually employ these tactics. Occasionally, people are put in a holding tank for several hours before charges are dropped and they are released.

The pavilion program in Dallas has been used as a justification for conducting sweeps of encampments. People who refuse to "relocate" to a pavilion are subject to arrest, or given bus tickets to leave the city.

Dallas enacted a law against drinking in public in conjunction with the aggressive panhandling and public lodging ordinances. It opened an "Inebriate Detention Center" at the rear of a police station and began to charge homeless persons under the law immediately. About one-half of those arrested and charged with a misdemeanor punishable by a fine up to $500 were homeless.

Homeless advocates contend that this law is neutral as it is written, but that it was enforced against homeless people in a discriminating manner. The City Council would suspend the ordinance during football season when thousands of college students would stream into town for the regular games and the Cotton Bowl. However, the ordinance is now being applied with less discrimination because the City Council agreed to "get tough" after an eruption of crowd violence following the Texas–Oklahoma football game.

For many years, police in Miami conducted homeless sweeps of the parade grounds before the Orange Bowl. During these sweeps, they confiscated and destroyed the possessions of homeless people, arrested them, and detained them in jail until the conclusion of the parade. At other times, Miami police may not arrest homeless people, but they continue to confiscate and destroy their belongings.

The Sheriff's Department of Orlando, Florida authorized a policy of destroying self-constructed homeless shelters in encampments. They could also destroy property and dump containers of food on the ground. After pressure from the state attorney's office and a local member of congress, the Sheriff agreed to refrain from continuing the policy.

Orlando now uses its pavilion program, the Coalition Campus, as a rationale for arresting or harassing people who do not agree to go there.

The City of Las Vegas has reversed its long standing policy of arresting or questioning homeless people without cause. One infamous incident occurred when police arrested a homeless man who was epileptic. Because he refused to identify himself during the arrest, the police destroyed his personal belongings, including his medication. He had his first epileptic seizure while he was being held in the police van, and during his 21-day stay in jail he had a second one requiring paramedical care. The man was subsequently released and the charges against him were dropped. This action reflected the city's policy of keeping all homeless people away from the downtown gambling and tourist area.

Security guards and librarians in Las Vegas were authorized to eject all people from public libraries who look homeless, bring personal belongings into the library, and emanate an odor within six feet.

Since the election of Mayor Jan Laverty Jones, Las Vegas has adopted a "kinder, gentler approach" to its homeless residents. It has built a day shelter and has trained two police officers to work with homeless people. Now, police officers refer homeless people to other resources rather than arrest them. Homeless advocates pressed for this policy and they report that there were only 10 arrests in 1993, in contrast to thousands of arrests per year before then.

Homeless sweeps in New York are routinely conducted when large conventions and other public events occur. During the 1992 Democratic National Convention, the police conducted an intense campaign to clean up midtown Manhattan by ridding homeless people from the streets. Under the national spotlight, as well as the scrutiny of a large coalition of homeless advocates, the police did not arrest anybody in this campaign, but directed them to other service centers set up by the city. A decade earlier, homeless people were arrested before the Democratic National Convention in New York.

Advocates in New York are closely monitoring any new signs of anti-homeless activity that might escalate arrests and other sweeps because Mayor Giuliani promised to crack down on homeless people during his election campaign. There are clear statements that signal a reversal of

New York's formerly humane approach to homeless people under the present city administration.

Police in Seattle conduct routine sweeps of the park areas. They do not arrest people unless they appear to be inebriated. More frequently, they use harassment and issue orders to move along. Police do keep records of people they stop and repeat violators usually receive a citation.

Seattle advocates are alarmed by the recent arrest campaign authorized under the city's "No Loitering Program." As described earlier, this program has established a partnership between the police and local merchants to enforce state laws prohibiting trespassing by one warning and subsequent arrest.

Homeless people in the District of Columbia are routinely subjected to random destruction of their belongings by police. Between June and October 1992, District police destroyed every encampment of homeless people living under the Whitehurst Freeway in the Northwest section of the city. Police routed the residents and told them to gather their belongings and eat all of their food within 5 minutes and leave. Any remaining goods or food were to be destroyed. One person even reported that a police officer took his eyeglasses and stepped on them.

The District police department has denied participating in any of this activity. Advocates, considering a legal challenge to the police department, decided against filing a suit. They feared that the reports of the homeless people involved would not be believed by a judge or a jury, thus establishing a legal precedent that could harm other homeless people or lawsuits.[5]

It is important to understand that the danger of homeless arrest campaigns rests equally on the legal sanctions governing them as well as any actions taken under the laws. The mere existence of statutes and codes prohibiting necessary and normal behavior and life styles of homeless people poses a constant threat of harassment or arrest and authorizes their further stigmatization. It also imposes what may be an impossible code of behavior on homeless people.

### Legal Challenges to Homeless Arrests

Every legal challenge to antihomeless ordinances, begging, sleeping, loitering, or camping, has implicitly challenged homeless arrests or property seizures where they are the designated punishment for violation of a law. However, there have been a series of cases that have explicitly addressed the constitutionality of arrests, sweeps, property seizures and harassment.

In his thorough analysis of official efforts to drive homeless people from American cities, Simon explained that homeless arrest campaigns violate many constitutional rights that are taken for granted by domiciled people. Furthermore, violation of these rights may effectively punish homeless people for their very existence.

Foremost among these rights is that of travel and freedom of movement, both interstate and intrastate. The Supreme Court in *Kolender v. Lawson* concluded that the arrest of an individual for vagrancy without identification implicated "Consideration of the constitutional rights of freedom of movement."[6] The opposite of freedom to travel is the freedom to remain in one place without being expelled.

Fourth Amendment principles hold that suspicion of future criminality is an insufficient ground for arrest. The Fourth Amendment requires that all arrests be based upon probable cause. Therefore, arrests of homeless persons on the grounds of prevention of a crime in the future cannot pass constitutional muster.

Arrests for sleeping and camping in public places are subject to constitutional challenge under the Eighth Amendment, which protects people from cruel and unusual punishment. This means that homeless arrests targeted only at homeless persons may be cruel and unusual punishment based solely upon their status. Moreover, arrest and conviction of homeless people for sleeping in public may punish them for a condition that they are powerless to avoid because of their status.

The Equal Protection Clause offers the clearest direction for challenges to homeless arrests. This clause has served as an instrument of government neutrality in the application of justice from its inception. It serves as a guarantee against the enactment of government hostility toward unpopular groups. Homeless arrest campaigns may be construed as official hostility toward homeless people and, therefore, subject to challenges under the Equal Protection Clause.

Property sweeps directed against homeless people may violate several constitutional protections of property rights. Three limitations on the government's right to seize and destroy personal property have existed since the ratification of the Constitution. First, they must be reasonable searches and seizures. Next, the Fifth Amendment prohibits the taking of private property for public use without compensation. Finally, official seizure or destruction of property without notice and an opportunity to be heard may violate due process protections. To the extent that local officials fail to provide these protections, property sweeps are subject to court challenges.

*Pottinger v. City of Miami* recognized the interests of the homeless in retaining their meager personal possessions and that this interest may outweigh the interests of public officials in preserving the aesthetic appeal of a public place. This indicates that property sweeps may be subject to challenge under the Fourth Amendment. The *Pottinger* decision also enjoined the city from arresting homeless people for eating, sleeping, bathing and congregating in public.[7]

The National Law Center on Homelessness and Poverty has identified 10 challenges to homeless arrests, sweeps, harassment and property seizures that have been brought before the courts between 1990 and 1993. The cases have all applied one or more of Simon's analyses.

Judged by compensatory rewards, the most satisfying challenge occurred in the City of Santa Ana where the city council agreed to pay $50,000 each to 17 homeless persons to settle a suit related to the confiscation and destruction of bedrolls and other personal property during cleanup sweeps of the parks and Civic Center. The city also entered into a settlement agreement related to the arrest, detention, and expulsion of the 64 homeless individuals in 1990 in which it paid $400,000 in damages to those arrested. Furthermore, the city agreed to stop detaining homeless people for minor infractions such as loitering or jaywalking in a discriminatory manner. The city also agreed not to shackle homeless persons to benches, mark their bodies with identification symbols, or threaten them with death or bodily harm.[8] As part of the settlement, the city admitted no prior wrongdoing.

In a District of Columbia case, filed by the Community for Creative Non-Violence, the plaintiffs challenged the constitutionality of a predawn raid on one of its shelters by the United States Marshals Service. The court found that the Marshals actions violated the Fourth Amendment rights to freedom from unreasonable searches and seizures and enjoined the Marshals from conducting searches without warrants, consent, or "dragnet-type" identity searches in the future.[9]

Advocates in Las Vegas successfully challenged the exclusion policies of the Las Vegas public libraries. The litigation resulted in a settlement agreement under which the librarians would not eject any homeless persons because they are homeless. The librarians also agreed to issue homeless persons library cards and not to eject them because of odors without consulting a homeless advocate. Unless the advocate agreed that the homeless person's odor was very offensive to other library patrons, the librarians could not force them to leave. Since the consent decree was entered into, no homeless person has been ejected from the Las Vegas public libraries.[10]

Las Vegas has also refrained from carrying out its policy of arresting or harassing homeless people for engaging in necessary life activities as part of a settlement agreement in *Benavides v. City of Reno*. The case was argued along the same lines as the Pottinger brief.[11]

Another case in Morristown, New Jersey challenged the constitutionality of library rules used against homeless people. The library rules prohibited loitering and limited the use of libraries to "normal activities associated with the use of a library." The rules also prohibited any behavior that disturbed other library patrons and established a "community standard" of hygiene and appearance while in the library.

The plaintiff in the case was ejected from the library for having an offensive body odor, disturbing the enjoyment of the library by other patrons, and behaving in a belligerent manner against the librarian. The court held that the library rules were constitutional and that the plaintiff had a constitutional right to receive the same information as any other library patron. However, the library was defined as a limited public forum in which people are permitted to exercise only rights associated with the nature and use of a library.[12]

In a class action suit filed in Huntsville, Alabama in 1993, four homeless men sought to enjoin the city from enforcing its policy of ejecting homeless people from its borders, harassing and arresting them for conducting routing daily activities, and using city building or licensing codes to lose private shelters for homeless people.

The court issued a preliminary injunction against the city's practice, finding that "While the City of Huntsville is under no constitutional duty to address the problems of its homeless citizens, it is under a constitutional duty not to discriminate against them solely because of their status as such."[13]

A suit filed in Oakland also affected the entire San Francisco Bay area and resulted in an important victory against homeless sweeps and property seizures. It resulted in a settlement agreement under which the California Department of Transportation agreed to refrain from discarding the possessions of homeless persons found in encampments under highway overpasses.

This suit was filed after seven homeless people complained that various government agencies had confiscated their belongings, including bedrolls, eyeglasses, medicines, and food stamps, during a series of homeless sweeps that had occurred without any prior notice. These homeless people were arrested for camping on California Public Transit Authority property, detained for up to 5 days without any arraignments or formal charges, and when released they returned to their former encampments to find that their possessions were no longer there.

Under the settlement agreement, the transit authority now warns people 48 hours prior to when they are to be forced off of its property or their possessions seized. Personal items must now be stored by the government for at least 20 days. After a sweep, notice must be posted at the sight with detailed instructions on where to retrieve any property. The settlement also required the Oakland Police Department to reimburse the seven plaintiffs in the suit $18,000 for the property that was destroyed.[14]

A San Francisco court delivered a setback to the protection of homeless people from arrests and property destruction. In *Stone v. Agnos*, a homeless man arrested for lodging in public complained that his First Amendment rights had been violated. He also complained that the destruction of his property after the arrest violated his due process rights.

The court decision held that First Amendment rights did not apply to sleeping because it is not an expression covered under First Amendment protections. Therefore, the police had not violated the plaintiff's rights. Nor could the plaintiff demonstrate that the police had behaved unreasonably to maintain a cause of action for violation of the plaintiff's due process rights.[15]

One extreme case actually resulted in the court's overturning a murder conviction because of a violation of search and seizure rights. A homeless man, convicted of murder, challenged the constitutionality of the search of his duffel bag and closed box located in his makeshift home under a highway.

The court held that the defendant had a reasonable right to privacy and that the police search of his bag and box after the arrest for evidence of crimes, without a warrant, violated his privacy and expectation of protection from unreasonable search and seizure.

Most of these cases, in conjunction with other decisions related to homeless activity in public arenas, have built a wall of protections for homeless people who seek to conduct routine activities associated with daily living. They serve as precedents for communities engaged in struggles between antihomeless sentiments and those that are sympathetic to the needs of homeless people. The court victories have asserted that homeless people have the same constitutional rights to protection from arrest, incarceration, and unreasonable searches and seizures of their property as domiciled people.

## Notes and References

1. Alice Baum and Donald Burns, *A Nation in Denial: The Truth About Homelessness* (Boulder: Westview Press, 1993).

2. Atlanta Task Force for the Homeless, *The Criminalization of Poverty*, September 23, 1993, 15; National Law Center on Homelessness and Poverty, *The Right to Remain Nowhere*, 30 (Part II, Note 1).

3. *Ibid.*, 37–39.

4. Simon, "Towns without Pity," 632 (Introduction, Note 6).

5. *Ibid.*, 70–122.

6. *Kolender v. Lawson*, 461 U.S. 352, 1983.

7. Simon, "Towns without Pity," 656–675 (Introduction, Note 6).

8. *Hinsley v. City of Santa Ana*, No. 636360 (Cal. Sup. Ct. Orange County 1990).

9. *Community for Creative Non-Violence v. U.S. Marshals*, 797 F. Supp. 7 (D.D.C. 1992).

10. *Bryant et al. v. Hunsberger et al.* Civil Action No. CV-S-91-549, Complaint, at 5.(Appendix B); National Law Center on Homelessness and Poverty, *The Right to Remain Nowhere*, 95 (Part II, Note 1).

11. *Benavidez v. City of Reno*, CVN 92-531HDM (1990).

12. *Kreimer v. Morristown*, 958 F.2d 1242 (3rd Cir. 1992).

13. *Church v. Huntsville*, No. CV-93-C-1239-S (N.D. Ala. 1993).

14. *Lee v. California Department of Transportation*, No. C-92-3131 SBA, Order Granting in Part and Denying in Part Defendants' Motion to Dismiss (N.D. Cal. October 26, 1992).

15. *Stone v. Agnos*, 960 F.2d 1242 (3rd Cir. 1992).

# 12

## THE LIMITATIONS OF
## JUDICIAL ADVOCACY

### After the Lawsuit Is Over

The central thesis of this book is that judicial advocacy has made it possible to advance and protect the interests of homeless people in the face of hostile legislation and public sentiment. Moreover, judicial decisions have filled the void created by scant legislation addressing the problems of homeless people. Most of the legal challenges described in the preceding chapters have effectively reinforced the constitutional rights of people who, though homeless, need to find ways to conduct their daily lives under a protective mantle of basic civil rights and citizenship entitlements.

Judicial decisions delivered by state and local courts, as well as some in the United States Supreme Court, have built a wall of protection for homeless people to ensure their right to at least the minimum standards of health, education, and welfare that governments are obligated to provide. The courts have overturned many legal and extralegal attempts of local government officials to criminalize and expel homeless people for their occupation and use of public spaces.

However, courts have also upheld local laws that openly state their intention to drive away homeless people. Some of the most controversial cases remain pending demonstrating the reluctance of some courts to issue politically unpopular decisions. Increasingly hostile communities are even seeking new and tougher approaches to eject homeless people, including lawsuits challenging prior court decisions constraining hostile official policies. Moreover, the impressive successes of homeless litigation have not reversed the proliferation of mass homelessness in the absence of legislation and appropriations required to redress the problem in terms of the numbers of homeless people or the complexity of the many situations that contribute to the problem.

This mixed record of judicial policy making on homelessness leads to questions about the implementation and impact of court decisions and the translation of law into action. The policy process is a complex web of interrelated tasks and stages with implementation fully as important as policy formulation. As such, court decisions are but one stage in the policy process. Many have characterized the policy process by its high degree of power diffusion. The politics of the courts must be viewed in the context of the larger sociopolitical system that governs and influences American social welfare policy.

Most research on judicial impact studies has focused on the record of compliance or noncompliance with decisions. More recently, scholars have turned their attention to questions of implementation. The problem with compliance studies is that the subject is frequently difficult to operationalize in terms of identifying what behavior constitutes compliance. But the greater limitation of this approach is that even when there is a high degree of judicial compliance, a decision may have relatively little social and political impact on the populace.

The history of civil rights legislation demonstrated this pattern. After 40 years of Supreme Court decisions on integrated schools and legislative reapportionment, local governments continue to circumvent the decisions. Justice Thurgood Marshall, who raised the defense of African American interests to a dramatic high, was so frustrated by the limited impact of his revolutionary court victories that he called for the arm-of-the-law approach to enforcement by the Department of Justice and the Federal Bureau of Investigation. Sadly, even the most aggressive enforcement actions do not alter public sentiment, values, and attitudes. Although social indicators reflect advances, social conditions remain difficult for the people represented by Thurgood Marshall. Racism undeniably continues to trouble the lives of African Americans

In the context of 1990s homelessness, communities in New York City, Berkeley, and New Haven are experiencing serious conflicts over the implementation of laws governing the housing rights of mentally ill people. Officials of the Department of Housing and Urban Development have been investigating the activities of opponents of community-based housing for mentally ill people under the authority of the Fair Housing Act in 32 cities across the United States. The Fair Housing Act, amended in 1988, protects housing rights of the disabled, including the mentally ill, drug addicts, alcoholics, and those suffering from AIDS.

Community opponents contend that these investigations are a witch hunt based upon rumors and that the Department is violating their free speech protections under the First Amendment. The Department defends these investigations as necessary to substantiate rumors of actions violating the Fair Housing Act.

These disputes offer contemporary evidence of the limited impact of the law. They reflect the nagging reality that placement of facilities to house and serve society's most troubled citizens is the subject of emotional debate almost everywhere, no matter what the law requires. They also reflect an even more profound problem with the research focus on judicial compliance. Most compliance studies have examined the responses of agencies charged with implementing a law. While this is an important subject of inquiry, it ignores what some allege is the most important measure of judicial impact, the change in attitudes and behavior of consuming populations. It is this problem that must be addressed in the face of increasing public hostility toward homeless people. This is also the arena of judicial policy implementation that social policy practitioners are probably more equipped to engage in than their legal colleagues.

Research that addresses judicial implementation reviews a broader array of responses and consequences within the different arenas of the sociopolitical policy process than compliance research. Nevertheless, compliance issues remain a central question within the larger endeavor. Research on judicial implementation investigates responses to judicial decisions within the legislative and executive arenas, as well as within the judicial court hierarchy. It also addresses responses from interest groups, public opinion, and the media.

Studies of congressional responses to the courts have tended to address decisions delivered by the Supreme Court. These responses fall into four categories: Congress may not respond, it may respond positively, it may respond with hostility, or it may respond in a negative manner without overt expressions of hostility. Most of the time Congress does nothing.

Positive responses occur when the Court–Congress relations are cooperative, which has not always been the case. This suggests that the Court retains a political role in fashioning public policy. Nor are court decisions necessarily viewed as sacrosanct. Congressional hostility tends to respond to a series of Court decisions that reflect a pattern of rulings that conflicts with congressional political positions rather than one ruling. Political parties are even likely to take stands on disputed court decisions because these matters become central political controversies. Under Congressional and political attack, the Supreme Court has backed down and reversed itself on numerous occasions.

State legislatures have no control over the Supreme Court, but they do respond to those decisions that affect local and state practices. The most dramatic example of state legislative attempts to overturn a Supreme Court decision rests in the numerous attempts of the southern states to resist compliance with *Brown v. Board of Education* outlawing racial segregation in public schools.

For the most part, however, there is little evidence of state resistance to United States Supreme Court decisions. At the state level, legislative–

judicial conflicts tend to be moderated by two factors. State supreme courts are generally deferential to the legislature and tend to take strict constructionist approaches to constitutions. State legislatures also meet for shorter periods of time than the federal legislature and they have more limited staff and other resources.

The executive branch has exercised more control over the Supreme Court than the legislature. The President possesses numerous formal and informal powers over the Court in spite of the doctrine of the separation of powers. The most obvious power of the presidency is the appointment of justices. Presidents may also influence legislative responses to court decisions in their role as the chief legislator of national politics. Similarly, they can mold public opinion. Finally, presidents may shape the Supreme Court agenda through the Office of the Solicitor General of the Department of Justice, which exercises considerable influence over the Supreme Court selection of cases for appeal.

All judicial policy is subject to review. The judicial hierarchy defines the role of appellate courts as review of the work of lower courts. Lower courts also have the authority to reverse appellate courts by virtue of their position as the implementing or interpreting agencies of the appellate courts. Lower courts can expand, selectively interpret, or evade appellate court decisions. Again, Southern resistance to civil rights court decisions reflects this pattern of noncompliance with the higher courts. In *Hawkins v. Board of Control,* Virgil Hawkins, an African American man, sued in the Florida state court to obtain admission to the University of Florida School of Law under the *Brown* decision. The Florida State Court simply dismissed the suit.

Appellate courts do have the power to discipline lower court judges in efforts to make them comply with judicial policy through the use of a writ of mandamus. This power is of limited consequence and is far less influential than that of professional norms as a compelling force for voluntary compliance.

Limited research exists on the influence of interest groups, public opinion, and the media on implementation of judicial decisions. Most research focuses on the extensive impact of these entities on the legislative and executive branches. Because of this, they clearly wield indirect influence on the implementation of judicial law.

They also wield direct influence on the judicial process because judges do heed public opinion and interests. However, studies explaining a direct link between public opinion, or the media, and judicial policy making have not delineated this connection. Public opinion is so commingled with legislative and executive forces that it is difficult to discern precisely what forces produce what clear outcome.

Interest groups also employ the more formal route of litigation to reverse or modify a court decision. Many of the NAACP Legal Defense Fund suits were filed for this purpose. Because such litigation is frequently expensive and lengthy, involving years not months, well-financed interest groups, rather than individuals or poor people's organizations, more commonly bring litigation before the lower courts attempting to persuade them to deliver contradictory or narrower interpretations of appellate court decisions.[1]

The doctrine of precedent inherent in case law plays a central role in the implementation of judicial decisions. Precedent expresses the legal principle that rules applied in one dispute are gleaned from earlier disputes so that similar cases should be decided similarly, regardless of the parties involved. The doctrine of precedent focuses on consistency of law.

The force of precedent in law should theoretically simplify judicial decision making and lead to predictable outcomes in the resolution of disputes, as well as interpretation of precedents in issues that do not come before the courts. Nevertheless, there is far more evidence of flexibility in court decision making than case law via precedent would lead us to believe. This helps to explain why there have been so many differing interpretations of First Amendment and Equal Protection rights in homeless decisions.

This flexibility is necessary to explain factual, as well as more subtle, differences between two seemingly similar situations. Although American courts more frequently invoke the doctrine of precedent than not, the exceptions provide an important legal protection.[2] On the one hand, they may curtail the implementation of court decisions, but they may also encourage challenges to precedent and enable litigants to extend the boundaries of legal precedents.

Studies of compliance or noncompliance and implementation of judicial decisions attest to the continuing political struggle after the lawsuit is over. The processes of interpreting, implementing, and administering policy are circular, locating the point of implementation at the center of the circle. Indeed, the circularity of the policy process helps explain why homelessness persists despite the impressive docket of favorable court decisions delivered at every judicial level. It also explains why even the most forthright moral imperative articulated in a judicial decision is only one factor in policy making.

This caveat serves as an important reminder that the courts are also agencies that implement or administer policy made elsewhere, most notably the legislature. Numerous homeless cases have been tried on this basis, for example, that of the *National Coalition for the Homeless v. Department of Education* to force implementation of the education requirements of the Stewart B. McKinney Homeless Assistance Act.[3]

This discussion of the impact and implementation of judicial decisions raises further questions about the limitations on judicial institutions in their policy making roles.


## Judicial Policy Making


Social science-oriented legal research has produced mixed perspectives on judicial policy making. The court system has been viewed as fundamentally unfair and unequal because of limited access and the tendency of the dispute resolution process to favor the "haves" over the "have-nots." Other analyses view judicial power, at least as exercised by the Supreme Court, as a legitimizing force that places a stamp of approval on broad policy tendencies abroad in the legislature and the general public.

Regarding the power of the judiciary to direct or redirect social advantage and disadvantage, there are two seemingly conflicting but interrelated assessments. The first contends that courts do, indeed, possess and wield this power. Those who disagree allege that the relationship between law and social change is too complex to point to one source of law. Others observe that the courts perform an inherently political role because they must function in accordance with the needs of the political ruling groups. Finally, some scholars have determined that the courts are the purveyors of the myth of law and justice, symbols that are necessary for any political regime to maintain its authority. In the final analysis, the central theme of most scholarship on judicial implementation is that the courts exist to distribute societal advantages and disadvantages in accordance with the values of those who control them.

Some have argued that the central ingredient of unfairness in the American judiciary system is inequality of access. *Gideon v. Wainwright* provided a constitutional guarantee of equality of legal representation for the poor in criminal cases.[4] The historic record of poor quality legal representation for poor people in contrast to the teams of legal experts assembled to represent wealthy clients in criminal cases attests to continuing inequality, despite the law.

Access problems point to a further illustration of unfairness, the tendency of courts to rule in favor of the "haves." Much of this is directly attributable to the superior quality of legal counsel available to the "haves." On a deeper level, there is considerable thought that courts placate the collective interests of the "haves" in dispute resolution. This may partially explain the large number of outstanding legal challenges to antihomeless policies that remain pending.

Class action impact litigation has offered the most direct resolution to problems of limited access to the courts and legal representation for poor people. Even class actions do not fully redress the problem of unfairness because informal court processes feature a high degree of bargaining. The Civil Litigation Research Project of the University of Wisconsin found that judges rarely reach decisions on the merits of the law. They actively intervene to encourage settlements and, in the process, avoid confronting issues of social reform.[5] The numerous consent decrees in homeless cases, including the *Callahan* settlement, demonstrate this judicial tendency to avoid ruling on controversial social reforms.

Nevertheless, courts have used their power to redirect societal advantages and disadvantages and have shown that they are capable of significant redistribution of values in the populace. Analyses have demonstrated the many constraints and external checks on judicial power and judges are keenly aware of these.

Despite any limitations on judicial power, the courts do retain a legitimizing force. Robert Dahl has suggested that the Supreme Court at least possesses the power to place its seal of approval on broad policy proclivities set out by the legislature and the polity.[6] At a minimum, this interpretation of the power of the judiciary delineates a rubber-stamping role. It is far more than that because the judiciary is a major partner with other branches of government. When the ruling coalition is indifferent or not united on certain issues, the Court can fill the void with its own interpretation of policies. The decade of homeless litigation has served just this purpose at national, state, and local levels. Judges have vetoed state and local government antihomeless actions in the scores of decisions documented throughout this book. Dahl viewed the courts as the conscience of the realm, or a guide and pioneer.[7]

The leaders of the civil rights movement and the Office of Economic Opportunity legal services program held this view of the judiciary as in instrument of directed social change. Homeless advocates have followed their lead. The results have been mixed.

The lot of African Americans and other racial minorities has considerably improved in the 40 years since the *Brown* school desegregation decision. However, it took more than the Supreme Court decision to achieve this. The President, Congress, and other significant public actors had to move forcefully to create the social and economic incentives for compliance with the *Brown* decision.

The lesson of the legal component of the War on Poverty is that the relationship between the law and social reform is complex and indirect. When poverty lawyers sought social change through litigation the results were limited. Even judicial victories were mitigated by political pressures of populations that opposed the laws and often obliterated them by their nonimplementation. The steady stream of successful cases against city and state governments proved to be no match for an increasingly conservative Congress, which eventually withdrew funding for legal service programs. Test case litigation, no matter how successful and constitutionally sound, could not stand up to popular antiwelfare perceptions that welfare recipients were the undeserving poor.

This theme is repeating itself in the context of the new rash of anti-homeless laws passed in the full knowledge of previous court decisions upholding the rights of homeless people.

These experiences support the view that attempts to employ legal challenges to bring about more fundamental social change are frequently premature if they run counter to the social values and behavior of a society. Legal decisions tend to reflect popular opinions rather than mold them. The judiciary then is an inherently political arbiter of the public and serves to channel public policy into popular paths that please the political elite but are often detrimental to "have-not" interests. This interpretation of judicial policy making leads to the disturbing conclusion that class-action impact litigation may not combat recent hostility toward homeless people.

A different paradigm for the judicial role, presented by Harry Stumpf, has been adopted in this book. It holds that the judicial function is that of a power broker. Rather than viewing the courts as authoritative decision makers based on principles, they are seen as genuinely political entities that can, and do, play many political roles. The tasks of government are multiple and frequently inconsistent. The judiciary preserves the appearance of a detached and neutral dispute resolution forum promising justice for all, especially minorities.[8]

A paradigm of the judiciary as both political and neutral provides it with what many believe is its most important sociopolitical role. Government requires more than the exercise of force and power. It requires the consent of the governed through moral and social sanctions. The courts offer these sanctions to government by legitimizing the political power structure through the diffusion of the myth of equal justice under the law. Under this paradigm, there is some room for optimism that impact litigation can combat hostility toward homeless people.

Surveys of public opinion about the courts consistently indicate that they have a high public approval rating that may even be out of proportion to the reality of their work. These data pertain to all social strata in American society and are not influenced by levels of education. If these surveys are correct, then the courts are succeeding in preserving the belief that law and justice prevail.

A summary assessment of judicial policy making leads to the conclusion that the courts are inevitably political entities that reflect and sanction the values and policy preferences of the government of which they are a part. When these values are in conflict, the courts play an important role of clarifying competing perspectives on issues. They act as arbiters in the search for neutral ground. As political instruments, courts exist to distribute societal advantages and disadvantages in accordance with the views of those who support them.[9]

## Legislative Advocacy or Judicial Advocacy

That the law is expected to fulfill many roles is both its limitation and its strength. Because the law can respond to evolving needs and attitudes, advocates may not find laws acceptable. Therefore, they must determine when to resort to the law. An equally important consideration is whether to advocate in the legislative, administrative, or judicial arena.

Most social advocacy has targeted legislatures. Advocates have chosen the legislative route because legislation can produce a solution applicable to a wider range of people than either the administrative or judicial route. This does not imply that one legal institution is necessarily better than another. The central question is what different expectations advocates have of the courts and the legislatures.

The history of collaboration between lawyers and social workers demonstrates strategies for differential approaches to the legislature and the judiciary. Progressive social reformers included lawyers and settlement house workers, the forerunners of the social work profession. Both groups joined forces in their sympathy for and moral outrage over the many victims of industrialization's harsher consequences and sought to reverse these destructive forces. They challenged unfair labor practices against women and children, unsafe working conditions, and the treatment of juvenile delinquents. Their impressive achievements were derived from protective legislation to eradicate the inequities and evils perpetrated by industrial society.

The early reformers resorted to the legislature because they considered it the better forum for changing conditions that affected the largest number of people in wide-ranging environments. At that time in history, the legislative process was quicker than the judicial process that involved intense and protracted deliberation. This is no longer the case given the persistence of contemporary government gridlock.

The early reformers also preferred legislation to judicial action because they viewed the courts as the enemy of reform and under the domination of industrial power interests. This view readily changed when it became apparent that even the strongest and clearest legislation could be challenged or mitigated through the implementation process. Despite their skepticism about the courts, they turned to them when the protective legislation they had sponsored was challenged.

Florence Kelly actually proclaimed her conviction that the new technology of social reform required many strategies. She joined forces with the progressive attorney Louis Brandeis in persuading other progressive reformers that the law could be responsive to social needs, as an instrument of social change. Brandeis expressed highly unorthodox views for his time by suggesting that legal rules had to bend to social needs, when prevailing wisdom held the opposite.

The "Brandeis brief" was a major innovation in appellate advocacy and was the first of many to be based on social data-based research produced by the National Consumers League. These briefs argued that the facts as well as the law were essential to the resolution of any court dispute. Facts combined with law were relevant to any determinants of community welfare and both were determined by the social environment in which the rules were shaped. Brandeis referred to this as the "living law." This principle forms the basis of every challenge to legal precedent and legislative action.

Nevertheless, social reformers continued to appeal to the legislature as a first line of attack through the New Deal. The growing reliance on government in assisting the poor, which culminated in the New Deal, justified such a legislative strategy.

The civil rights efforts of the 1950s convinced all social reformers that multiple strategies were essential to achieve the goals of equity and justice. This was exemplified in the multifaceted approach of the War on Poverty and the establishment of the Office of Economic Opportunity, which included the legal services program. The Legal Services Corporation, designed to increase the access of poor people to the courts and to use the courts as instruments of social change through class-action litigation, was as central to the War on Poverty as any of the legislation that it passed. These legal services offered myriad opportunities for lawyers and social workers to collaborate on every level, representing individual clients or welfare rights organizations, or mounting judicial class-action challenges.[10]

This summary of the historical antecedents for collaboration between lawyers and social workers has attempted to explicate some principles that advocates can apply when deciding between judicial and legislative approaches to reform. The lessons of history can never be exact because the context changes even among parallel situations. What was true for the early social reformers is not as readily applicable to the contemporary political environment, most notably the efficiency of the legislature in contrast to that of the judiciary.

One strategy applied in the progressive era remains viable today. Undoubtedly, the legislature offers the most effective route to social change. Its power to set policy relevant to large groups of people is clearly greater than that of the judiciary. For this reason alone, advocates must investigate the likelihood of success in the legislative arena before pursuing any other strategy.

Perhaps the most compelling reason for seeking social reforms in the legislature lies in the peculiar nature of impact litigation. It seeks relief in the form of institutional reform, rather than individual damages. As such, judicial decisions are subject to the hazards of implementation. In deciding impact litigation, judges are frequently cast in the role of social service administrators. They must cast their decisions in terms that force the compliance of unwieldy bureaucracies. The *Callahan* consent decree was highly specific in the standards it established for shelters so that advocates have frequently turned to the courts to enforce compliance. Similarly, conditions governing the daily activities of mentally ill people in custodial facilities were carefully spelled out by the courts when deciding on their right to care, and protections under involuntary commitment laws.

The lessons of the civil rights movement and the War on Poverty are fundamental. They teach that social problems on the massive dimensions of racial inequality and poverty must be addressed on every accessible front.

Not to be overlooked in the rush to seek justice in the courts is the rigor of bringing legal challenges. They are inordinately time consuming and costly. The exemplars of test case litigation have generally been tried under the financial auspices of privately funded charitable organizations, interest groups, or the government. Only a few cases have received the support of private law firms that have agreed to offer *pro bono* services. A major example is the *Callahan* case, tried by Robert Hayes when he was an associate in a private corporate practice. This means that the funding base for judicial policy making is always precarious.

Because litigation is inevitably a protracted affair, quick remedial action such as the opening of a shelter or continued permission for use of public parks for sleeping is seldom possible. For many homeless people, "A loss of time may well mean the loss of lives."[11]

The legislative process, however, is equally lengthy. So it is expensive considering the costs of mounting a successful advocacy campaign. Paid lobbyists, public relations and advertising, the deployment of agency staff from other responsibilities, communications, and other organizing tasks add up to large sums.

The central focus on homeless litigation as an instrument to redress

the problem has occurred because there has been such limited legislation and budgetary appropriation addressing the problem. Homeless
advocates also opted to focus on judicial challenges to the injustices
associated with homelessness because they saw little discernible interest
in legislative solutions to the problem during the 1980s. Indeed, the
tendency to ignore or underestimate the broad dimensions of homelessness among the elected leaders of the 1980s was far greater than any
interest in solving the problem. Even the Stewart B. McKinney Act
offered limited emergency relief and budgetary appropriations for the
Act were always far lower than needed. Judicial action was even necessary to enforce the law's requirement that homeless children be allowed
to attend public school.

Under President Clinton's administration, the legislative arena has
emerged as a far more promising one for solutions to homelessness. In
spite of growing public hostility to homeless people, the Clinton Administration's ambitious plan to break the cycle of homelessness and prevent future homelessness included an unprecedented $1.7 billion. This
would have more than quadrupled the funds now available to cities that
are heavily impacted by homelessness. The Administration's homeless
initiative remains expensive because the team responsible for its design
acknowledges the broad scope of homelessness and the complexity of
meeting the multiple challenges.

This request for significant new funds has already been reduced in the
legislative budgetary process. Money has, however, been allocated to
cities under the initiative, so that cuts in HUD will not affect it. But the
long overdue comprehensive plan of action to reverse homelessness
holds some promise that possible failures in the courts will be redressed
by a sympathetic administration.

In addition to the presidential homeless initiative, momentum to address homelessness by addressing its underlying causes is continuing to
build across the nation. It may even serve as a countervailing force
to hostile government actions. Advocates are using this opportunity to
press for substantive change using the Beyond McKinney: Policies to
End Homelessness Task Force policy proposals. To abet this process, a
joint effort of HUD and the Interagency Council resulted in the conven-
ing of 18 "Interactive Forums" across the United States to follow up on
the recommendations of the Beyond McKinney Task Force policy proposals. These groups may have facilitated renewed energy among
homeless advocates, as well as hope that the policy proposals can result
in legislation. This may be too sanguine a view, but it does not obviate
the fact that the Clinton homeless initiative responded to the proposals
that emanated from the "Interactive Forums."

## Collaboration between Law and Social Work

Saltzman and Proch have presented a series of convincing arguments supporting the value of law and social work collaboration. They emphasize the fact that social workers have been learning about the law and applying it in the best interests of their clients for the following reasons. The law shapes and regulates all social work practice. It also regulates the lives and actions of social workers' clients through restrictions and social controls, as well as the articulation of entitlements. Knowledge of the law also enables social workers to recognize that certain problems of their clients are legal.[12] Practically speaking, many of the concrete problems that arise in the context of law and society may be defined as *sociolegal*.

For these reasons alone, social workers must be able to communicate effectively. On a deeper level, lawyers and social workers who espouse concern for redistribution and social reform share an ideology that can be more productively put into action through cooperative, rather than separate, endeavors. Each group brings different knowledge and skills to its common value systems. This interplay between law, social policy, and social problems can be concretely conceptualized by examining the methodologies and knowledge bases that each profession brings to its collaborative efforts. Albert notes that this task is complicated by the fact that clinical social workers, agency administrators, social planners, and community organizers tend to identify problems differently. This need not imply that different methodological approaches to practice need alter the professional social workers' value base and professional commitment to equity, social justice, and beneficence.

Whatever the methodology, social workers bring intimate knowledge of the law's responsiveness to client needs and social issues. Their encounters with clients, groups, communities, and social service organizations provide them with more awareness of private troubles and public problems than most human service professionals and other people, except service consumers. Social workers occupy a unique position to provide the necessary social data to use as evidence in litigation.

Despite their unique knowledge and insight, social workers must acknowledge the legal boundaries of their work. Their respect for constitutional rights does not restrain lawyer's concern for their clients interests. It merely guides them in interpreting laws. Issues of due process, equal protection, confidentiality, and every other civil right are more frequently ambiguous than clear. Legal education and experience offer a sounder basis for clarifying the legal dimensions of a sociolegal problem.

The expansive role of the law in social policy formulation and implementation compels interprofessional collaboration. It suggests, more-

over, that social workers engaged in policy practice need to add several
critical legal skills to their framework for identifying and analyzing problems, as well as their formal and informal advocacy roles. Foremost
among these are investigation, legal research, legal writing, preparation
of case materials, and knowledge of discretionary decision making.[13]
Attainment of these skills does not require a law degree, merely the
addition of a new analytical perspective to social policy practice.

Albert offers a comprehensive set of current organizational models for
social worker–lawyer collaboration demonstrating the convergence of
law and social work in public and private sector direct services, as well
as public and private indirect services. Each of these models depicts
instances where the two professions work within a shared goal of concern for the client or client group.[14]

The clearest, and perhaps most pervasive, model of interprofessional
collaboration resides within the public child welfare policy arena. Responsibility for protecting children from abuse and neglect falls within
the domain of public child welfare agencies. Lawyers, usually in the
Office of the City Solicitor or State Attorney General, are responsible for
enforcing this protective legislation. Social workers are responsible for
reporting violations as well as counseling children and their families.
They perform a dual function as the arm-of-the-law and service provider.

Child advocacy units have emerged in many public child welfare
agencies. They are staffed by attorneys, social workers, psychologists
and pediatricians and seek to provide sociolegal counsel to parents and
children. These teams are most effective in instances where the interests
of parents and their children conflict. The Child Advocacy Unit of the
Defender Association of Philadelphia exemplifies this model.

Family courts have also developed public sector models of social work
and legal collaboration in direct service. Conciliation programs have
been established to counsel parents and children who are in the throes
of divorce and custody conflicts. Social workers tend to administer and
staff the conciliation programs in cooperation with lawyers. To serve
their clients, they must know the relevant law, interpret it, or even
challenge it.

Again, the Legal Service Corporation of the Office of Economic Opportunity provided a major testing ground for sociolegal collaboration.
Drawing on settlement house models, storefront law offices were situated in poor communities. Lawyers and social workers shared authority
and responsibility, joining with other community activists. Lawyers
handled the legal troubles of clients and social workers handled their
nonlegal problems.

In the private arena, domestic violence has set the stage for extensive
collaboration between lawyers and social workers in direct service. The

Women's Law Center in Los Angeles and Women Organized Against Rape (WOAR) in Philadelphia are but two examples. WOAR works in conjunction with the District Attorney's Office to improve its services to rape survivors. The partnership has led to the establishment of a special child sexual abuse unit in the District Attorney's office. The Women's Law Center represents abused women in police and court cases but it also draws upon social workers and other direct service practitioners with expertise in domestic violence to counsel and provide continuing social support for its clients.

Private practitioners have begun to form close working relationships with lawyers to resolve problems in divorce and child custody cases. Divorce mediation has rapidly evolved to become a common practice in the resolution of emotionally charged financial and legal settlements. Some jurisdictions actually require mediation as a condition of divorce.

Public sector indirect services denote interventions that emphasize social policy and social change. Lawyers and social workers share an orientation to sociopolitical change. All of the homeless litigation presented in this book falls within this category.

Here too, the legal services model of the War on Poverty prevails. In her insightful analysis of lawyers and the welfare rights movement, Davis contends that assessmentss of the ultimate failure of the litigation strategy in the movement overshadow the positive aspects of lawyer–activist collaboration. One factor in the failure of the poverty program's litigation strategy was the short duration of the effort. Whereas the NAACP Legal Defense Fund labored for 25 years, the welfare rights movement, an integral component of the War on Poverty, lasted for only 5 years between 1965 and 1970. More profoundly, the social isolation and unpopularity of poor people may have frustrated broad reform through litigation. Sparer acknowledged this problem and taught that litigation on behalf of poor people was doomed to failure if it was cast in the context of the War on Poverty. He drew upon the principle of universal coverage articulated in the campaign to pass the Social Security Act.[15]

Every private social service agency that engages in advocacy in relation to clients and their social environment engages in collaborative initiatives with lawyers. Many engage legal consultants or staff on a continuing basis. At the national level, the exemplar of private sector indirect service legal–social work collaboration is the Children's Defense Fund. In the states and municipalities, agencies that serve and represent sexual minorities, racial minorities, women, children, and elderly people have tended to engage in interprofessional initiatives around impact litigation.

Conversely, private legal defense organizations have sought the counsel of social workers in carrying out their mission. The ACLU, National

Law Center on Homelessness and Poverty, Western Center on Law and Poverty, and Legal Aid Society have featured prominently in homeless litigation constructing their arguments in concert with social workers and other human service providers, activists, and homeless people.

In contrast to their 1960s counterparts, numerous contemporary proponents of social justice who seek to make the American legal system responsible and accessible to low-income people contend that the private sector offers the answer to the problem of equal access. In this spirit, a new Legal Corps has been formed in the City of Los Angeles.

The Legal Corps will be staffed by young professional volunteers who will spend at least 1 year of full-time service in South-Central Los Angeles, the seat of the 1992 civil uprisings. They will practice law, serving on boards of community-based organizations and acting as catalysts for community progress. This new organization may be a harbinger of a national domestic Peace Corps for lawyers.

In adopting this model of private sector direct and indirect sociolegal service, the private law firms and corporations spearheading the Legal Corps have combined the earliest legal aid model with the progressive era efforts to use the law as an instrument of social change. It shares the same weaknesses of previous private sector initiatives and provokes lament for a concept of legal services as citizenship entitlements. On a more optimistic note, the new organization signals a renewed spirit of professional responsibility for keeping justice alive. It also offers an opportunity for young lawyers who want to engage in public service law.

## Different Perspectives on Law and Social Justice

Having presented the case for interprofessional initiatives based largely upon the mutual concern for social justice among lawyers and social workers, it is important to qualify this position. Despite their common goal, lawyers and social workers may bring different views of social justice and its attainment to problem solving.

The social work profession practices on the basis of a longstanding commitment to advocacy at both the case and class levels. This is a central component of the NASW Code of Ethics. It features prominently in the curricula of schools of social work, and is one of the key measures of competent social work practice. For social workers, their main concern is for effective client advocacy. As a central intervention strategy, advocacy brings social workers into partnerships with lawyers.

The meaning and interpretation of advocacy strategies are less clear than its intent among social workers. Frequently, they advocate in haste without sufficient regard for legal constraints or the legal system's capacity to respond. Politicians and political theorists frequently note that single interest advocates are valuable catalysts for change but are too impatient to take the necessary steps to achieve their agenda. Inspired by a passionate sense of injustice, social workers tend to believe that "there ought to be a law" and focus on making this happen. This is an understandable position, given the ethical commitment of the profession and the frustration that many practitioners and their clients experience in the social service bureaucratic maze of indifference.

Lawyers are also committed to client advocacy, but they are equally concerned about reform of the law. Yale Law School Emeritus Professor Thomas Emerson distinguished between law as an occupation and law as a mission. The occupation of law means that it is an instrument to maintain the social order operating within the boundaries of the status quo. As a mission, law seeks to achieve social goals.[16]

This dual orientation of lawyers, compared to the single orientation of social workers, reflects their commitment to the highest principles of dispute resolution. As advocates, they seek to ensure that justice will emerge from the application or modification of legal rules. Their concern for social reform therefore is mitigated by their interest in the conditions under which social change is determined. Attorneys must operate within a Code of Professional Responsibility that articulates a dual responsibility to the client and the legal system. The NASW Code of Ethics articulates a singular responsibility, the best interests of the client.

These perspectives are clearly compatible but they can also produce conflict or disagreement between the two professions when they collaborate. Albert recommends that the best route to resolving such real or potential conflict lies in mutual recognition of the different value premises, as well as the shared concerns. Recognition of the different perspectives can preserve the partnership in efforts to represent client interests.[17]

Whatever the differences, the history of collaboration among lawyers, social workers, and, in the best cases, recipient activists demonstrates that class-action impact litigation, as well as direct service law, can involve far more than access to justice. It can be a powerful instrument of social reform. This rich history demonstrates that the goal of social justice can be attained through interprofessional initiatives designed to challenge the multilayered complexities of contemporary private troubles and public problems.

The record of homeless impact litigation represents another stage in the history of using the law as an instrument of social change and protection of citizen entitlements. It takes its place among the earlier efforts to ensure "Equal Access Under Law," emblazoned across the facade of the United States Supreme Court. It serves as the most recent reminder of Chief Justice Earl Warren: "It is the spirit and not the form of the law that keeps justice alive."

## Notes and References

1.   Harry P. Stumpf, *American Judicial Politics* (New York: Harcourt, Brace Jovanovitch, 1988), Chapter 12, "Judicial Policies: Compliance, Implementation, and Impact." This chapter provided the basis for *After the Lawsuit Is Over*. It presents numerous examples of court decisions that have not been identified in this section because they would digress from the central point of the book and the chapter.

2.   Albert, *Law and Social Work Practice*, 11–12 (Chapter 1, Note 2).

3.   Karger and Stoesz, *American Social Welfare Policy*, 372–373 (Chapter 4, Note 9).

4.   *Gideon v. Wainwright*, 372 U.S. 335 (1963).

5.   David M. Trubeck et al., "The Costs of Ordinary Litigation," *UCLA Law Review*, 31(1):122 (October 1983).

6.   Robert A. Dahl, *Pluralist Democracy in the United States: Conflict and Consent* (Chicago: Rand McNally, 1967), 154–170.

7.   *Ibid.*

8.   Stumpf, *American Judicial Politics*, Ch. 2.

9.   *Ibid.* Ch. 13.

10.   Albert, *Law and Social Work Practice*, 206–210 (Chapter 1, Note 2).

11.   Hopper and Cox, "Litigation in Advocacy for the Homeless," 312 (Chapter 1, Note 7).

12.   Saltzman and Proch, *Law in Social Work Practice*, xi–xii (Introduction, Note 11).

13.   Albert, *Law and Social Work Practice*, 204 (Chapter 1, Note 2).

14.   *Ibid.*, 210–214.

15.   Davis, *Brutal Need*, 142–145 (Chapter 1, Note 8).

16.   Raymond Albert, *Integrating Legal Content into the Social Work Curriculum* 1985, mimeograph, 2–3.

17.   *Ibid.*, 218–220.

# CASES CITED

# INDEX